INTANGIBLES

INTANGIBLES

Management, Measurement, and Reporting

Baruch Lev

BROOKINGS INSTITUTION PRESS
Washington, D.C.

Library of Congress Cataloging-in-Publication data
Lev, Baruch.
Intangibles : management, measurement, and reporting / Baruch Lev.
    p.   cm.
Includes bibliographical references and index.
    ISBN 0-8157-0094-6 (cloth : alk. paper)—
    ISBN 0-8157-0093-8 (pbk. : alk. paper)
    1. Corporations—Valuation—United States. 2. Business
enterprises—Valuation—United States. 3. Intangible
property—Valuation—United States. I. Title.
    HG4028.V3 L485 2001   2001001834
    658.15—dc21   CIP

9 8 7 6 5 4 3

The paper used in this publication meets minimum requirements of the
American National Standard for Information Sciences—-Permanence of Paper
for Printed Library Materials: ANSI Z39.48-1992.

Typeset in Sabon and ITC Oficina Sans

Composition by Circle Graphics
Columbia, Maryland

Printed by R. R. Donnelley and Sons
Harrisonburg, Virginia

Foreword

While economists, business people, and policy analysts continue to debate the question of what is "new" about the so-called "New Economy," one important feature of modern economies in the early twenty-first century seems clear: intangible factors are playing an increasingly dominant role in wealth creation. A growing share of economic activity today consists of exchanges of ideas, information, expertise, and services. Corporate profitability is often driven more by organizational capabilities than by control over physical resources, and even the value of physical goods is often due to such intangibles as technical innovations embodied in the products, brand appeal, creative presentation, or artistic content.

But intangible assets, despite their importance, are poorly measured, if at all, and their implications for public policy are not understood. The Brookings Institution Project on Intangibles attempted to address this problem by initiating a wide-ranging national conversation about the role of intangibles in the economy. As one part of that project, codirectors Margaret M. Blair and Steven M. H. Wallman asked New York University professor Baruch Lev to draft a report on the status of research in this area and to offer his recommendations for reform of accounting and financial disclosure rules to provide better information about intangibles. Professor Lev's report evolved into this book, which includes his proposals for a new reporting model for corporations to use in providing information to investors and others about what they are doing to create and manage their critical intangible assets.

At the end of the volume, five scholars and practitioners comment on the issues raised by Lev and his proposed solutions.

The author would like to thank Joshua Livnat, James Ohlson, Mark Bothwell, Steve Waite, Bronwyn Hall, and Katherine Schipper for comments on earlier drafts of this book. Stephen Gates, Brian Hackett, Boyan Jovanovic, Jack Triplett, and Wayne Upton provided the formal comments for publication here. Margaret Blair and Steven M. H. Wallman commissioned the book and organized the symposium where the early draft was presented. Lisa Chavez helped to organize the symposium, and Nancy Kleinrock provided early editorial assistance with the manuscript. At the Brookings Institution Press, the book was edited by Diane Hammond, verified by Catherine Theohary, proofread by Inge Lockwood, and indexed by Julia Petrakis.

The authors also wish to thank the following for their financial support of this project: American Society for Training and Development; Arthur Anderson; Dickstein, Shapiro, Morin and Oshinsky; Dow Chemical; Ernst and Young; IBM; Kenichi Ikeda; Pfiser; PricewaterhouseCoopers; Skandia AFS; Alfred P. Sloan Foundation; Steelcase; Thermo Electron; University of Southern California, Leventhal School of Accounting; and Valuation Research.

The views expressed here should not be ascribed to the trustees, officers, or staff members of the Brookings Institution or the organizations with which the author and those commenting are affiliated, nor to any individual or organization listed above who generously supported the work of the task force.

MICHAEL H. ARMACOST

President, Brookings Institution

Washington, D.C.

May 2001

Contents

Introduction   **1**

1 **What, Why, and Who?**   **5**

2 **The Economics of Intangibles**   **21**

3 **The Record**   **51**

4 **Intangibles in the Dark**   **79**

5 **What Then Must We Do?**   **105**

6 **The Road Ahead**   **129**

Appendixes   **135**

    A. Accounting Rules and
       Regulations for Intangibles   135
       Shyam Vallabhajosyula

    B. Intellectual Capital Management
       Best Practices   155
       Suzanne Harrison, Patrick H. Sullivan Sr.,
       and Michael J. Castagna of ICMG

References   **167**

Comments

Brian Hackett   177
Stephen Gates   180
Boyan Jovanovic   183
Jack E. Triplett   189
Wayne Upton   194
References   200

Index   **203**

INTANGIBLES

Introduction

Wealth and growth in today's economy are driven primarily by intangible (intellectual) assets. Physical and financial assets are rapidly becoming commodities, yielding at best an average return on investment. Abnormal profits, dominant competitive positions, and sometimes even temporary monopolies are achieved by the sound deployment of intangibles, along with other types of assets. It is therefore hardly surprising that in recent years intangibles have occupied an ever larger niche in the mushrooming management literature, both popular and academic.[1]

Central among the issues discussed in this volume is the optimal use of intangibles, which requires quality and timely information about these assets. Accordingly, I discuss the information deficiencies that arise from the shortcomings of the tra-

This book advances the literature on intangible assets in four dimensions:

—the economics of intangibles

—the empirical record of intangibles

—the harms from lack of information regarding intangibles

—the proposed value chain scoreboard

---

1. For example, Stewart (1997) was among the first comprehensive books in the area and still is an excellent source on intangible (intellectual) assets.

1

ditional accounting system to reflect the value and performance of intangible assets, including the consequent harms to firms, investors, and society. Prescriptions to improve information on intangibles follow.

This book advances the literature on intangible assets in four dimensions: the economics of intangibles, the empirical record of intangibles, the harms from lack of information regarding intangibles, and the proposed "value chain scoreboard."[2]

Chapter 1 addresses the three questions, What are intangible assets? Why the current interest in them? And who should be concerned about intangibles? I trace the meteoric rise over the past two decades in the value and impact of intangibles to fundamental changes in the structure and scope of business enterprises. Specifically, the relentless competitive pressure induced by the globalization of trade, far-reaching deregulation, and technological changes (most recently the Internet) forced companies in the last two decades to increasingly rely on continuous innovation (of products, processes, and organizational designs) for survival and growth. Innovation, in turn, is primarily achieved by investment in intangibles (research and development [R&D], information technology, employee training, customer acquisition)—hence the steep rise in the role of these assets in the production functions of businesses. A major theme of this book is linking intangibles to innovation.

Innovation is primarily achieved by investment in intangibles.

What are the economic laws governing intangible assets? I address this fundamental question in chapter 2. Much of the management literature extols the upside of intangibles, primarily their ability to create value by scalability and network effects. Often missing from the discussion is the counterweight: the challenges of managing intangibles and achieving scalability and network externalities. Accordingly, I present an economic framework for analyzing issues concerning intangibles that encompasses both value drivers and value detractors: scalability (nonrivalry), increasing returns, and network effects versus partial excludability (the general lack of full control over the benefits of intangibles), inherent risk, and nontradability (absence of organized markets in intangibles). I then demonstrate how this economic framework for intangibles—a cost-benefit

2. The author is in the process of applying for a trademark for the concept "value chain scoreboard."

analysis—facilitates and enriches the discussion of managerial, investment, and policy issues concerning intangible (intellectual) assets.

Research on various issues concerning intangible (knowledge) assets, both conceptual and empirical, is quite extensive, yet it is scattered in the economics, organization, strategy, finance, and accounting journals. In chapter 3, I survey and synthesize much of this research, focusing on the contribution of intangibles to corporate value and growth. This record taking encompasses the three major nexuses of intangibles: discovery (for example, R&D), organizational capital (for example, brand names), and human resources. The dominant theme of the surveyed research is the establishment of empirical linkages between inputs (investment in R&D, information technology, customer acquisition) and outputs (earnings, productivity, shareholder value). Accordingly, chapter 3 can be viewed as bringing the evidence to bear on the economics of intangibles discussed in chapter 2.

Information, or the lack thereof, centrally impacts the management of and investment in intangibles. Superficially, the information deficiencies regarding intangibles are the result of accounting shortcomings (expenditures on intangibles are expensed, while those on physical and financial assets are capitalized). In fact, the information failures concerning intangibles are deeply rooted in their economic attributes (the economics of intangibles). Prescriptions for improvement in the information available about intangibles are obviously predicated on an understanding of those root causes as well as on an appreciation of the current motives and incentives of the information providers: managers, auditors, and financial analysts.

In chapter 4, I trace the measurement and reporting problems of intangibles to the unique attributes of these assets: high risk, lack of full control over benefits, and absence of markets. I then show how this analysis, focusing on root causes, can be used to shape proposals for improved information disclosure. Relatedly, I discuss the politics of intangibles' disclosure, that is, the fact that corporate executives and auditors currently have few if any incentives to expand the information available about intangibles. This rarely discussed incentives issue presents a major stumbling block to any improvement in the information environment surrounding intangibles.

All this would matter little if the information deficiencies concerning intangibles were not causing serious private and social harms. Accordingly, the major share of chapter 4 is devoted to a theoretical and empirical analysis of the harms (damages) associated with deficiencies in intangibles' disclosure. I show that economic theory predicts—and empirical evidence confirms—that deficiencies in intangibles' disclosures are associated with the following:

—Excessively high cost of capital, particularly for enterprises in dire need of financing, namely early-stage, knowledge-intensive companies.

—Systematic undervaluation by investors of the shares of intangibles-intensive enterprises (the "lemons discount"), particularly those that have not yet reached significant profitability. Undervaluation and high cost of capital hinder investment and growth.

—Excessive gains to officers of R&D-intensive companies from trading in the stocks of their employers (insider gains). Such gains come at the expense of outside investors and may erode confidence in the integrity of the market.

—Continuous deterioration in the usefulness of financial information, possibly leading to volatility and excessive riskiness of securities.

—Manipulation of financial information through intangibles.

The documented harms are indeed serious. Absent publicly available data on specific corporate decisions and their consequences, one can only speculate that intangibles-related information deficiencies adversely impact business operations and governance as they impact external constituencies.

Finally, the Tolstoyan question: What then must we do? Chapter 5 advances a coherent information system encompassing the core of modern business enterprises: the value (innovation) chain. I thus return to the book's main theme: the role of intangible investments, along with other forms of capital, in firms' innovations—the lifeline of the modern corporation. The proposed information system is comprehensive, covering the major phases of the value chain—discovery, implementation, and commercialization—and enumerates quantifiable, linked-to-value indicators for each aspect of the value chain.

The literature and commentary on intangible assets has reached a certain level of maturity. Several key issues beg taking stock: the accumulated knowledge about intangible (intellectual) assets, with particular emphasis on the economic laws governing intangibles; the lessons to be drawn from the extensive research on intangibles; the private and social harms related to information deficiencies concerning intangibles; and ways to overcome these deficiencies. This volume provides such a stocktaking and a road map into the future in the concluding chapter 6.

CHAPTER ONE

What, Why, and Who?

B elow I address the questions posed in the introduction. What are intangible assets? Why the current interest in these assets? And who should care about them?

What Are Intangible Assets?

Merriam Webster's International Dictionary defines *intangible* as "incapable of being defined or determined with certainty or precision." I believe that intangible assets can be defined, but I certainly agree with Webster that they cannot be determined with certainty or precision. Here is the definition: Assets are claims to future benefits, such as the rents generated by commercial property, interest payments derived from a bond, and cash flows from a production facility. An intangible asset is a claim to future benefits that does not have a physical or financial (a stock or a bond) embodiment. A patent, a brand, and a unique organizational structure (for example, an Internet-based supply chain) that generate cost savings are intangible assets.

Throughout this volume I use the terms *intangibles, knowledge assets,* and *intellectual capital* interchangeably. All three are widely used—*intangibles* in the accounting literature, *knowledge assets* by economists, and *intellectual capital* in the management and legal literature—but they refer essentially to the same thing: a nonphysical claim to future benefits. When the claim is legally secured (protected), such as in the case of patents, trademarks, or copyrights, the asset is generally referred to as *intellectual property.*

There are three major nexuses of intangibles, distinguished by their relation to the generator of the assets: discovery, organizational practices, and human resources. The bulk of

The three major nexuses of

intangibles are discovery,

organizational practices,

and human resources.

Merck and Company's intangibles was obviously created by Merck's massive and highly successful innovation effort partially reflected by R&D expenditures ($1.82 billion in 1998), conducted internally and in collaboration with other entities.[1] In contrast, Dell's major value drivers are related to the second nexus, a unique organizational design, implemented through direct customer marketing of built-to-order computers via telephone and the Internet. Cisco's Internet-based product installation and maintenance system, which generated $1.5 billion in savings during 1996–98, is another example of an intangible created by a unique organizational design.[2]

Brands, a major form of intangible assets prevalent particularly in consumer products—electronics (Sony), food and beverages (Coca-Cola), and more recently in Internet companies (America Online, Yahoo! and Amazon), are often created by a combination of innovation and organizational structure. Coke's highly valuable brand is the result of a secret formula and exceptional marketing savvy. The unique products created and acquired by AOL during the 1990s are responsible for its brand, along with massive marketing (customer acquisition) costs.

The third nexus of intangibles, those related to human resources, are generally created by unique personnel and compensation policies, such as investment in training, incentive-based compensation, and learning through collaborations with universities and research centers. Such human resource practices enable employers to reduce employee turnover, provide positive incentives to the work force, and facilitate the recruitment of highly qualified employees (such as scientists). Specific organizational designs such as Xerox's Eureka system, which is aimed at sharing information among the company's 20,000 maintenance personnel, enhance the value of the human resource–related intangibles by increasing employee

1. For 1998 data, see Merck's 10-K report (1998). By a recent count, Merck has more than a hundred R&D and marketing alliances. See Thomson Financial Securities Data, "Joint Ventures and Strategic Alliances Database," December 2000.
2. The Cisco information is from *Business Week*, September 13, 1999, p. 140.

productivity.[3] Thus although it is convenient to classify intangibles by their major generator—discovery, organizational design, or human resource practices—the assets are often created by a combination of these sources.

Finally, it should be noted that the demarcation lines between intangible assets and other forms of capital are often blurry. Intangibles are frequently embedded in physical assets (for example, the technology and knowledge contained in an airplane) and in labor (the tacit knowledge of employees), leading to considerable interaction between tangible and intangible assets in the creation of value. These interactions pose serious challenges to the measurement and valuation of intangibles. When such interactions are intense, the valuation of intangibles on a stand-alone basis becomes impossible.

To summarize: intangible assets are nonphysical sources of value (claims to future benefits) generated by innovation (discovery), unique organizational designs, or human resource practices. Intangibles often interact with tangible and financial assets to create corporate value and economic growth.

Intangibles: Why Now?

In a recent hearing of the Senate Committee on Banking, Housing, and Urban Affairs, "Adapting a 1930s Financial Reporting Model to the Twenty-First Century," each of the five testifying experts ascribed the deficiencies of information in corporate financial reports primarily to the growth of intangible assets and the inadequate treatment of these assets by the traditional accounting system.[4] Intangible assets, it was argued, surpass physical assets in most business enterprises, both in value and contribution to growth, yet they are routinely expensed in the financial reports and hence remain absent from corporate balance sheets. This asymmetric treatment of capitalizing (considering as assets) physical and financial investments while expensing intangibles leads to biased and deficient reporting of firms' performance and value.[5] This argument, while perfectly valid, is not new. With a few exceptions, intangible investments have always been expensed in financial reports. What, then, explains the current focus on

3. Bobrow, Cheslow, and Whalen (2000).
4. Hearing held on July 19, 2000. Testifying experts (alphabetically) were Robert Elliott (KPMG), Baruch Lev (New York University), Steve Samek (Arthur Andersen), Peter Wallison (American Enterprise Institute), and Michael Young (Willkie Farr & Gallagher).
5. I elaborate on these biases in chapter 4.

these assets? Why are intangibles more important now than in the 1960s, 1970s, and 1980s?

The market-to-book value (that is, the ratio of the capital market value of companies to their net asset value as stated on their balance sheets) is frequently invoked to motivate the focus on intangibles. As indicated by figure 1-1, the mean market-to-book ratio of the Standard and Poor (S&P) 500 companies (among the largest 500 companies in the United States) has continuously increased since the early 1980s, reaching the value of ~6.0 in March 2001. This suggests that of every six dollars of market value, only one dollar appears on the balance sheet, while the remaining five dollars represent intangible assets.[6] Hence, some argue, the current focus on intangibles is warranted.

This, however, raises various issues. Stock prices are very volatile, and many decreased sharply in 2000–01. Stock prices can therefore not solely support an interest in intangibles. Moreover, a longer historical perspective reveals that in the 1950s and 1960s market-to-book ratios also substantially exceeded 1.[7] So, what is new? Finally, as figure 1-1 indicates, the market-to-book ratio hovered near unity in the late 1970s and early 1980s. Where were intangible assets then? Surely firms possessed some intangibles (patents, brands) before the mid-1980s. Merck had significant pharmaceutical patents, and Coca-Cola had a precious brand name. Are recent intangibles different from previous ones or more valuable now than in the 1970s? What is unique about current intangibles?

The Fundamental Changes Driving Intangibles

Intangibles existed, of course, in the 1970s and much earlier, dating back to the dawn of civilization. Whenever ideas were put to use in households, fields, and workshops, intangibles were created. Breakthrough inventions such as electricity, internal combustion engines, the telephone, and pharmaceutical products have created waves of intangibles. Intangibles (intellectual capital or knowledge assets) are surely not a new phenomenon.

---

6. This, of course, is an oversimplification, since physical assets and some financial assets are presented on the balance sheet at historical cost. Market values will reflect the difference between the current and historical costs of these assets. However, even when this difference is accounted for by computing Q-ratios (market values to replacement cost of assets), this ratio currently surpasses 3 (see Hall [2000]), indicating that the value of intangible assets is approximately three times larger, on average, than the current value of physical assets.

7. Hall (1999).

FIGURE 1-1. Average Price-to-Book Ratio of the S&P 500 Companies, December 1977–March 2001[a]

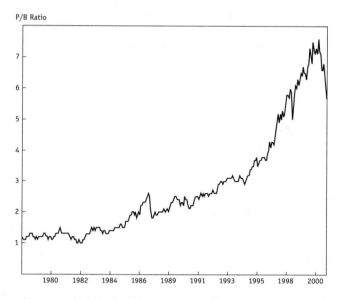

Source: Compustat, Standard and Poor, McGraw Hill.
a. Ratio recorded every month.

What is new, driving the recent (since the mid-1980s) surge in intangibles, is the unique combination of two related economic forces. One is intensified business competition, brought about by the globalization of trade and deregulation in key economic sectors (for example, telecommunications, electricity, transportation, financial services). The second is the advent of information technologies, most recently exemplified by the Internet. These two fundamental developments—one economic and political, the other technological—have dramatically changed the structure of corporations and have catapulted intangibles into the role of the major value driver of businesses in developed economies. The following case of the Ford Motor Company, as told in *Forbes*, demonstrates both the dramatic change in corporate structure and the consequent growth of intangible investments, typical of twenty-first-century businesses.[8]

8. I do not find popular clichés such as *new economy* and *information revolution* particularly useful in the discussion of intangibles, and they are used sparingly if at all in this volume.

Ford Remaking Itself into a Cisco

Ford [Motor Company] announced in April 2000 that it would return $10 billion to shareholders, capital that would not be needed by the new, leaner Ford. It was already in the process of spinning off most of its parts plants into Visteon. Henceforth, it would be just another supplier to Ford. . . . While shedding physical assets, Ford has been investing in intangible assets. In the past few years, it has spent well over $12 billion to acquire prestigious brand names: Jaguar, Aston Martin, Volvo, and Land Rover. None of these marquees brought much in the way of plant and equipment, but plant and equipment isn't what the new business model is about. It's about brands and brand building and consumer relationships. In the "new economy," quite deliberately, Ford has been selling things you can touch and buying what exists only in the consumer's mind. . . . The Internet facilitates these changes in two big ways. In a B2B sense, it facilitates the substitution of an outside supply chain for company-owned manufacturing. In a B2C sense, it facilitates a continuous interaction with consumers that offers myriad ways to enhance the brand value. . . . Decapitalized, brand-owning companies can earn huge returns on their capital and grow faster, unencumbered by factories and masses of manual workers. Those are the things that the stock market rewards with high price/earnings ratios.[9]

Ford is thus restructuring itself, in particular deintegrating vertically (spinning off the manufacturing of automotive parts), shedding physical assets, investing heavily in intangibles, and facilitating these changes by increased reliance on the Internet. The emergence of intangibles (mainly brands, in Ford's case) as the major driver of corporate value at Ford is thus the direct result of the two forces mentioned above: competition-induced corporate restructuring facilitated by emerging information technology.[10]

9. *Forbes*, July 17, 2000, pp. 30–34. (B2B means business to business; B2C means business to consumer.)

10. Movement up the value chain, such as Ford's outsourcing and spinning off car components, pushes suppliers down the value chain: "Lear Corp. doesn't make Internet switching gear in Palo Alto, Calif. Instead, the Southfield, Mich., company makes seats, electrical systems and other interior parts for the cars and trucks that New Economy millionaires rush out to buy with their stock gains—and Lear gets precious little respect from Wall Street. . . . Despite growth profiles and profits that put many Internet companies to shame, Lear seems to have a permanent lease in the Dow's Doghouse." *Wall Street Journal*, July 21, 2000, p. B4.

Ford is not an aberration. Driven by severe competitive pressures (globalization), rapid product and service innovation, and the deregulation of key industries (telecommunications, financial services, and electrical utilities), companies in practically every economic sector started in the early to mid-1980s to restructure themselves in a fundamental and far-reaching manner. Vertically integrated industrial-era companies, intensive in physical assets, were primarily designed to exploit economies of scale.[11] However, these production-centered economies were sooner or later exhausted and could no longer be counted on to provide a sustained competitive advantage in the new environment: "Traditional economies of scale based on manufacturing have generally been exhausted at scales well below total market dominance, at least in the large U.S. market. In other words, positive feedback based on supply-side economies of scale ran into natural limits, at which point negative feedback took over. These limits often arose out of the difficulties of managing enormous organizations."[12]

Intangibles are not a new phenomenon. From the dawn of civilization, whenever ideas were put to use in households, fields, and workshops, intangibles were created. Breakthrough inventions such as electricity, the internal combustion engine, the telephone, and pharmaceuticals have created waves of intangibles.

Once economies of scale in production have been essentially exhausted, production activities, intensive in physical assets, became commoditized and failed to provide a sustained competitive advantage and growth. Companies responded to this commoditization of manufac-

---

11. "It [the industrial-era corporation] was asset-intensive, because the first companies in each sector that could exploit the economies of scale and scope gained a formidable advantage vis-à-vis new entrants. At the same time, it was very highly vertically integrated, because the need to ensure the right level of throughput, at a time when the market for intermediate goods was just developing, forced companies to take direct control of their suppliers and distribution systems." Zingales (2000, p. 28). See also Chandler (1977, 1990).

12. Shapiro and Varian (1999, p. 179).

turing in two ways: by deverticalizing themselves, namely outsourcing activities (for example, Ford's parts production) that do not confer significant competitive advantages; and by strengthening the emphasis on innovation as the major source of sustained competitive advantage. These two fundamental changes in the structure and strategic focus of business enterprises gave rise to the ascendance of intangibles.[13]

In the twenty-first-century corporation the vertical integration of industrial-era companies is increasingly substituted by a web of close collaborations and alliances with suppliers, customers, and employees, all facilitated by information technology, with special attention given to the Internet.

Intangible Linkages and Human Resources

While less vertically integrated than its predecessors, the twenty-first-century corporation is much more connected than the industrial-era enterprise. The vertical integration of industrial-era companies is increasingly substituted by a web of close collaborations and alliances with suppliers, customers, and employees, all facilitated by information technology, with special attention given to the Internet. Traditional economies of scale are complemented and sometimes substituted by economies of network, where the economic gains are primarily derived from relationships with suppliers, customers, and sometimes even competitors (for example, the Ford and General Motors plan to launch a joint Internet-based supplies exchange).

Whereas the linkages among parties (or corporate divisions) in the

---

13. "Physical assets, which used to be the major source of rents, have become less unique and are not commanding large rents anymore. Improvements in capital markets, which have made it easier to finance expensive assets, have certainly contributed to this change, as has the drop in communication costs, which reduced the importance of expensive distribution channels, which favors the access to the market of newly formed companies. Increased competition at the worldwide level has increased the demand for process innovation and quality improvement, which can only be generated by talented employees. Thus, the quest for more innovation increases the importance of human capital." Zingales (2000, p. 29).

industrial-era, vertically integrated companies were mostly physical (such as conveyor belts connecting auto parts divisions to assemblers and railway networks), the current essential linkages between firms and their suppliers and customers are mostly virtual and reliant upon intangibles: Cisco's web-based system of product installation and maintenance, linking the company to its customers; Merck's hundred research and development (R&D) alliances; and Wal-Mart's computerized supply chain are examples of such intangible linkages. These highly valuable intangibles, often termed *organizational capital*, were not major assets (value drivers) before the 1980s. In the modern corporation, these organizational intangibles are among the most valuable corporate assets.

The twenty-first-century corporation is not only more connected than its industrial-era predecessor, it is also more dependent on its employees. Economic developments have considerably weakened firms' control over human resources. "At the very time human capital has become more important, firms' grip on it weakened for two reasons. First, the easier access to financing has increased employees' outside options [going to work for a start-up company, for example]. Second, the opening up of world trade created the space for many independent suppliers. This generated many alternative employment opportunities, making employees' human capital less specific to their current employer."[14] The increasing rate of employee turnover across many economic sectors testifies to the deteriorating bonds between employers and employees. Obviously, firms that are able to maintain a stable labor force and secure (or appropriate) a significant portion of the value created by employees possess valuable employee-related intangibles.

The enormous loss from employee turnover is demonstrated by the finding that 71 percent of the firms in the Inc. 500 list (a group of young, fast-growing companies) were established by persons who replicated or modified innovations developed within their former employers.[15] This suggests the magnitude of the loss from failure to retain key employees and to secure the value created by them. Specific training programs, compensation practices (such as substantial stock-based compensation awarded deep down the corporate hierarchy), and innovative arrangements (such as the establishment of entrepreneurial centers within corporations) are effective in stabilizing the work force. Like organiza-

14. Zingales (2000, pp. 29–30).
15. Bhide (2000).

tional capital, such employee-related intangibles were not prominent in industrial-era enterprises, which exerted significant control over their employees. Human resource intangibles are now pronounced in successful corporations.

The Urgency to Innovate

Innovation has always been an important activity of individuals (Thomas Edison, Alexander Graham Bell) and business enterprises. The prospects of abnormal profits or monopoly rents, protected for a certain period by patents or "first-mover advantages," have always provided strong incentives to innovate. The great scientific and industrial inventions of the nineteenth and twentieth centuries—electricity, the internal combustion engine, chemical and pharmaceutical discoveries, new communications and information technologies—attest to the age-long strong incentives to innovate. Clearly, innovation is not unique to the current economic environment.[16]

What is unique to the modern corporation is the urgency to innovate. Given the decreasing economies of scale (efficiency gains) from production discussed above, coupled with the ever increasing competitive pressures, innovation has become a matter of corporate survival. This urgency to innovate is reflected in the sharp increase in the number of professional workers engaged in innovation (creative activities). Table 1-1 indicates that during the first seventy years of the twentieth century the number of creative workers increased by 2.4 million, while during the next thirty years the increase was 5 million. Note also the corresponding increase of creative workers in proportion to all employees, from 3.8 percent in 1980

---

16. Robert Gordon, for example, argues that recent information-related innovations do not measure up to many previous ones: "I have argued that the current information technology revolution does not compare in its quantitative importance for MFP [multifactor productivity—productivity gains generally ascribed to innovation and technological change] with the concurrence of many great inventions in the late nineteenth and early twentieth century that created the modern world as we know it. There are four major clusters of inventions to be compared with the computer, or chip-based IT [information technology] broadly conceived. These are . . . electricity, including both electric light and electric motor . . . the internal combustion engine, which made possible personal autos, motor transport, and air transport . . . petroleum and all the processes that 'rearrange molecules,' including petrochemicals, plastics and pharmaceuticals . . . the complex of entertainment, communication and information innovations that were developed before World War II [telephone, radio, movies, television, recorded music]." Gordon (1998, pp. 33–36).

TABLE 1-1 Professional Creative Workers, 1900–99

Units as indicated

Year	Professional creative workers (millions)	Proportion of all employment (percent)
1999	7.6	5.7
1990	5.6	4.7
1980	3.7	3.8
1970	2.6	3.3
1960	1.6	2.3
1950	1.1	1.9
1900	0.2	0.7

Source: Nakamura (2000, p. 17). 1900–80, *U.S. Census of Population*; 1990 and 1999, U.S. Census Bureau, *U.S. Census Bureau, Employment and Earnings*, January 1991 and January 2000.

to 5.7 percent in 1999. If one expands Leonard Nakamura's definition of creative workers (architects, engineers, mathematicians, computer scientists, urban planners, writers, artists, entertainers, athletes) to include financial sector employees engaged in the development of products and services (derivative and option products, risk management tools), the recent growth in the number of people directly engaged in innovation would be higher still.

Raghuram Rajan and Luigi Zingales provide an example of the "urgency to innovate" in banking.

> While the credit evaluation skills of the loan officer mattered, they were of secondary importance to the funds that the bank placed in her hands to lend. Without the funds, the officer had little value. . . . Competition from [capital] markets and other institutions has meant that the ability to channel funding is no longer the critical asset it once was. As a result, the importance of the loan officer has changed. Rather than simply keeping her hand on the spigot controlling the flow of funds, she has to create new ideas for structured financing for firms that will attract their attention in an increasingly competitive and crowded market. Innovative and customized deals are the source of profit now rather than the old plain-vanilla loan that is now a commodity.[17]

17. Rajan and Zingales (2000, p. 14).

While many nineteenth- and early twentieth-century innovations were made by individuals (electricity, telephone, and television, to name a few) and were subsequently developed by corporations, by the second half of the twentieth century, innovation became a major corporate activity, with massive resources devoted to it (for example, U.S. corporate expenditures on R&D, one of several forms of investment in innovation, reached $145 billion in 1998).[18] Success and leadership, even in traditional industries, can now be secured only by continuous innovation. Enron (electricity and gas production), Wal-Mart (retail), and Corning (previously producing housewares) are prime examples of companies that leverage major innovations to gain leading positions in their industries and sometimes even creating new fields (energy and bandwidth trading, in Enron's case).

Innovations are created primarily by investment in intangibles. When such investments are commercially successful, and are protected by patents or first-mover advantages, they are transformed into tangible assets creating corporate value and growth.

Innovations are created primarily by investment in intangibles. The new products, services, and processes generated by the innovation process (new drugs, automatic teller machines, Internet-based distribution channels) are the outcomes of investment in such areas as R&D, acquired technology, employee training, and customer acquisition costs. When such investments are commercially successful, and are protected by patents or first-mover advantages, they are transformed into tangible assets creating corporate value and growth.[19]

18. The emergence of innovation as a major economic activity is also reflected in the development of growth theory in the economic literature. Early models, such as Solow (1956), considered innovation, or technological change, as exogenous—outside the scope of the economic system (manna from heaven). Recent growth models, in contrast, consider innovation as endogenous—an economic activity on par with the employment of capital and labor; on endogenous growth models, see Romer (1998, 1990). The data on corporate R&D in 1998 are derived from NSF (1998).

19. Nakamura (2000, pp. 19–20) writes: "Schumpeter . . . argued that what is most important about a capitalist market system is precisely that it rewards change by allowing those who create new products and processes to capture some of the benefits of their creations in the form of short-term monopoly profits. . . . These monopoly profits provide entrepreneurs with the means to fund creative activities . . . [and] widen and

Summary

Figure 1-2 provides a graphic answer to the question, Why the current interest in intangibles? The intensified competition in practically all business sectors brought about by the globalization of trade, far-reaching deregulation, and technological changes (like the Internet) forces business enterprises to radically change their operating models. Most of these changes revolve around deverticalization (for example, outsourcing) and innovation. Intangibles are the fundamental drivers of both: deverticalization is achieved by a substitution of intangibles (like Internet-based supply chains) for physical assets, and innovation is achieved primarily by investment in intangibles. Hence the recent growth of and focus on intangible assets.

So What? (Who Should Care about Intangibles?)

True, intangible capital is large and fast growing, but so too are the physical and financial (stocks and bonds) investments of the corporate sector. Why should policymakers, managers, and investors be particularly concerned about intangibles? What justifies a wide public discourse on the issue? Books and treaties on intangibles (intellectual capital) often focus on the deficient accounting and reporting of intangible investments in corporate financial statements and argue that these information deficiencies call for certain remedies. Others argue that the inadequate internal information systems dealing with intangibles adversely affect managerial decisions, and they too offer remedies.

Generally missing from these claims concerning information deficiencies and the suggested remedies are two important elements: a thorough examination of the reasons for the information deficiencies and a careful empirical documentation of the adverse private and social consequences or failures due to the presumed deficiencies. Why is it that, despite the growing awareness of the importance of intangible assets, they remain almost universally ignored in accounting and reporting procedures? Obviously, any useful prescriptions concerning intangibles-related information require a thorough understanding of the impediments to change.

---

deepen their sales networks so that new products are quickly made known to a large number of customers. . . . Thus, while Adam Smith saw monopoly profits as an indication of economic inefficiency, Joseph Schumpeter saw them as evidence of valuable entrepreneurial activity in a healthy, dynamic economy."

FIGURE 1-2. **The Ascendancy of Intangibles**

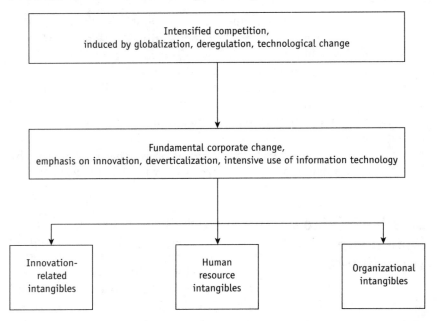

Shortcomings of a specific information system, in this case accounting for intangibles in internal and external corporate reports, will not result in adverse consequences if decisionmakers (managers, investors) can obtain the required information from other sources. Investors may, for example, obtain information about intangibles through meetings or conference calls with corporate officers or from research reports issued by analysts.[20] Managers too may supplement the deficient internal accounting system with specific information on intangibles (like patents per R&D or employee retention indicators). Accordingly, convincing prescriptions

---

20. After all, the accounting for physical assets in financial statements is as deficient as the accounting for intangibles. True, physical assets are capitalized (recognized as assets), but they are recorded at historical costs and depreciated by ad hoc, unrealistic schemes (for example, ten-year straight-line depreciation). What economic inferences about value and performance of physical assets can be drawn form their balance sheet values? Essentially none. For the sake of concreteness, consider the relevance to current managerial or investors' decisions of the cost of commercial property constructed in New York ten years ago—or of mainframe computers acquired five years ago.

for change in the management and measurement of intangibles should be based on documented deficiencies, or harmful consequences, rather than on ad hoc arguments about information shortcomings.

These two themes—a fundamental understanding of the attributes and the sociopolitical context of intangibles and an empirical documentation of adverse consequences related to intangibles—are explored in chapters 2, 3, and 4. The former outlines the economics of intangibles, while the latter two elaborate on the managerial and capital market impacts of the recent prominence of intangibles in firms' production functions, as well as on documented harms. This analysis clarifies the relevance of intangibles to wide constituencies, with the following groups having primary interest in intangibles:

—*Corporate managers and their shareholders.* Evidence indicates that intangible investments are associated with excessive cost of capital (lemons' discount, in the economic parlance), beyond what is called for by the higher-than-average risk of these investments. The excessive cost of capital, in turn, hinders investment and growth. Managers and investors should, therefore, be interested in mechanisms aimed at alleviating the excess cost of capital.

—*Investors and capital market regulators.* Research documents the existence of above-average information asymmetry (differences in information about firms' fundamentals between corporate insiders and outsiders) in intangibles-intensive companies. Economic theory suggests that large and persistent information asymmetries between parties to a contract or a social arrangement lead to undesirable consequences, such as systematic losses to the less informed parties and thin volume of trade. Investors and policymakers should, therefore, be interested in systematically decreasing the intangibles-related information asymmetries.

—*Accounting standard setters, corporate boards.* Empirical evidence indicates that the deficient accounting for intangibles facilitates the release of biased and even fraudulent financial reports. This should obviously be of concern to regulators of financial information (the Securities and Exchange Commission, the Financial Accounting Standards Board) and to corporate board members who rely heavily on accounting-based information to monitor managerial activities.

—*Policymakers.* The information from corporate financial statements is a major input into the national accounts and policy deliberations. The various intangibles-related deficiencies in financial information adversely affect public policymaking in key areas, such as the assessment of fiscal policy (for example, R&D tax incentives) supporting innovation, optimal protection of intellectual property (the scope of patents, for example), and the desirability of industrial policy.

Thus a thorough examination of the attributes of intangibles (the economics of intangibles), as well as the evidence on specific harmful consequences related to intangibles, points at wide constituencies that should be concerned about the ensuing consequences.

Synopsis The recent prominence of intangible assets is the result of the confluence of two major forces: substantive changes in the structure of business enterprises and far-reaching information technology and scientific innovations.

A productive discourse on intangibles should be based on
—analysis of the economics of intangibles
—an understanding of the incentives and motives of the major players
—documentation of the economic consequences of the rise of intangibles

Intangibles are inherently different from physical and financial assets. Managerial and regulatory systems are slow to adapt to these differences, resulting in widespread adverse private and social consequences that should be of concern to managers, investors, and policymakers. A productive discourse on intangibles should be based on a thorough analysis of the economics of intangibles, an understanding of the incentives and motives (particularly aversion to change) of the major players (executives, financial analysts, accountants), and a careful, empirical documentation of the economic consequences of the rise of intangibles.

CHAPTER TWO

The Economics of Intangibles

The extensive and fast-growing literature on intangibles (intellectual capital) generally extols the potential of these assets to create value and generate growth. Scalability, network effects, and increasing returns are the major themes (some would say buzzwords) of these writings. Often overlooked is the fact that intangibles, like physical and financial assets, are subject to the fundamental economic laws of balancing benefits and costs. The benefits from scalability, network effects, and other virtues of intangibles come at a price—sometimes a steep one. To enhance the scalability of a software program, for example, it is often necessary to relinquish some control over it (for example, open source systems).

The fundamental cost-benefit tension underlies the economics of intangibles, as it does the economics of other forms of capital. A thorough understanding of the managerial, valuation, and policy issues related to intangibles, therefore, requires a careful analysis of this tension. Below I outline the essentials of the economics of intangibles, opening with a discussion of the two major drivers of benefits from intangibles—nonrivalry (nonscarcity) and network effects—and continuing with the discussion of the three major cost drivers (value detractors), namely, partial excludability, inherent risk, and nontradability. This unified cost-benefit approach to the analysis of intangibles is my definition of the economics of intangible capital.

> *Intangibles, like physical and financial assets, are subject to the fundamental laws of balancing benefits and costs.*

Nonrivalry (Nonscarcity), Scalability

Physical, human, and financial assets are rival assets in the sense that alternative uses compete for the services of these assets. In particular, a specific deployment of rival assets precludes them from simultaneously being used elsewhere. Such rivalry leads to positive opportunity costs for rival assets, where the cost is the opportunity forgone, namely the benefit from deploying the asset in the next-best alternative. Thus, for example, when United Airlines assigns a Boeing 747 plane to the San Francisco–London route, that airplane cannot be used at the same time on the San Francisco–Tokyo route. Likewise with the airplane's crew and the capital used to finance its acquisition. Physical, human, and financial assets are thus rival or scarce assets, in which the scarcity is reflected by the cost of using the assets (the opportunity forgone).

In contrast, intangible assets are, in general, nonrival; they can be deployed at the same time in multiple uses, where a given deployment does not detract from the usefulness of the asset in other deployments. Accordingly, many intangible inputs have zero or negligible opportunity costs beyond the original investment. Thus while United's airplanes and crew can be used during a given time period on one route only, its reservation system (a knowledge-intensive asset) and its frequent flyer program (organizational capital) can serve, at the same time, a potentially unlimited number of customers. Stated differently, nothing is given up (no opportunity forgone) when the reservation system fulfills a customer's order. Once an airline reservation system has been developed, its usefulness is limited only by the potential size of the market—and of course by competitors' actions—but not by its own use.[1]

Physical, human, and financial assets are rival or scarce assets. In contrast, intangible assets are, in general, nonrival; they can be deployed at the same time in multiple uses. Herein lies their scalability.

A major contributor to the nonrivalry of intangibles is the fact that these assets are generally characterized by large fixed (sunk) cost and neg-

---

1. Romer (1994, 1998) elaborates on the nonrival, or nonscarcity, attribute of intangibles (*software*, in his terminology), particularly in the context of economic growth theory.

ligible marginal (incremental) cost. The development of a drug or a software program generally requires heavy initial investment, while the cost of producing the pills or software diskettes is negligible.[2] Many such intangible investments are not subject to the diminishing returns characteristic of physical assets. For example, doubling the volume of production generally requires heavy investment in plant and machinery, but quadrupling the volume of drugs sold does not require any change in the underlying patents or research and development (R&D).

Intangibles are often characterized by increasing returns to scale. The usefulness of the ideas, knowledge, and research embedded in a new drug or a computer operating system is not limited by the diminishing returns to scale typical of physical assets.

The nonrivalry (or nonscarcity) attribute of intangibles—the ability to use such assets in simultaneous and repetitive applications without diminishing their usefulness—is a major value driver at the business enterprise level as well as at the national level. Whereas physical and financial assets can be leveraged only to a limited degree by exploiting economies of scale or scope in production (a plant can be used for at most three shifts a day), the leveraging of intangibles to generate benefits—the scalability of these assets—is generally limited only by the size of the market.[3] The usefulness of the ideas, knowledge, and research embedded in a new drug or a computer operating system is not limited by the diminishing returns to scale typical of physical assets (as production expands from two to three shifts, returns decrease due, for example, to the wage premium paid for the third shift and to employee fatigue). In fact, intangibles are often characterized by increasing returns to scale. An investment in the development of a drug or a financial instrument (a risk-hedging mechanism,

2. *Sunk cost* means that if the product fails the market test, the initial investment has no alternative use.
3. Good management can, of course, extract considerable efficiency gains from physical assets, too. *Economist* (November 13, 1999, p. 72) describes the experience of Ryanair minimizing service cost and turnaround time of airplanes by using secondary airports, thereby gaining three hours from six turnarounds and letting each aircraft make two more flights a day than otherwise possible. Such gains, though significant, ultimately reach decreasing returns.

for example) is often leveraged in the development of successor drugs and financial instruments. Information is cumulative, goes the saying.

The case of Sabre, American Airlines' reservation and information system, illustrates the unique value creation potential of intangibles in contrast to that of tangible assets.[4] On October 11, 1996, AMR Corporation, the parent company of American Airlines, sold (an equity carve out) 18 percent of its Sabre subsidiary in an initial public offering that valued Sabre at $3.3 billion. On the previous day, AMR had a total market value (including Sabre) of about $6.5 billion. Thus a reservation system generating income from travel agents and other users of its services constituted half of the market value of AMR, equaling the value of the world's second largest airline, owning 650 airplanes (in 1996) and other physical and financial assets, including valuable landing rights. A $40 million R&D investment in Sabre during the 1960s and 1970s mushroomed into a market value of $3.3 billion in the mid-1990s. By October 30, 1999, Sabre's share in the total market value of AMR increased to 60 percent, demonstrating the value creation potential (scalability) of intangibles relative to that of tangibles.[5]

Intangible capital takes various forms. It can be protected by legal rights (often termed *intellectual property*), such as patents and trademarks, or it can be in an unprotected, know-how state. It can be embedded in durable products such as software operating machine tools, or it can stand alone—for example, as brands. Intangible capital is increasingly present in the form of organizational assets—the unique organizational and managerial designs of business enterprises. Here, too, the ability to leverage organizational capital to achieve efficiencies and create value far exceeds the value creation ability of physical assets. Consider the case of Cisco Systems, as told by the *Economist*.

> The first bottleneck [to fast growth] was in after-sales support. The equipment that Cisco sells, however good, does not just run first time out of the box. Networks have to be carefully configured, and each mix of kit ordered is highly customized. Customers expected continuous support, yet highly trained engineers

4. This case was prepared in 1998 by Bruce Weber, Baruch College, City University of New York.
5. In December 1999, AMR announced its intention to distribute to shareholders its 83 percent ownership interest in Sabre, thereby transforming Sabre to a 100 percent publicly traded company.

who could deal with the full range of technical problems were hard to find. Besides, they were being submerged by the daily flood of relatively trivial queries.

The answer turned out to be the Web. Cisco decided to put as much of its support as possible online so that customers would be able to resolve most workaday problems on their own, leaving the engineers free to do the heavy lifting. It was an almost instant success, becoming in Mrs. Bostrom's [head of Cisco's Internet Solutions Group] words, a "self-inflating balloon of knowledge." Cisco's customers did not just go to the website to get information, they started using it to share their own experiences with both Cisco itself and other customers.[6]

Here, then, is a case in which a scarce, rival input (Cisco's engineers and maintenance personnel) was replaced to a large extent by a nonrival intangible asset (online software and instruction programs), which was then leveraged to a balloon of knowledge and fortune, estimated by Cisco's chief financial officer to save $1.5 billion over three years (an amount close to Cisco's entire 1998 net income).

The benefits of intangibles (knowledge) often exhibit "increasing returns to scale," as Gene Grossman and Elhanan Helpman note. "Knowledge is cumulative, with each idea building on the last, whereas machines deteriorate and must be replaced. In that sense, every knowledge-oriented dollar makes a productivity contribution on the margin, while perhaps three-quarters of private investment in machinery and equipment is simply to replace depreciation."[7] Thus investment in drug or software development, even if failing the market test, often guides and benefits future drug or software development, which is yet another scalability aspect of intangibles.

The scalability of intangibles, emanating from their properties of nonrivalry and increasing returns, is reflected in, among other things, the market dominance of many intangibles-intensive enterprises. At the end of 1999 Intel Corporation had a 77 percent market share of personal computer microprocessors, Cisco Systems had 73 percent of the router market, while 78 percent of Internet users accessed it through America Online, and eBay conducted ~70 percent of online auctions.[8] Such market domi-

6. *Economist*, June 26, 1999, p. 12 of survey.
7. Grossman and Helpman (1994, p. 31).
8. *Forbes*, November 29, 1999, p. 54.

nance is unheard of in traditional, capital asset–intensive sectors, where even the most efficient and well-managed enterprises (like Exxon, General Electric in appliances, or Ford) have market shares of less than 25 percent.

In sum, the nonrivalry attribute of intangibles—the fact that a specific deployment of an intangible asset does not detract from its concurrent usefulness in other deployments (the use of Amazon.com's website by customer A does not preclude customer B from using it at the same time)—is a major value driver of intangible assets. This value creation potential, often referred to as the scalability of intangibles, is limited only by the size of the market. In contrast, the rivalry of physical assets—the preclusion of these assets from multiple, concurrent uses—significantly restricts their scalability. The increasing returns that characterize some intangibles further enhance their scalability.

Network Effects

The economics of networks can be succinctly summarized: One's benefit from being part of a network increases with the number of other persons or enterprises connected to it. In networks, bigger is better.[9] Networks can be physical, like landline telephone and railroad networks, or virtual, like Windows 2000 or the VHS videocassette networks of users. The benefits from a network increase with its size, primarily because there are more people with whom to interact or conduct business. Thus the benefits from a cellular phone system whose reach is limited to the Manhattan borough are substantially inferior to the GSM cellular system that can reach any place in Europe. Furthermore, the larger the size of the network, the greater the benefits derived from the development of applications (software programs, compact disks, videocassettes). The payback from Java, for example, is still restricted because some application writers are not convinced that Java will become a sufficiently universal system. Increased network size also enhances the rate of learning and adoption of new technologies, further enhancing the benefits (network externalities) in network markets.[10]

The fact that benefits in network markets increase with the size of the network often creates positive feedback, in which success begets success. A

9. See Shapiro and Varian (1999, chap. 7) for an illuminating discussion of network effects.
10. See Goolsbee and Klenow (1998) for the positive network effects on the adoption of home computers (people are more likely to buy their first home computer in areas where a high fraction of households already own computers).

technology that gains an initial, even small, lead may quickly expand and dominate the market, because users, with their eyes on the future, select technologies they expect to prevail. Users' expectations of success are crucial in network markets, enhancing ever more the positive feedback effect.[11]

The Sabre case discussed in the previous section demonstrates the potency of network effects versus traditional economies of scale characteristic of physical assets. American Airlines obviously attempts to take advantage of every economy of scale opportunity in its airline operations, yet its market share is relatively stable, approximately 16–17 percent.[12] Sabre, on the other hand, exploiting network effects, had a 40–50 percent market share in the North American market in 1998.[13] The large market share of Sabre is largely due to the network effect. When it became travel agents' preferred reservation system, airlines, hotels, car rental companies, and other suppliers of travel-related services joined the Sabre network.

> *A technology that gains an initial, even small, lead may quickly expand and dominate the market, because users select technologies they expect to prevail.*

Large networks are facilitated by standards.[14] Compatibility with an accepted standard is key to success in network markets.[15] Classic standards are the VHS system for videotapes, the three-inch standard for computer disks, and the Dow Jones industrial average for stock market data. "Standards expand network externalities, reduce [consumer] uncertainty, and reduce consumer lock-in. Standards also shift competition from a winner-take-all battle to a more conventional struggle for market share, from the present to the future, from features to prices, and from systems to components."[16]

11. See Economides (1996) for a survey of network effects.
12. From testimony on the state of competition in the airline industry before the Committee on the Judiciary, House of Representatives, May 19, 1998.
13. From sabre.com, investor relations.
14. See Shapiro and Varian (1999, pp. 208–23) for fascinating case histories of the evolution of standards in railroad gauges, the alternating current (AC) system of electrical power, color television, and high-definition television.
15. Assuredly, a certain degree of standardization is desirable for most products, not just intangibles. For example, a standard height for car bumpers will help reduce damage in minor collisions.
16. Shapiro and Varian (1999, p. 258).

Network effects are prevalent in computer, software, telecommunications, and consumer electronics markets. Similar, but informationally induced, network effects exist in pharmaceutical markets, when "the use of a drug by others [doctors] influences one's perceptions about its efficiency, safety, and 'acceptability,' and thus affects its valuation and rate of adoption."[17] Thus demand for a pharmaceutical product by patients and physicians, like demand for a software program or a computer operating system, depends in part on the number of other patients using the drug, thereby creating a network effect.

Network markets are sometimes characterized by "tipping," in which even a small real or perceived advantage of a product or system can lead to a very large future advantage if the product or system becomes the standard. It is often argued that standards or dominant positions, once established, are difficult to change even with superior technology, since consumers are locked into the standard.[18] The possibility of tipping generally leads to intense competition at the early stages of market evolution, as firms struggle to win a dominant position by such means as moving first, using penetration pricing (low or zero prices) to quickly gain customers (for example, AOL's early strategy of offering free subscriptions), or merging with providers of complementary products (AOL's acquisition of Netscape).[19] The winner-take-all nature of network markets increases the uncertainty facing producers: The fierce competition during 1999–2000 in e-commerce to gain market share and dominant position manifested the characteristics of network markets. In such markets, it is sometimes argued, the best product does not always become consumers' preference. Being locked into an inferior product and reluctant to sustain the cost of switching to an improved one, consumers may stay with the inferior product.[20]

17. Berndt, Pindyck, and Azoulay (1999, pp. 1–2).

18. See, for example, Farrell and Shapiro (1988); Katz and Shapiro (1986).

19. Nevertheless, the number of first-mover success stories is almost matched by the number of first-mover disasters. The $5 billion Iridium project, a pioneer of satellite service, is now in bankruptcy. Similarly, the Newton, Apple's pioneering entrant in the hand-held computer market, is now defunct.

20. The generality of the positive feedback (path dependence) and the lock-in phenomena is contested by Liebowitz and Margolis (1999). Based on careful research, the authors argue that even the classic lock in—the QWERTY keyboard arrangement of typewriters and computers, where an allegedly inferior arrangement survives because of lock in—is in fact unsubstantiated. There is no evidence, according to the authors, that competitor systems were more efficient than QWERTY. They argue that lock-in cases in which inferior technologies survive are rare and perhaps nonexistent.

The essence of network effects and positive feedback is demonstrated by the Nintendo example:

> When Nintendo entered the U.S. market for home video games in 1985, the market was considered saturated, and Atari, the dominant firm in the previous generation, had shown little interest in rejuvenating the market. Yet by Christmas 1986, the Nintendo Entertainment System (NES) was the hottest toy on the market. The very popularity of the NES fueled more demand and enticed more game developers to write games to the Nintendo system, making the system yet more attractive. Nintendo managed the most difficult of high-tech tricks: to hop on the positive-feedback curve while retaining strong control over its technology. Every independent game developer paid royalties to Nintendo. They even promised not to make their games available on rival systems for two years following their release![21]

What does all this have to do with intangibles? Surely, network effects are present in tangibles-intensive industries too. Transportation networks (railroads, trucking, airlines, shipping), fixed-line telephones, car rental companies, and automatic tellers are but a few examples of tangible-intensive industries in which network effects can be exploited. In recent years, however, intangibles are at the core of most industries and sectors characterized by network effects. Here is the reason.

Network effects arise primarily in situations in which consumers and users value large networks. As a Lexus owner, I do not care much about the size of the Lexus owners' network. However, as an owner of a fax machine, cellular phone, or high-definition television, I do care a lot about the size of the network. The usefulness to me of a fax machine, a cellular phone, or a computer operating system increases with the number of other users: more people to communicate and transact with, more applications developed for the network. So quite simply network effects exist where there are networks of users. But increasingly, at the core of an important network lies an innovation that was subsequently developed into a product or service, and for which property (ownership) rights are secured by patents, trademarks, or a strong brand.[22] In other words,

---

21. Shapiro and Varian (1999, p. 178).

22. In some cases, first movers can secure temporary monopoly rents even without a patent. AOL is a case in point.

at the core of a network market lies an intangible, characterized by the triplet idea-product-control. Examples of such intangibles propelling network markets are the Nintendo Entertainment System mentioned above, Microsoft's operating systems, Lotus spreadsheets, the wireless application protocol for mobile browsers, Intel's Pentium chips, and Visa credit cards.

Intangibles are present not only at the core but also at the periphery of network markets. I refer to the intangibles formed by alliances and collaborations that contribute to the network effects: "An alliance formed by a group of companies for the express purpose of promoting a specific technology or standard . . . an alliance built like a web around a sponsor, a central actor that collects royalties from others [or makes the technology freely available to alliance members but not to others], preserves proprietary rights over key components of the network and maintains control over the evolution of the technology."[23] An example of an alliance aimed at securing a competitive advantage and reaping network effects is the following:

At the core of a network market lies an intangible, characterized by the triplet idea-product-control.

In September, Palm announced an agreement with Nokia Corporation, the Finnish mobile-phone maker, followed by another licensing deal in October with Japanese consumer electronics giant Sony Corporation. The deal provided Palm's new partners with Palm technology for their phones and other hand-held gadgets.

The two high-profile deals had a domino effect on software developers. Suddenly realizing how serious large consumer electronics firms were about the market for hand-held devices, developers began flocking to Palm in late 1999, asking to create applications for the gadget. "Those licensing deals made it clear to us that Palm was a company with legs," says Jason Devitt, chief executive of Vindigo, a New York firm that has since created a local restaurant-and-event-finder for the Palm. Thousands of other software developers flocked to Palm, including Pocket

23. Shapiro and Varian (1999, pp. 201–02).

Sensei, which makes user interface software, and Actioneer Incorporated, which makes a notes-reminder program.[24]

In sum, network effects are a hallmark of advanced technology, information-based industries. While network markets exist in many physical-intensive industries, they are prominent in technology and science-based sectors due to the fundamental changes in the nature of the corporation—less dependent on vertical integration yet more dependent on networks of employees, suppliers, and customers—and the dramatic decreases in the cost of communication (ease to network). Networks are increasingly characterized by product-related intangibles (unique products and services protected as intellectual property) at the core and alliance-related intangibles at the periphery. Network effects, accordingly, are often predicated on intangibles assets.

If It's So Good . . .? In the preceding two sections, I elaborate on the substantial value creation (scalability) potential of intangible assets that result from the nonrivalry (nonscarcity), the increasing returns, and the positive feedback (network effects) attributes that often characterize these assets. Such value creation potential is the subject of numerous "new economy" books and articles exhorting the wonders of intellectual capital or knowledge assets. A serious discussion of intangibles, however, must tackle the "If it's so good . . ." conundrum:

If intangibles are such potent value creators, what limits the expansion of these assets? Why are not all firms virtual, in the sense of having only, or primarily, intangible capital, with no or only negligible physical capital? To be sure, a growing number of firms are pretty close to virtual. Microsoft's net physical and financial assets in June 2000, for example, constituted less than 10 percent of its market value, and Cisco's physical and financial assets accounted for 5 percent of its market value, rendering these companies almost virtual. However, companies in most economic sectors—chemicals, transportation, and manufacturers of durable goods—are far from virtual. Such companies have significant investments in physical assets (property, plant and equipment, inventories), and many are intangibles-poor. Even more surprising, among the most notable successes in online (Internet) selling are

24. *Wall Street Journal*, August 8, 2000, p. A1.

physical-heavy behemoths like J. C. Penny Company.[25] Why are these companies not substituting intangibles for physical assets? What limits the growth of intangibles?

An important limiting factor is the size of the relevant market and growth potential. As is made clear in the preceding sections, the scalability of intangibles is predicated on the size of the market. Sabre's value and growth potential is substantial because of the huge travel and related services market. Similarly, the potential of some business-to-business Internet exchanges derives from the enormous size of the market they plan to service, such as chemicals, auto parts, and aerospace parts. However, in relatively small or low-growth markets—such as apparel, certain luxury food products (wine and liquors), and home appliances—the usefulness of intangibles is restricted. Thus market size and potential growth limit the expansion of intangible assets.

However, the major limitation on the use and growth of intangibles is managerial diseconomies. Intangible assets are, in general, substantially more difficult to manage and operate than tangible assets. For one, the well-defined property rights of physical and financial assets, relative to the often hazy property rights of intangibles, considerably facilitate the management of the former. American Airlines' executives, for example, do not lose sleep about competitors misappropriating their planes and facilities, but preventing competitors from imitating American's leading reservation system (Sabre) is a major and continuous challenge. The virtual nature of intangibles further complicates their management. For example, identifying unused physical capacity (half-empty airplanes) and taking corrective actions (changing price policy) are straightforward tasks, whereas optimizing network effects from a new technology is a harrowing challenge.[26]

> *Cost accounting is almost exclusively geared to industrial-age physical and labor inputs. Such information systems are wholly inadequate for the management of knowledge-based enterprises.*

---

25. "Penny Wise," *Forbes*, September 4, 2000, p. 72.

26. Consider for example the complicated and risky strategies discussed by Shapiro and Varian (1999, chaps. 7 and 9) for success in network markets.

Contributing to the difficulties of managing intangibles is the fact that managerial information systems (cost accounting), which provide managers with information on costs, revenues, and deviations from budgets, are almost exclusively geared to industrial-age physical and labor inputs. The costs commonly allocated to products, processes, or activities (activity-based costing) are raw materials, labor, and overhead (for example, depreciation). Intangible inputs, such as R&D and customer acquisition costs, are considered period expenses and are not allocated to products and processes. Such tangibles-based managerial information systems are wholly inadequate for the management of knowledge-based enterprises.

Diseconomies resulting from limited capacity to manage intangibles are the major factor restricting the use and growth of these assets. On the other hand, overcoming such diseconomies by improving information systems and the management of intangibles promises enormous rewards. This is the essence of the economics of intangibles—the cost-benefit tension. The following three sections elaborate on the unique attributes of intangibles, which create the challenges of managerial diseconomies.

Partial Excludability and Spillovers

The benefits of tangible and financial assets can be effectively secured (appropriated) by their owners. For example, investors in securities or commercial real estate enjoy to the fullest the benefits (or sustain the losses) of these investments. The well-defined property rights of physical and financial assets enable owners to effectively exclude others from enjoying the benefits of these assets.

In the case of intangible investments, however, nonowners can rarely be precluded from enjoying some of the benefits of the investments. For example, when a company invests in training its employees (on-the-job training or tuition payment for a master's in business administration), other companies (and society at large) will benefit from such investments when the trained employees switch employers. The investing company cannot effectively exclude others from the benefits of such training.[27] Even in the case of patented inventions, for which property rights are legally well defined, there are substantial benefits to nonowners, generally termed

27. Only when the training is perfectly company-specific (for example, training in a production system unique to the company) does the investing company exclude others from the benefits of training. Such company-specific human capital is, of course, rare.

spillovers. Obviously, after patent expiration (twenty years from application in the United States), the invention can be used freely by nonowners, such as in generic drug manufacturing. But even before patent expiration, there are often significant spillovers through imitation (product reengineering) by competitors.

The large number of patent infringement lawsuits attests to the considerable difficulties and the high cost of appropriating the benefits of patents. Indeed, one survey concludes that the effectiveness of patents as a means of appropriating returns on R&D has declined since the early 1980s, despite the strengthening of patent protection.[28] U.S. manufacturing firms, the survey reports, rely more on secrecy and lead time (first to market) to recoup investment than on the protection of the legal patent.[29] Furthermore, significant international spillovers occur primarily because property rights protection is not effectively enforced in many countries, resulting in uninhibited copying and imitation of R&D products (drugs, software). The Amazon.com 1999 10-K report attests to the seriousness of international spillover: "Effective trademark, service mark, copyright, patent and trade secret protection may not be available in every country in which our products and services are made available online. The protection of our intellectual property may require the expenditure of significant financial and managerial resources." Innovation spillovers, and the consequent loss of benefits, thus result from the imperfectly defined and enforced property rights of intangibles.

A striking example of the partial excludability characteristic of intangibles, and the existence of significant spillovers, is provided by the transistor, which was invented at the Bell Laboratories.[30] Bell's investment in R&D during the 1950s and 1960s leading to the transistor's invention is estimated at approximately $160 million.[31] However, Bell's basic patents in transistors were made available to other enterprises for a paltry payment of $25,000 advance royalty because of an antitrust lawsuit against Bell. Licensing income earned by American Telephone and Telegraph (AT&T) on transistors thus amounted to an insignificant fraction of its R&D costs.

---

28. Cohen, Nelson, and Walsh (2000).

29. See Hall and Ham (1999) for a reconciliation of this survey evidence with the significant rise in the rate of patenting in the past decade.

30. Bell Laboratories (Bell Labs) was a subsidiary of AT&T until the spin-off of Lucent Technologies by AT&T in September 1996. Bell Labs is now a subsidiary of Lucent.

31. The data for this example are taken from Freeman and Soete (1997, p. 178).

Obviously, of the huge private and social values created by the transistor for a large number of technology and consumer product companies, AT&T—its inventor—appropriated only a negligible fraction.

True to its tradition, AT&T managed more recently to miss out on the benefits of another major invention: cellular (wireless) phone technology. This technology was developed at Bell Labs in the late 1970s but was deemed by AT&T and its outside consultants commercially useless. Consequently, AT&T abandoned the development of cellular telephony, allowing wireless companies since the mid-1980s a free use of the technology. In 1994 AT&T paid approximately $13 billion to acquire McCaw Cellular, thereby gaining a foothold in the cellular phone market.

Individuals too rarely appropriate the full benefits of their inventions. For example, Philo Farnsworth, the inventor of television technology, died destitute and in obscurity, while David Sarnoff and RCA-NBC reaped much of the television benefits.[32]

Nowhere is the inability to fully secure the benefits of ideas and developments as serious and consequential as when employees endowed with knowledge and experience leave the enterprise to work for competitors or to form their own companies. The business folklore is replete with examples of key employees leaving a company to form a dominant player in the same industry (such as Intel's founders coming from Fairchild). In fact, in excess of 70 percent of the companies in the Inc. 500 list (young, entrepreneurial enterprises) were founded by people who applied, often with some modifications, ideas developed by themselves and others in their previous employment.[33] This enormous spillover is, of course, due to partial excludability—the inability of owners of intangibles to exclude others from enjoying the benefits of intangibles.

The partial excludability (fuzzy property rights) characteristic of most intangible investments creates unique and considerable managerial challenges.[34] Exploiting the potential of a machine to the fullest is a manageable engineering task. Making full use of the tacit knowledge residing in the brains of employees is considerably more challenging. Only when such knowledge is coded (in manuals or artificial intelligence programs) and systematically shared with other employees, is the value of this knowledge

32. For elaboration on the television patents and major actors, see "Who Really Invented Television?" *Technology Review* (September–October, 2000): 96–106.

33. Bhide (2000).

34. See appendix B for case studies of the management of intangibles.

fully exploited to the benefit of the company. Yet setting up such coding and information-sharing systems is a major challenge.[35] Maximizing revenues from patents and know-how that are not used by the enterprise to develop products also presents a challenge and requires taking an inventory of knowledge and finding customers (licensees) for these intangible goods.[36]

Spillovers from intangibles create significant opportunities to learn from others (reverse engineering, for example). But this requires special managerial attention and capacity, termed *adaptive capacity* by economists. This is what knowledge management is all about: appropriating maximal benefits from one's own innovations and exploiting to the fullest the discoveries of others (within legal boundaries).

> *Knowledge management is about appropriating maximal benefits from one's own innovations and exploiting to the fullest the discoveries of others (within legal boundaries).*

The fuzzy property rights of most intangibles exert significant effects on the public disclosure of firms' investments in these assets. The recognition of an asset for financial reporting purposes, namely the accounting rules for recording and reporting asset values in financial statements, requires, among other things, that the enterprise has effective control over these assets.[37] Since a business enterprise does not exercise strict legal control over most intangibles—such as human capital, nonpatented know-how, and customer acquisition costs—accounting regulators are reluctant to qualify such intangibles as assets, leading to the immediate expensing of corporate investment in most intangibles. This indiscriminate bundling of true expenses (those having no future benefits) and intangible investments is a major cause for the deterioration in the usefulness of financial information to managers and investors.[38]

The partial excludability and spillovers characteristics of most intangibles also raise weighty policy issues. Most fundamentally, the gap

35. An information-sharing system of this type—Eureka—was developed by Xerox for its 20,000 technicians. Such formal systems, however, are still rare.
36. Until 1993, when Louis Gerstner became chief executive officer of IBM, patent licensing income was negligible ($30 million in 1990). Gerstner set up a licensing operation estimated to have generated more than $1 billion in revenues in 1999. See Rivette and Kline (2000b, p. 58).
37. For control as related to asset recognition, see FASB (1985a, para. 26).
38. For discussion, see Lev and Zarowin (1999).

between the private return (to investors and owners) in intangibles and the social return enjoyed by society should be neither too large nor too small. Too narrow a gap (for instance, achieved by a perfect and infinite protection for patents) will deny society the full benefits of innovations, whereas too wide a gap (no patent protection) will diminish incentives to innovate.[39] Fiscal policies (tax incentives and direct subsidies to R&D and employee training) and laws establishing and protecting property rights over intangibles (patent law, trademark law) are aimed at optimizing the social-private return differential. However, effective public policy in this area is seriously hampered by lack of sufficient information on intangible investments and their benefits.

Summarizing: intangibles differ from physical and financial assets in the ability of owners to exclude others from enjoying the full benefits of investments. Nonowners can rarely be perfectly excluded from sharing the benefits of intangibles. Such partial excludability or nonexcludability gives rise to spillovers (benefits to nonowners) and absence of control in the strict legal sense over most intangibles. These in turn create unique and significant challenges in managing and reporting on intangible assets, leading to a constant tension between the value creation potential of these assets (scalability) and the difficulties of delivering on the promise through full appropriation of benefits.

The Inherent Risk of Intangibles

Intangibles such as R&D, human capital, and organizational assets are the major inputs into firms' innovation or creativity processes. While our understanding of the origins, drivers, and circumstances conducive to innovation processes is in its infancy, it is widely recognized that innovation is highly risky relative to other corporate activities, such as production, marketing, and finance.[40]

---

39. Nakamura (2000, p. 20) writes: "The more valuable the product, the greater the reward to its creator [private return] should be. And that's exactly what a patent or copyright does. . . . At the same time, it remains true that the temporary monopoly [from a patent] itself deprives society of the full value of the creation, since, to secure their monopoly profits, firms limit supply. Thus, the full value of the creation is realized only when the monopoly ends."

40. In statistics and decision theory, risk is distinguished from uncertainty. Risk is the situation in which the random variable is defined by a reasonably known probability distribution, such as the distribution of the rates of return on stocks. Uncertainty is the case in which even the distribution of the random variable (for example, the payoffs from a radically new drug under development) is unknown. Despite this

Clayton Christensen's in-depth study of the disk drive industry demonstrates the extent of risk associated with innovation.[41] During 1976–93, the development period of the disk drive industry, a total of eighty-three companies entered the U.S. disk drive sector. Thirty-five entrants were diversified companies, such as 3M and Xerox, engaged in other lines of business; while forty-eight companies were independent disk drive startups. Of these forty-eight, only ten (21 percent) generated $100 million in disk drive revenues in at least one year since commencing operations—a modest measure of success in an explosive industry with total revenues of $65 billion during 1976–94. Of the thirty-five established companies, only five (14 percent) reached the $100 million annual revenue target. The low overall success rate of both diversified and pure-play companies (18 percent) in this fast-growing industry attests to the high level of risk associated with the innovation process.

> *A few products or processes are blockbusters, while the rest are duds. Herein lies the inherent riskiness of the innovation-creativity process and of the underlying investment in intangibles.*

Other research corroborates the high risk associated with innovation and intangibles. For example, F. M. Scherer and coworkers examined a heterogeneous sample consisting of German patents, bundles of U.S. patents licensed by seven universities, and the capital market experience of U.S. startup companies.[42] The major conclusion of the study was that "in all cases, a relatively small number of top entities [patents, startups] accounted for the lion's share of total invention or innovation value." For example, the top 10 percent of patents (both in Germany and the United States) accounted for 81–93 percent of total patent value, clearly implying that the majority of patents were essentially worthless, rendering the investment in those patents a loss. Even among the initial public offerings examined by Scherer, which were backed by venture capitalists and had

conceptual distinction, I use—in the Bayesian tradition—the terms *risk* and *uncertainty* interchangeably.

41. Christensen (1997, pp. 128–32).
42. Scherer, Harhoff, and Kukies (1998).

at the time of going public products on the market and a certain level of revenues, the top 10 percent of entities accounted for approximately 60 percent of the total market values of the companies.

These and other empirical studies demonstrate the skewness of the innovation process: a few products or processes are blockbusters, while the rest are duds. Herein lies the inherent riskiness of the innovation-creativity process and of the investment in intangibles underlying this process.

Assuredly, all investments and assets are risky in an uncertain business environment. Yet the riskiness of intangibles is, in general, substantially higher than that of physical and even financial assets. For one, the prospects of a total loss common to many innovative activities, such as a new drug development or an Internet initiative, are very rare for physical or financial assets.[43] Even highly risky physical projects, such as commercial property, rarely end up as a total loss. The huge Canary Wharf project in London, for example, virtually bankrupt in the mid 1990s, revived later and is now considered a commercial success.[44]

A comparative study of the uncertainty associated with R&D and that of property, plant, and equipment confirms the large risk differentials: The earnings volatility (a measure of risk) associated with R&D is, on average, three times larger than the earnings volatility associated with physical investment.[45] Focusing on volatility of earnings is important in reminding the reader that risk is not limited to potential losses. The concept of risk encompasses both positive and negative outcomes—the possibility of either gaining or losing more than one expected. A total loss is just one possible outcome in the range of future realizations.

What drives the high risk of intangibles? The answer becomes clear when the role and location of intangibles in the innovation process, spanning from discovery to commercialization, is considered: "The driving process in these increases in value, these increases in GDP [gross domestic product] and in wealth, is the *discovery* of new and better formulas, recipes, instructions for rearranging things. Of course, it's not just the dis-

---

43. The total loss prospects of intangibles are often driven by the winner-take-all characteristic of many information and high-tech sectors; see Shapiro and Varian (1999, chap. 7). Where winners take all, losers take nothing.

44. For the Canary Wharf saga, see Homer-Dixon (2000, chap. 3).

45. For the study, see Kothari, Laguesse, and Leone (1998). Since R&D is the only major intangible investment that is separately reported by public companies, much of the empirical research on intangibles naturally focuses on R&D.

covery of these formulas and processes that creates value; it's also the carrying out of those instructions, the reworking of that knowledge into physical forms that allow for practical application."[46]

Along the innovation process, from discovery to the commercialization of physical products or services, the level of risk concerning future outcomes is continuously decreasing.

It is important to note that during the innovation process, which typically starts with discovery (new ideas, knowledge) and ends with the commercialization of physical products or services, the level of risk concerning future outcomes (sales, profits) is continuously decreasing. Basic (radical) research, which often takes place at the very beginning of the innovation process, is of the highest risk regarding technological and commercial success.[47] The prospects of applied research, or product innovation, which generally involves the modification of existing technologies, are obviously less uncertain than those of the preceding basic research. Further along the innovation span and descending in the level of risk, one encounters process innovation—efforts to improve the efficiency of the production process—which is less risky than basic research and product innovation, since there is no commercialization risk associated with process R&D, being aimed as it is at internal use. Finally, the production of physical assets (computers, machine tools, consumer electronic products), which together embody the implementation stage in the innovation chain, is obviously less risky than earlier innovation stages, since the technological uncertainty of earlier stages has been resolved.[48] The uncertainty associated with a ready-to-market CT scan-

---

46. Romer (1998, p. 10).

47. The place of basic research in the innovation process is actively debated and clearly varies across industries and technologies. The linear model, in which basic research initiates the R&D process, does not always represent reality.

48. Shapiro and Varian (1999, p. 21) note: "The dominant component of the fixed costs of producing information are *sunk costs*, costs that are not recoverable if production is halted. If you invest in a new office building and you decide you don't need it, you can recover part of your costs by selling the building. But if your film flops, there isn't much of a resale market for its script. If your CD is a dud, it ends up in a pile of remainders at $4.95 or six for $25. Sunk costs generally have to be paid up front, *before* commencing production." These comments apply equally well to many intangibles, such as R&D and investment in brands and human capital.

ner, for example, is substantially lower than that associated with the development efforts that preceded the production of the scanner.[49]

The decreasing level of risk along the innovation process clarifies the reason for the inherently high risk of intangible investments. These investments, such as R&D, employee training, acquired technologies, and research alliances, are most intensive at the early, high-risk stages of the innovation process. Much of the investments at later, lower risk stages of the process are in physical assets, such as machine tools and distribution channels.[50]

The inherently high risk associated with intangibles has important managerial, capital market, and policy consequences (elaborated on in chapters 3–5). Managerial mechanisms for reducing and sharing the risk of intangibles, such as R&D alliances and diversified portfolios of innovative projects, are at the core of managing the innovation process. The risk assessment of intangibles-intensive firms is (or should be) at the core of investment analysis, particularly given the deficient public information about intangibles. Policymakers are often concerned with the prospects of underinvestment in risky yet socially important innovations (like genome codification), given that corporate-based risk aversion may prevent an optimal investment in innovation. Risk, of course, plays a major role in the accounting treatment of intangibles. The widely held belief that the prospects of most intangible investments are highly uncertain and not

---

49. CT is computer-aided tomography. The decreasing risk along the innovation process was quantified by Mansfield and Wagner (1977, pp. 22–32) more than twenty years ago. Examining the outcomes of individual R&D projects in sixteen chemical, pharmaceutical, electronics, and petroleum companies, these authors estimated the following mean probabilities of success (evaluated across companies and projects):
   —Probability of technical success: 0.57
   —Probability of commercialization (selling a product), given technical success: 0.65
   —Probability of financial success (return on investment equal to or higher than the firm's cost of capital), given commercialization: 0.74
As noted by Scherer, Harhoff, and Kukies (1998), these success probabilities are probably overstated, since the projects examined were mostly from large, well-established enterprises. Nevertheless, Mansfield and Wagner's estimates corroborate the general phenomenon of decreasing level of risk (or increasing prospect of success) as products move along the innovation path.

50. Uncertainty is also higher at the firm or project level than at the economy or society level. For example, a specific firm faces the risk that its developed technology will be imitated by competitors. Society will often gain from such imitation (for example, in lower product prices). Bell Labs' development of the transistor, cited above, demonstrates this point.

amenable to reliable valuation (for example, computation of the present value of cash flows) underlies the decision of accounting authorities to immediately expense such investment (R&D, employee training, customer acquisition costs, and so on).

Under proper management, the high risk of intangibles can be leveraged into considerable value.

Summarizing: investment in intangibles is generally intensive at the early (discovery) stages of the innovation process. It is in these early stages that the risk concerning the technological and commercial success of the innovation is highest. Consequently, the level of risk associated with intangibles is, in general, substantially higher than that associated with most physical and financial assets. Risk, however, is not all bad. In fact, as options models indicate, risk (volatility) creates value when the downside loss is constrained. Under proper management, therefore, the higher risk of intangibles can be leveraged into considerable value.

Markets in Intangibles

The absence of organized and competitive markets in intangibles sets these assets apart from most financial and physical assets. This nontradability of intangibles has far-reaching consequences for management and investment: "A piece of equipment is sold and can be resold at a market price. The results of R&D investments are by and large not sold directly . . . the lack of direct measures of R&D output introduces inescapable layers of inexactitude and randomness into our formulation."[51] In the policy domain, nontradability is often invoked to disqualify intangibles from being recognized as assets in corporate financial reports: "It is the same line of reasoning, that a cost can be an asset, that leads some people to suggest that the FASB [Financial Accounting Standards Board] should reconsider FASB Statement No. 2 and allow for recognition of R&D costs as an asset. Note that in none of the cases is the asset [proposed to be] represented on the balance sheet *exchangeable*."[52]

Markets perform numerous vital economic and social functions: They provide producers of goods and services with liquidity and with signals

---

51. Griliches (1995, p. 77).
52. Scheutze (1993, p. 69); emphasis mine. Walter Scheutze was a chief accountant with the Securities and Exchange Commission.

concerning consumers' preferences, in addition to enabling risk sharing and specialization (for example, inventors could specialize in inventing and then sell the invention to developers). Primarily, market prices provide information about values of goods and services that is vital to optimal resource allocation. Consequently, the absence of organized markets in intangibles has serious consequences.[53] For example, the measurement and valuation of intangibles (patents, brands) is restricted by the scarcity of comparables, namely prices of assets in similar transactions. In some peoples' minds, the absence of such comparables disqualifies intangible investments from consideration as assets in both corporate and national accounts. The absence of markets in intangibles also challenges the management of these assets. Illiquidity and restricted risk-sharing opportunities (like the securitization of the firm's R&D operations) increases the risk of intangible investments and restricts their growth. The absence of markets in intangibles, therefore, may create a role for government to improve resource allocation and the transparency of intangible investments.

Markets, however, come in different forms and shapes and are constantly evolving. Many companies sell or license their patents (some even donate patents to universities), trades of brands and trademarks are quite frequent, several top performers (David Bowie, for instance) have securitized their song catalogs, and there have been attempts to issue stocks in R&D entities.[54] Most important, the advent of the Internet ushered in a host of web-based exchanges in intangibles (intellectual property). The tradability of intangibles is obviously a considerably more complex issue than what appears on the surface: that there is no markets in intangibles. Accordingly, the following discussion examines various key aspects and developments related to the marketability of intangibles.

Are Intangibles Inherently Nonmarketable?

The absence of organized markets in intangibles is, according to some economists, a consequence of the inability to write "complete contracts" with respect to the outcomes of intangible investments; that is, the difficulties in specifying in advance the actions of the parties to the contract

53. I emphasize organized markets because, in principle, markets exist whenever trade takes place. Accordingly, when firm A licenses a patent to firm B, a market exists. What distinguishes intangibles from most other assets is the absence of organized, active exchanges with numerous participants and transparent prices (e.g., stock and commodity exchanges).

54. Lev and Wu (1999).

(for example, the seller and the buyer of an incomplete R&D project) and how these outcomes (research findings) will be shared. As David Teece states, "It is inherent in an industry experiencing rapid technological improvement that a new product, incorporating the most advanced technology, cannot be contracted for by detailed specification of the final product. It is precisely the impossibility of specifying final product characteristics in a well-defined way in advance that renders competitive bidding impossible in the industry."[55]

The ability to clearly specify actions and sharing of outcomes between the parties to a trade is an essential prerequisite of active markets. For example, the high-volume market in mortgage-backed securities (bundles of individual mortgages) is mainly due to the clearly defined property rights (ownership) of mortgages (who assumes the default and prepayment risks) and the ability to specify in advance how the benefits—streams of interest and principal payments—are to be shared among investors (some receive the interest, others the principal). In contrast, it is difficult to conceive similar contracts in bundles of corporate R&D projects, given the considerable difficulties (and cost) of specifying outcomes as well as in allocating in advance investors' rights and responsibilities. Suppose, for example, that a specific pharmaceutical research idea developed by Merck is included in an R&D bundle sold to investors. Suppose further that the research project is subcontracted by investors to Merck for development and that the project subsequently fails clinical testing, resulting in terminated development. Nevertheless, the experience and knowledge gained by Merck in the development process of this drug will most probably benefit future developments at Merck or other drug companies. Who then owns these benefits? The investors in the R&D bundle? Or Merck? Clearly, writing a complete contract that specifies all eventualities (*states of the world*, in the economic jargon) and the associated rights and responsibilities of the parties involved would be prohibitively expensive.

The cost structure of many information-related intangibles, which is characterized by large (and often sunk) initial investment and marginal-to-zero production costs, further undermines the operation of a conventional price system for such products. Carl Shapiro and Hal Varian demonstrate this attribute of information-related intangibles with the case of *Encyclopedia Britannica:*

55. Teece (1988, p. 260).

A few years ago a hardback set of the thirty-two volumes of the *Britannica* cost $1,600. . . . In 1992 Microsoft decided to get into the encyclopedia business . . . [creating] a CD [compact disk] with some multimedia bells and whistles and a user friendly front end and sold it to end users for $49.95. . . . *Britannica* started to see its market erode. . . . The company's first move was to offer on-line access to libraries at a subscription rate of $2,000 per year. . . . *Britannica* continued to lose market share. . . . In 1996 the company offered a CD version for $200. . . . *Britannica* now sells a CD for $89.99 that has the same content as the thirty-two volume print version that recently sold for $1,600.[56]

The negligible marginal costs of producing the outcomes of many intangible investments prevent a stable price system and market in such assets.[57] The often fuzzy property rights over intangibles also impede the establishment of markets and organized trade. Questions concerning ownership of the human capital resulting from firms' investment in training, or the distinction between the firms' ownership of a brand and the part that belongs to its founder (for example, Microsoft and Bill Gates), complicate the trade in intangibles. Even with respect to patents, arguably the intangible with the best defined property rights, the proliferation of infringement lawsuits attests to the fuzziness of such rights. Markets cannot, of course, function without clearly defined property rights of parties to a trade.

The impediments to markets in intangibles, as stated above—contracting difficulties, negligible marginal costs, and fuzzy property rights—do not preclude the existence of markets in intangibles. They do, however, indicate that such markets will have to incorporate specific mechanisms and arrangements to alleviate the inherent problems. Indeed, recent web-based exchanges in intellectual property (pl-x.com, for example) provide valuation and insurance services that are not common in financial or physical-asset markets.

What Does History Tell Us?

Records of active U.S. markets in patented technology exist since the passage of the first patent law in 1790. Naomi Lamoreaux and Kenneth

---

56. Shapiro and Varian (1999, pp. 19–20).
57. "But on the whole, particularly in the case of 'general knowledge,' the unimportance of marginal costs compared to average costs of producing new knowledge leads to a nonfunctioning of competitive market mechanisms." Nadiri (1993, p. 16).

Sokoloff, examining trade patterns in patents during the nineteenth and early twentieth centuries, come to the following conclusion:

> We have shown not only that there was a high volume of trade in patented technologies, but also that such commerce and patenting activity were closely associated with each other. Indeed, a broad variety of evidence seems consistent with what theory would suggest, that improvements in the capabilities to trade in technology would stimulate increases in specialization at invention by those with a comparative advantage in that activity, as well as increases in the rate of invention more generally.[58]

Lamoreaux and Sokoloff also document that the rise of intermediaries, such as registered patent agents in the late nineteenth century, facilitated the growth of technology markets. That market, which was characterized by a dichotomy between inventors and developers, changed at the turn of the twentieth century, "with a decrease in the proportion of arm's length transactions and a corresponding increase in the assignments made at issue by patentees who were officers or other principals in the companies specified as assignees."[59] Thus rather than being developed by inventors and sold at arm's length to developers, most innovations since the early twentieth century have been invented and developed within corporations or research centers. The market in inventions is currently of marginal importance. Apparently, there are substantial economies in developing intangibles within corporations relative to external markets.[60]

The huge volume and varied nature of intangibles developed and owned by the corporate sector naturally seeks a trading outlet. Since not all ideas and discoveries can be fully developed and operated internally, attempts are made to sell, license, or outsource patents and know-how. Incentives to sell or license or outsource intangibles have led to an increasing volume of patent licensing, to a large number of mergers and acquisitions where the main asset traded is R&D or technology in the development process, and to a proliferation of alliances and joint ventures aimed at the development and marketing of innovations.[61] There is clearly

58. Lamoreaux and Sokoloff (1999, p. 35).
59. Lamoreaux and Sokoloff (1999, p. 24).
60. Coase (1937).
61. For patent licensing, see Rivette and Kline (2000a); for mergers and acquisitions, see Deng and Lev (1998); for alliances and joint ventures, see Lerner and Tsai (2000). As an example regarding technology acquisitions, on August 25, 1999, Cisco Systems

substantial trade in intangibles, but it lacks the main characteristic of markets: transparency. Details of licensing deals and alliances are generally not made public, and acquired intangibles are usually bundled with other assets. Consequently, while liquidity and risk-sharing prospects of intangibles have considerably improved, the benefits of observable prices in facilitating measurement and valuation still elude intangibles.

Internet-based markets in intangibles (intellectual capital) may provide the missing transparency, along with liquidity and risk sharing.[62] Not surprisingly, the assets traded in these exchanges are mostly patents—again, the intangibles with the most clearly defined property rights. Such exchanges, however, are in their infancy, and the volume of trade is still very low. It is too early to predict whether and when these exchanges will develop into full-fledged markets in intangibles. We have thus gone a long way from the individual inventor market of the nineteenth century to Internet exchanges in intellectual capital.

Summary

Intangibles are inherently difficult to trade. Legal property rights are often hazy, contingent contracts are difficult to draw, and the cost structure of many intangibles (large sunk cost, negligible marginal costs) is not conducive to stable pricing. Accordingly, at present there are no active, organized markets in intangibles. This could soon change with the advent of Internet-based exchanges, but it will require specific enabling mechanisms, such as valuation and insurance schemes. Private trades in intangibles in the form of licensing and alliances proliferate, but they do not provide information essential for the measurement and valuation of intangibles.

Synopsis   The economics of intangibles, like that of other forms of capital, boils down to an analysis of the tension between costs and benefits. In the realm of intangibles, the major benefits are scalability, increasing returns, and network effects (externalities). The costs

---

announced the acquisition of Cerent Corporation, a maker of devices that route telephone calls and Internet traffic on and off fiber-optic lines. Cerent posted a mere $10 million in sales in the six months ending June 1999 and was acquired by Cisco for an astounding price of $6.9 billion. Obviously, Cisco was after Cerent's technology. The extent of the market in technology is demonstrated by the fact that Cerent is the fortieth acquisition of Cisco, itself a young company (established in 1986).

62. For a survey of such exchanges, see "Technology Licensing Exchanges" (2000).

include the usual costs involved in any physical or financial asset-investment (acquisition, maintenance) as well as the costs unique to intangibles (partial excludability, high risk, nontradability). (This economics of intangibles is depicted in figure 2-1.)

Decisions concerning the acquisition, management, valuation, and reporting of intangibles involve a careful consideration of the benefits expected from these assets against the difficulties to fully secure these benefits. The management of intangibles (knowledge) is aimed at maximizing

FIGURE 2-1. The Economics of Intangibles: Value Drivers versus Value Detractors

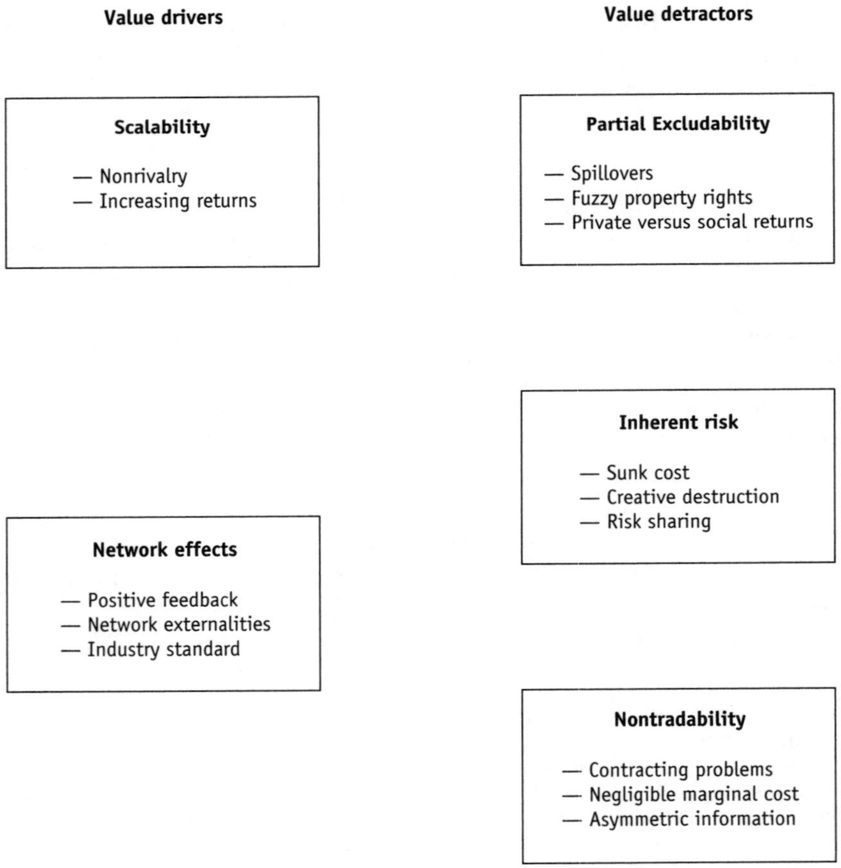

Value drivers

Value detractors

Scalability

— Nonrivalry
— Increasing returns

Partial Excludability

— Spillovers
— Fuzzy property rights
— Private versus social returns

Inherent risk

— Sunk cost
— Creative destruction
— Risk sharing

Network effects

— Positive feedback
— Network externalities
— Industry standard

Nontradability

— Contracting problems
— Negligible marginal cost
— Asymmetric information

the benefits and identifying ways to overcome the difficulties.[63] Patenting, cross-licensing, trademarking, moving first, or establishing an industry standard are ways to appropriate most of the benefits of intangibles. R&D and marketing alliances, trading in futures markets (as in energy or bandwidth), and securitization are means of managing the risk of intangibles. Furthermore, the formulation of appropriate exit strategies, such as licensing, initial public offerings, or sale on an Internet exchange, is aimed at mitigating the nontradability restriction.

The above framework for the economics of intangibles is also useful in analyzing measurement and reporting issues. To qualify as an asset for financial reporting, for example, it has to be shown, first, that the corporation exercises a considerable (though not necessarily complete) degree of control over the asset (namely, it is able to appropriate most of the benefits); second, that the risk concerning commercial success has been considerably reduced (that technological feasibility has been established, for example); and third, that market mechanisms are available to trade the asset or its consequent cash flows. Thus a convincing case for recognizing an intangible as an asset on the balance sheet can be made if it is shown that the firm will appropriate most of the benefits from the asset, that its risk is relatively low (for example, a drug has passed clinical tests), and that opportunities to license the technology exist.

In the following chapters I demonstrate the use of the economics of intangibles framework in analyzing managerial, investment, and policy issues and in advancing recommendations.

---

63. Appendix B provides examples of specific procedures used by companies in the management of intangible (intellectual) capital.

CHAPTER THREE

The Record

C hapter 2 outlines the major economic principles governing intangible investments. To advance knowledge, theoretical principles should be subjected to empirical examination and observation. Accordingly, this chapter is devoted to an analysis of the record of intangible investments, that is, the empirical findings concerning the nature of intangible assets and their impact both on the operations and growth of business enterprises and on investors in capital markets.[1]

Evidence is here presented on the contribution of research and development (R&D) to corporate growth and how it is directly related to the scalability (nonrivalry) and network attributes of intangibles. Evidence on the more recent and fast growing form of intangible assets—organization capital—is examined, and the nascent evidence on the contribution and valuation of human capital is considered.

The Value Created by Intangibles: A Case Study

On average, investments in intangibles clearly create value (that is, yielding a return above the cost of capital). Why else would business enterprises invest heavily and consistently in R&D, employee training, brand creation and maintenance, organizational change, and other forms of

1. The macroeconomic implications of intangibles for national growth and welfare are by and large beyond the scope of this book. For a comprehensive treatment of intangibles (technology) in the context of macroeconomic growth theory, see Aghion and Howitt (1998).

intangible assets?[2] The questions requiring research are subtler ones: What is the magnitude of the value created by intangibles relative to other assets? Are there systematic differences in the contribution to value among various types of intangibles (for example, between the return on basic R&D versus the return on applied R&D)? Which of the firm's attributes (size, diversification) and economic circumstances (such as a booming economy) primarily affect the productivity of intangibles? And how do investors assess intangibles' value, particularly given the deficient public reporting about these assets? To highlight the relevance of research on intangibles, I open with a discussion of a specific research project, namely the productivity of chemical R&D.[3]

The chemical industry was one of the earliest sectors to invest substantial resources in R&D. Results were quick to follow, with chemical R&D in the twentieth century generating an impressive array of pathbreaking scientific discoveries and innovative products in fertilizers, petrochemicals, synthetic materials, and pharmaceutics.[4] Currently, however, chemical companies are only moderate investors in R&D, and the industry is not considered particularly innovative when compared with the likes of computer, biotechnology, and telecommunications companies.[5] It appears that the productivity of chemical R&D has stagnated in recent years. Moreover, there are widespread public concerns about the environmental impacts of some chemical products and the safety of others (like genetically engineered crops). This inimical public and investor opinion motivated the Council for Chemical Research to sponsor a series of studies on the contribution of chemical R&D to business enterprises and to society at large. In the following, I briefly report on one aspect of this effort: the assessment of the rate of return on corporate investment in R&D.[6]

2. In 1999, for example, according to COMPUSTAT, U.S. public companies' expenditures on R&D were 4.8 percent of their total revenues on average.

3. The research on the contribution of R&D in the chemical industry described here was sponsored by the Council for Chemical Research.

4. See Freeman and Soete (1997, chap. 4) for a discussion of the development and contribution of chemical R&D.

5. The mean R&D intensity (R&D-to-sales ratio) of chemical companies in 1999 was 4.7 percent, compared with 12.1 percent for pharmaceutical companies, 11.1 percent for software companies, and 4.8 percent for all companies with R&D expenditures. See Aboody and Lev (2001).

6. Aboody and Lev (2001).

A sample of eighty-three publicly traded chemical companies was used in the analysis, which covered the period 1980–99. The return on (contribution of) R&D to the investing companies was measured by statistically estimating the contribution of one R&D dollar spent in a given year to the company's operating income in that year and the subsequent ten years, controlling for the contribution to income of physical assets

A dollar invested in chemical R&D increases, on average, current and future operating income by two dollars.

(property, plant, and equipment) and of brands (advertising). The focus on the contribution of R&D to current and subsequent income derives from the fact that successful R&D projects have sustained, long-term impact on profitability. This analysis yielded the following conclusions:

—A dollar invested in chemical R&D increases, on average, current and future operating income by two dollars.[7] Translated to annual rate of return on investment, the before-tax rate of return on chemical R&D is 27 percent, or ~17 percent after taxes.

—A 17 percent after-tax return indicates a very substantial contribution of chemical R&D to corporate value, given that the weighted average (equity and debt) cost of capital of most chemical companies is 8–10 percent. This annual cost-benefit differential of about 7 percent indicates that R&D is an important value driver for chemical companies (positive economic value added), even considering the above average risk of R&D. Indeed, in stock performance, chemical companies collectively outpaced the Standard and Poor's 500 companies during the 1985–98 period.[8]

—The significant value contribution of chemical R&D is obviously of importance to managers of chemical companies, who are engaged in the allocation of scarce resources to R&D and other corporate activities, as well as to investors in chemical companies and to policymakers, given government support for R&D (such as tax incentives).

—There exist significant economies of scale (size advantages) in chemical R&D: The return to R&D of companies investing considerable

7. Operating income is defined as income before general, financing, and income tax expenses.
8. See Aboody and Lev (2001).

resources in R&D (R&D-intensive companies) is substantially higher than the R&D returns of low investors in R&D. The implications of these findings for corporate acquisitions and diversification (exploiting R&D synergies), as well as R&D alliances, are straightforward.

—In contrast to the abnormal (above-cost-of-capital) return on chemical R&D, the study documents only average return on physical assets (~8 percent) and advertising expenses. Physical assets behave like commodities, earning the cost of capital. Here, too, important implications can be drawn concerning the desirability of additional investment in physical assets—and the benefits from outsourcing manufacturing activities—which decreases reliance on these assets.[9]

—With respect to the capital market valuation of chemical R&D, investors were found to fully appreciate (price) the prospects of R&D. This stands in contrast to what is seen in the faster changing technological areas (telecommunications, computers), where investors appear to systematically underestimate the contribution of R&D in certain types of companies (see chapter 4). This finding about the fair valuation of chemical R&D should alleviate managers' concerns with negative investor reaction to R&D increases.[10]

> Nondisclosure of most expenditures for intangibles is a major impediment to the advancement of knowledge about intangibles in particular and corporate performance in general.

The chemical R&D study demonstrates the breadth of issues of concern to managers, investors, and policymakers that can be addressed by systematic research on the contribution of intangibles. In the next section, I summarize the major findings in the economic, finance, and accounting literature regarding the contribution of R&D to corporate performance and growth. Much of the research in the field of intangibles deals with R&D, which is just one—albeit important—form of intangibles. The reason for the R&D focus of researchers is simple: R&D is the only intangible that is reported separately (a line item) in corporate finan-

---

9. Recall the discussion in chapter 1 about the deverticalization of integrated companies and the general move toward the outsourcing of manufacturing operations.

10. I refer here, of course, only to R&D increases that are economically justified and well explained to capital markets.

cial statements.[11] Expenditures on other forms of intangibles (employee training, information technology, brand creation) are generally aggregated with other expenses in the financial reports. This nondisclosure of most expenditures for intangibles—which constitutes, of course, a different issue from the measurement (expensing versus capitalization) of intangibles and is simpler to solve—is a major impediment to the advancement of knowledge about intangibles in particular and corporate performance in general.[12]

R&D and the Growth of Business Enterprises

The contribution of R&D to the performance and growth of business enterprises can be estimated by relating a performance measure (profits, sales) statistically to R&D expenditures—in the current and previous periods to allow for the delayed effect of R&D on business performance—and by controlling for the effect of other investments (physical assets) on business performance. This statistical approach to empirically address issues concerning intangibles and their private and social impact was frequently used by economists and researchers in related areas. The empirical work started with extensive historical case studies and proceeded to large sample (cross-sectional) analyses of the impact of R&D on firms' productivity and growth. This research effort yielded several important findings:[13]

—R&D expenditures contribute significantly to the productivity (value added) and output of firms, and the estimated rates of return on R&D investment are quite high—as much as 20–35 percent annually—with the estimates varying widely across industries and over time.[14]

—The contribution of basic research (work aimed at developing new science and technology) to corporate productivity and growth is substantially larger than the contribution of other types of R&D, such as product development and process R&D (where the latter is aimed at enhancing the efficiency of production processes).[15] The estimated contribution

11. This is the case in the United States. In many other countries, firms are not required to single out even R&D in their financial reports. See appendix A.
12. For more on this issue, see chapters 4 and 5.
13. For a discussion of these findings and the methodological (statistical) issues involved in analyzing the cost-benefit relationship of R&D, see Griliches (1995).
14. See Hall (1993).
15. See Griliches (1995). Related findings concern the importance of university research to industrial innovation; see Mansfield (1991); Acs, Audretsch, and Feldman (1994).

differential of approximately three to one in favor of basic research is particularly intriguing, given the widespread belief that public companies

The contribution of basic research—aimed at developing new science and technology—to corporate productivity and growth is substantially larger than that of other types of R&D, such as for product development and process.

have been recently curtailing expenditures on basic research, in part as a response to the skepticism of many financial analysts and institutional investors about the commercialization prospects of basic research.[16] Basic research is, of course, more risky than applied R&D (see chapter 2), but it is inconceivable that risk differentials by themselves account for a three-to-one productivity superiority of basic research.

—The contribution of corporate-financed R&D to productivity growth is larger than that of corporate-based—but government-financed—R&D (granted primarily to government contractors). The fact that most contracts with the government are based on cost-plus terms may partially explain this finding. This result should not detract from the significant contribution to the industrial and technological infrastructure of publicly funded research conducted by government agencies and in federal laboratories (such as the contribution by the National Institutes of Health to pharmaceutical and biotech companies) as well as the substantial contribution of university research to technology.[17]

It should be noted that much of the research summarized above was based on survey data and industry aggregates, due to severe limitations in corporate published data. In fact, most of the examined variables and

16. First-hand evidence of adverse analyst attitudes toward basic research can be found in an article by Richard Mahoney, former chairman and chief executive officer of the Monsanto Company. He describes how, over an extended period, Monsanto developed its biotechnology capacity, while analyst "naysayers offered a constant drumbeat of advice: reduce R&D, sell off any asset that wasn't nailed down and use the cash proceeds to buy back shares." *New York Times*, May 31, 1998.

17. See Mansfield (1991). Striking examples of major contributions of government-sponsored R&D to industry are the Internet, funded originally by the Department of Defense as a bomb-resistant communications network and later developed by the National Science Foundation; and the human genome project, which was initiated by the National Institutes of Health.

attributes—such as basic versus applied research and company versus government-sponsored R&D—cannot be directly estimated from information publicly disclosed to investors. Thus an important implication of these and similar findings is to suggest which kinds of currently unavailable information and data would be useful to managers, investors, and policymakers.

Alternative Output Measures: Market Value and Patents

The research presented above relates R&D inputs (intensity, capital) to firms' productivity, sales, or profit growth, in an attempt to estimate the return on corporate investment in innovation as well as to examine macroeconomic issues, such as the productivity decline in the United States in the 1970s and early 1980s.[18] This methodological approach encounters various problems; in particular the time lag between the investment in R&D and the realization of benefits (such as sales) is often long (particularly for basic research) and generally unknown, increasing the uncertainty about the estimated R&D contribution. Furthermore, biases and distortions in reported profits—arising from firms' attempts to "manage" investors' perceptions (see chapter 4)—might cloud the intrinsic relationship between R&D and its subsequent benefits.

These measurement difficulties have prompted a search for alternative and more reliable indicators of R&D output than reported sales and profitability measures. Two output indicators have received considerable attention: capital market values of corporations and patents.[19] Believers in efficient capital markets argue that stock prices and returns provide reliable signals of enterprise value and performance; hence R&D contribution can be evaluated using market values. Patents, and particularly citations in patent applications, provide an additional indication of the value of R&D and firms' technology.

Concerning capital market studies, the research persuasively indicates that investors regard R&D as a significant value-increasing activity. For example, a number of event studies register a significantly positive investor

18. R&D intensity is the ratio of R&D expenditures to sales; R&D capital, which is not reported on corporate balance sheets, is generally measured by economists using estimates of annual R&D amortization rates, which have a range of 10–15 percent; see Hall (1993).
19. The research using patent counts and citations as R&D output measures is voluminous; it is summarized in Griliches (1990); Hall, Jaffe, and Trajtenberg (2000).

reaction (stock price increases) to corporate announcements of new R&D initiatives, particularly of firms operating in high-technology sectors and using cutting edge technology.[20] When information is available, investors distinguish among different stages of the R&D process—such as program initiation and ultimate commercialization—most significantly rewarding mature R&D projects that are close to commercialization.[21] Furthermore, econometric studies that relate corporate market values or market-to-book ratios to R&D intensities consistently yield positive and statistically significant association estimates.[22] Further probing of the data suggests that investors value an R&D dollar spent by large firms more highly than that spent by small firms, probably a reflection of economies of scale in R&D.[23] For example, large companies may benefit from lessons of failed R&D projects as they pursue the development of other projects.

The evidence thus indicates unequivocally that investors view R&D expenditures as on average enhancing the value of firms and that they also demonstrate some ability to differentiate the contribution of R&D across industries, firm sizes, and stages of R&D maturity. Investors' ability to fine-tune R&D valuations is obviously hampered by the absence of detailed information on these attributes in corporate financial reports.

Data on R&D expenditures available in financial statements are crude indicators of R&D contribution and value creation: there is productive R&D and wasteful R&D (Motorola and partners' $5 billion investment in the Iridium satellite communications project, currently in bankruptcy, is an example of the latter). The R&D productivity estimates discussed above obviously averaged the good and the bad, missing considerable information in the process. In an attempt to improve the estimation of R&D contribution, researchers experimented with patents, which can be

20. See, for example, Chan, Kesinger, and Martin (1992). It was widely believed in the 1980s and early 1990s that, prodded by investors' "obsession" with quarterly earnings, U.S. managers routinely sacrificed the long-term growth of their firms by curtailing investments such as R&D, yielding long payoffs but immediate hits to earnings. The evidence of investors' positive reaction to R&D increases, despite the negative effect of such increases on near-term earnings (due to the immediate expensing of R&D), largely dispels the allegation of investor myopia, at least with respect to R&D.

21. Pinches, Narayanan, and Kelm (1996). I return to this important finding in the proposed information system (see chapter 5).

22. Ben Zion (1978); Hirschey and Weygandt (1985); Bublitz and Ettredge (1989).

23. Chauvin and Hirschey (1993). Recall the large difference in return on R&D of large and small companies in the chemical industry study reviewed above.

considered an intermediate output measure of R&D (the final output measure is, of course, the benefit—sales, cost savings—generated by the R&D expenditure). Patents are only partial indicators of R&D output, since not every R&D project is patented. Yet patent research provides interesting insights.

The Findings of Patents Research

Various attributes of patents, such as the number of patents registered by a company (patent counts), patent renewal and fee data, and citations of and to patents were examined by researchers. Both patent counts and the number of innovations emerging from a company's R&D program were found to be associated with the level of corporate investment in R&D (the higher the R&D expenditures, the larger, on average, the number of consequent patents and innovations) as well as with firms' market values (the larger the number of patents and innovations, the higher the market value, on average). Patents are thus related to both inputs (R&D) and outputs (market values) of the innovation process and, therefore, are meaningful intermediate value measures.

It is clear, however, that patents and innovations are noisy measures of R&D contribution, due to the skewness of their value distributions—that is, the tendency of a few patents or innovations to generate substantial returns (blockbusters), while the majority turn out to be virtually worthless.[24] Citations (references) to a firm's patents included in subsequent patent applications (forward citations) offer a more reliable measure of R&D value, since such citations are an objective indicator of the firm's research capabilities and the impact of its innovation activities on the subsequent development of science and technology.[25]

Various studies show that patent citations capture important aspects of R&D value. For example, Manuel Trajtenberg reports a positive association between citation counts and consumer welfare measures for CAT scanners; Hilary Shane finds that patent counts weighted by citations (the

24. See, for example, Patel and Pavitt (1995).
25. The list of citations to previous patents or scientific studies in patent applications ("prior art," in the legal jargon) is of considerable importance and is checked carefully by patent examiners, since patent citations assist in delineating the claims, or property right boundaries, of the invention. Indeed, patent citations are used as evidence in patent infringement lawsuits; see Lanjouw and Schankerman (1997). For a detailed example of patent citations and citation-based indicators, see Deng, Lev, and Narin (1999).

firm's number of registered patents divided by the number of citations by others to these patents) contribute to the explanation of differences in Tobin's q measures (market value over replacement cost of assets) across semiconductor companies; and Bronwyn Hall and colleagues report that citation-weighted patent counts are positively associated with firms' market values (after controlling for R&D capital).[26] Patents and their attributes thus reflect technological elements used by investors to value companies.

In a direct test of the usefulness of patent citation measures as indicators of value, studies have been conducted to examine the ability of various citation-based measures to predict subsequent stock returns and market-to-book values of public companies.[27] Three measures were found to possess such predictive ability: the number of patents granted to the firm in a given year, the intensity of citations to a firm's patent portfolio by subsequent patents, and a measure based on the number of citations in a firm's patents (backward citations) to scientific papers (in contrast with citations to previous patents).

Three patent-related measures are predictive of subsequent stock returns and market-to-book values of public companies:

—number of patents granted to the firm in a given year

—intensity of citations to a firm's patent portfolio by subsequent patents

—number of citations in a firm's patents to scientific papers

The third measure reflects the scientific intensity of a patent and may provide a proxy for the extent of basic research conducted by the company. The fact that patent indicators are associated with subsequent stock prices and returns suggests that investors are not fully aware of the ability of these measures to convey useful information about firms' innovation processes and capabilities. This is

---

26. Trajtenberg (1990); Shane (1993); Hall, Jaffe, and Trajtenberg (2000). In related studies, Austin (1993) reports that patents identifiable with end products tend to be more highly valued by investors than the average patent; and Megna and Klock (1993) find that the number of patents of rival firms (technologically strong competitors) has a negative effect on a company's q ratio.

27. See Deng, Lev, and Narin (1999); Hirschey, Richardson, and Scholz (1998).

of course not surprising, given the novelty of patent-related measures as indicators of enterprise value.

Patents are the intangible assets most actively traded in markets (see chapter 2), in the form of licensing and sale of patents. An examination of firms' royalties from the licensing of patents indicates that the volume of royalty income is swiftly increasing and that investors value a dollar of patent royalties (the implicit market multiplier of royalty income) two to three times higher than a dollar of regular income.[28] The reason for the high valuation of patent royalties probably lies in the stability of this income source (patents are usually licensed for several years) relative to other more transitory components of income. Patent royalties also impact investors' valuation of R&D, namely the market value they assign to a dollar of R&D expenditures. The valuation of the R&D of firms with royalty income is higher than the valuation of the R&D of firms that do not license patents, probably due to investors' belief that the quality and prospects of the R&D of firms able to license patents is relatively high.[29]

Summary

R&D, a major form of corporate intangible investment, is found to be an important contributor to firms' productivity, growth, and capital market value. The magnitude of this contribution—return on R&D investment—varies across industries and over time but is, by and large, considerably higher than firms' cost of capital; hence the value creation capability of R&D. The research record, therefore, strongly supports the assertions made in chapter 2 concerning the scalability of intangibles due to their nonrivalry and increasing returns properties as well as the existence of positive network effects (externalities) of many intangibles.

> *The return on R&D investment is, by and large, considerably higher than a firm's cost of capital; hence the value creation capability of R&D.*

In addition to the general findings about the positive contribution of R&D to corporate value and growth, the empirical record indicates the following:

---

28. For royalty volume data and analysis, see Rivette and Kline (2000a).
29. The last two findings are from Gu and Lev (2000).

—The return on basic (fundamental) research is substantially higher than that of applied or process R&D.

—Despite the expensing of R&D outlays in financial reports, investors consider R&D an important asset.

—Even for Internet companies, where the uncertainty regarding future benefits is currently considerable, investors value much of the R&D (product development) as an investment (asset) rather than an expense.[30]

—Patents and their attributes (for example, citations) constitute useful intermediate output measures of R&D value.

—In recent years, internal R&D has been complemented by acquired R&D and technology under development, where the latter often surpasses the former in volume of expenditure.[31]

—Royalties from patent licensing are a potent (in terms of creating market value) source of corporate income.

Organizational Capital

The extensive research focusing on R&D provides important insights about the organization of R&D activities (such as economies of scale), the private and social returns on R&D, the appropriation of R&D benefits (such as the effectiveness of patent protection), and investors' valuation of innovation activities. R&D, however, is but one component of firms' intangible capital (knowledge assets), which is of course particularly pronounced in the technology- and science-based sectors. Other components of intangibles—human and organizational capital—have received substantially less research attention than R&D. Consequently, our knowledge concerning these important intangibles is rudimentary at best.[32]

While no reliable data on firms' investment in organizational capital are available, it stands to reason that the size of these investments—and their contribution to growth—was substantial over 1980–2000. One indication is the relatively small size and slow growth of R&D expenditures

30. See Demers and Lev (2000).
31. See Deng and Lev (1998).
32. Research is, of course, predicated on data availability. Since public corporations do not provide systematic data regarding human and organizational capital, there is scant research on these assets. For example, in a recent study of intangibles, R&D and advertising expenditures are the only intangibles-specific items on which data are provided because these are the only intangibles-related items routinely disclosed by public companies; see Nakamura (1999).

compared with the explosive growth in the market value of corporations. For example, R&D (as a proportion of nonfinancial corporate gross domestic product) increased from a mean value of 2.3 percent in 1980–89 to 2.9 percent during 1990–97, which represents a modest increase indeed. Fixed tangible investment (as a percent of corporate gross domestic product) in fact decreased from 14.1 percent in 1980–89 to 12.6 percent in 1990–97.[33]

In contrast to these relatively small changes in R&D and tangible investment, the S&P 500 index, reflecting the market value of the major U.S. corporations, surged from 135.76 at the end of 1980 to 1320.28 on January 1, 2001—a nearly tenfold increase.[34] This imbalance suggests that other investments besides R&D and tangible assets created the bulk of the growth in corporate value over these two decades. Organizational and human capital are prominent among those value creators.[35] Indeed, since the mid-1980s, corporate restructuring—which is a prime creator of organizational capital—became a major managerial activity. So what do we know about organizational capital?

Computer-Related Organizational Capital

Erik Brynjolfsson and Shinkyu Yang statistically associated (regressed) the market values of 1,000 large companies to their tangible assets, R&D expenditures, and investment in computers.[36] Estimation results are striking: while a dollar of physical investment (property, plant, equipment) is valued in the capital market at approximately one dollar on average (yet more evidence of the commoditization of tangible assets), each dollar of computer capital is associated with close to ten dollars of market value! If this were literally true—one dollar invested in information technology creates ten dollars of market value—computer purchases would have been many times larger than they are. The explanation of the high valuation associated with computers is that they reflect the value (contribution) of organizational capital, not just of computers. Stated differently,

33. Data from Nakamura (1999, table 1).
34. Even this tenfold increase is an understatement, since the S&P index does not include dividends.
35. Hall (1999, p. 6) writes: "Firms produce productive capital by combining plant, equipment, new ideas, and *organization*." Emphasis mine.
36. Brynjolfsson and Yang (1999). Data on computer capital were derived from the Computer Intelligence Infocorp database, which details information technology spending for Fortune 1000 companies.

computers are a proxy for the extensive corporate investment in organizational change. Brynjolfsson and Yang explain as follows:

> Our deduction is that the main portion of the computer-related intangible assets comes from the new business processes, new organizational structure and new market strategies, which each complement the computer technology. . . . More recent studies provide direct evidence that computer use is complementary to new workplace organizations. . . . As IT [information technology] is a new technology still being developed rapidly, IT investment may accompany considerable changes in the structure and behavior of organizations. . . . Wal-Mart's main assets are not the computer software and hardware, but the intangible business process they have build around those computer systems. . . . Amazon's website and the computer hardware infrastructure are only a small portion of their total assets, but the accompanying business model and business process that support the model are quite valuable . . . the value of the business data about customer information, supplier information and business knowledge is several times as large as the cost of disk storage itself.[37]

This is the strongest evidence I am aware of concerning the substantial contribution of organizational capital to corporate value.[38] Relatedly, evidence shows that corporate diversification across both industries and countries enhances the value of an enterprise in the presence of intangibles.[39] This is intriguing evidence, since diversification (conglomeration) has fallen out of favor since the early 1980s. The management mantra since then has been, "Focus on core operations, and spin off unrelated activities." Empirical research indeed supports the virtues of corporate focus by documenting the existence of a 15–20 percent diversification discount: the market values of diversified companies are lower on average than those of similar, "pure-play" (single-industry) companies.[40]

37. Brynjolfsson and Yang (1999, pp. 30–31).
38. Recall that the ten-to-one contribution multiple of information technology is evaluated after accounting for the contribution to market value by both physical assets and R&D.
39. See Morck and Yeung (1999).
40. See, for example, Berger and Ofek (1995); Daley, Mehrotra, and Sivakumar (1997).

Thus Randall Morck and Bernard Yeung's evidence on the positive contribution of diversification to corporate value seems inconsistent with both corporate practice (focus on core operations) and empirical evidence. In fact, however, there is no inconsistency. Morck and Yeung's findings about the contribution of diversifi-

> *Corporate diversification across both industries and countries enhances the value of an enterprise only in the presence of intangibles.*

cation to value relate only to companies that posses substantial intangibles. Here is the explanation:

> Consider a company like 3M, which possesses a wealth of knowledge in adhesive material. It profitably branches into businesses that can tap into its technological know-how, like stationery (e.g., stick up notes and adhesive tapes) and cassette tapes (attaching electromagnetic particles to plastic tapes). . . . Firms diversify into businesses, some appear to be unrelated, which use some common information-based assets . . . [such as] production knowledge and skills, marketing capabilities and brand name, and superior management capabilities. Information-based assets, once developed, can be applied repeatedly and simultaneously to multiple businesses and locations in a non-rivalry manner to generate extra returns.[41]

Although diversification across unrelated operations often detracts from enterprise value, when the diversification is aimed at scaling intangibles it results in considerable value added. Such leveraging of intangibles across industries and countries obviously requires considerable organizational capital, such as the Intranet systems of pharmaceutical and chemical companies aimed at sharing information among R&D personnel, the capacity to value patents and identify potential buyers and licensees (such as the system used by IBM in its Internet-based technology exchange), and the development of exchanges in new goods and services, such as Enron's energy and bandwidth trading activities.[42] These forms of organizational capital are potent value creators. Diversification enhances the value creation potential of intangibles.

41. Morck and Yeung (1999, pp. 6–8).
42. For the IBM system, see patents.ibm.com.

Summary

Available research clearly indicates that the contribution of organizational capital to an enterprise value is substantial.[43] This, however, is only the tip of the iceberg. Questions abound: What exactly are those value-enhancing organizational assets? Under what circumstances do they contribute to value? How can such contribution be enhanced? While anecdotal stories in the managerial–new economy literature proliferate (Dell's innovative distribution system, Federal Express's efficient package-tracking system, Gap's exploitation of its brand portfolio, and Williams Company's installation of fiber-optic lines in gas transmission pipelines, to name a few), systematic research on specific types of organizational capital is scarce.[44] In the following section, I analyze the relevant available evidence on customer-related intangibles.

> *The contribution of organizational capital to an enterprise is evidently substantial.*

Brands, Franchises, and Customer-Related Capital

The value chain of knowledge-based enterprises generally starts with discovery (ideas, inventions), proceeds through the technological development of the new products and services under development, and ends up with the commercialization of the innovation outputs. For example, the value chain phases of drug development are as follows: basic research, drug testing and approval by the Food and Drug Administration (FDA), and finally marketing and sales. Considering the research available on the various phases of the value chain, there is substantial research on discovery-related intangibles (R&D, acquired technology, adaptive capacity), some research on technological feasibility (patents, investor reaction to FDA approvals), and only scant

---

43. In fact, Hall (1999, p. 30) attributes the entire difference between market values of companies and the value of their physical assets to organizational capital. "Because the hypothesis makes the total capital stock of corporations observable as the total value of securities, it is possible to quantify otherwise elusive concepts that appear to be central to the modern economy. These are technology, organization, business practices, software, and other produced elements of the successful modern corporation." For a skeptical view of the validity of attributing the difference between market and capital asset values to intangibles, see Bond and Cummins (2000).

44. For sample anecdotes, see Boulton, Libert, and Samek (2000).

systemic research on commercialization-related intangibles. I survey in this section the major research findings concerning the final phase of the value chain: customer-related intangibles, which is a specific form of organizational capital.[45]

Customer Acquisition Costs

It has been noted earlier that discovery-related intangibles can be measured by input indicators, such as R&D, acquired technology, and investment in information technology, and by output indicators, such as number of patents and their attributes (citations) and number of innovations generated by the R&D process. In a similar vein, measurement of customer-related intangibles can be based on input data or on outcome (output) measures. Following are several examples.

Practically all business enterprises have customers and spend considerable resources on increasing their customer base, stabilizing it (reducing customer turnover, or "churn"), and extracting maximum value from customers. Internet companies spent more in the late 1990s on customer acquisition than most other enterprises. Network effects are paramount in the various Internet sectors (business to business, business to consumer, and so on), rendering first-mover advantages often decisive. A widely known case of quick and effective penetration is AOL's drive during 1994–96 to acquire new customers by massive advertising and by providing free service and other incentives.[46]

Are such customer acquisition costs an intangible—that is, an asset expected to generate future benefits—or just a regular marketing expense? Acquisition costs are an intangible asset if, based on the past experience of the industry and the specific company and current outlook, customers can be expected to stay with the company well beyond the current year and contribute to revenues. A case in point is the cellular (wireless) phone industry. Cellular phone operators pay substantial commissions ($250–$300 per customer) to retailers for linking them with customers. For large companies, which add hundreds of thousands or even millions of customers a year, these commissions are the major administrative expense item, amounting to hundreds of millions of dollars annually. During

45. I do not venture into the extensive consumer research in marketing, since my focus is intangibles.

46. Data on AOL's customer acquisition costs and increases in the number of subscribers are provided in AOL's annual 10-K reports.

the early to mid-1990s, the U.S. cellular industry stabilized; industry statistics indicate that customers stay, on average, about three and a half years with a cellular operator.[47] A case could thus be made that the commissions paid for cellular customer acquisitions are indeed an investment in an intangible asset, since the payoffs of this investment stretch considerably longer than one year (a single year is a common accounting cutoff between an expense and an asset).

Indeed, an empirical study associating returns on stocks of cellular companies with commissions paid for acquiring customers, earnings before these commissions, and other control variables indicates that these commissions are considered an investment by shareholders.[48] Specifically, despite being expensed in the financial report, these commissions are positively and significantly associated with stock returns (changes in stock prices).[49] Thus when it can be established based on past experience and industry trends that the acquired customers will, on average, stay with the company over a multiyear period, the cost of acquiring these customers is indeed an intangible asset.[50] This is also the case for commissions paid by lenders for acquiring loans and for commissions for life insurance contracts.

Acquisition of Internet Customers

As noted above, Internet companies, particularly electronic retailers, or e-tailers (business to consumers) and portals, spent substantial resources on customer acquisition (advertising, free service, other "freebees") during the nascent period of these sectors (the late 1990s). Getting first to the market and quickly capturing a large market share were (and in many cases still are) essential components of the Internet company business model. However, applying the asset recognition criteria—a reasonable expectation of a multiyear stream of benefits from customers and a history demonstrating some stability of the customer base—the customer acquisition costs of most Internet companies would not qualify as an asset (AOL, Yahoo!, and perhaps Amazon are the exceptions). The jury on the persistence of benefits from customer acquisition by Internet companies is still out.

47. Amir and Lev (1996).
48. Amir and Lev (1996).
49. A true expense, like wages or rent, is negatively associated with stock returns; the higher the expense, other things equal, the lower the stock value.
50. On the accounting treatment of customer acquisition costs, see appendix A.

Hope (some will say delusion) nevertheless ruled the day in the late 1990s, and investors indeed considered customer acquisition costs as an investment rather than as a regular business expense. Several empirical studies indicated that in 1998 and 1999 these costs were positively related to market values of Internet companies.[51] Investors thus perceived Internet customer acquisition costs to be an asset.

The situation concerning customer acquisition costs of Internet companies, however, changed dramatically in the first half of 2000. Investors' euphoric perceptions of the potential of e-tailers turned to pessimism, resulting in a collapse (particularly during March and April 2000) of stock prices of most Internet companies. Empirical studies focusing on this shakeout period clearly indicate that investors no longer consider customer acquisition costs an asset.[52] The positive and significant association between market values of companies and customer acquisition costs, present during 1998–99, vanished in the first half of 2000.[53] This confirms the validity of the asset recognition criteria outlined above: customer acquisition costs qualify as an asset if experience and current industry outlook provide a solid basis for an expectation of a stable, multiyear customer base. This is clearly not currently (late 2000) the case for business-to-consumer Internet companies.

Customer-Related Output Measures

Customer acquisition costs and related indicators (advertising expenses, commissions) are input—or cost—measures. They, like R&D expenditures, are generally situated in the early phase of the valuation chain, where uncertainty about economic success (commercialization) is relatively high.[54] For management and investment purposes, as well as for

51. See Hand (2000); Demers and Lev (2000). In contrast, cost of sales, which is a regular expense, was found by researchers to be negatively related to market values of Internet companies.

52. Demers and Lev (2000).

53. Investors' skepticism of the validity of customer acquisition costs as assets is also due to the manipulation of this item by some Internet companies. As reported, for example, in "Fess-Up Time" (*Forbes*, September 18, 2000, pp. 80, 84), several companies included various shipping costs and discounts given to customers in reported marketing expenses. This was done in an effort to reflect a higher gross margin (these costs should have been included in costs of sales, rather than in marketing expenses). Obviously, when such accounting games are played by companies, the validity of reported items becomes questionable.

54. For example, the customer acquisition costs of business-to-consumer companies that folded in 2000 are by and large lost. *Wall Street Journal* (November 15,

accounting recognition of assets in financial reports, it is useful to expand the scope of customer indicators to include output measures, capturing the value of intangibles in advanced phases of the value chain, where uncertainty about commercial success is substantially reduced. In an analogy to discovery intangibles, in which patents and innovation sales are considered output measures, brands and trademarks are examples of customer-related output indicators.[55] Similarly, customer satisfaction measures also indicate intangibles' values in an advanced phase of the value chain.

Brand valuation and management is big business, practiced by many corporations and consultants and researched extensively by marketing and management academics.[56] The current discussion is restricted to empirical work on the value creation potential of brands and their property rights protectors, which are manifest as trademarks.

Customer satisfaction is, of course, a driver of brand value. One study reported that various measures of customer satisfaction—some developed internally by firms, others by an independent polling institute—are associated with firms' market values.[57] The usefulness of customer satisfaction measures for management and investing, where benchmarking against competitors is essential, is limited, however, since these indicators are not yet standardized and publicly reported, and therefore cannot be compared across firms. Relatedly, it was also found that estimates of corporate brand values published by *Financial World* are associated with market values.[58] These and similar studies thus establish that various methodologies aimed at quantifying brand values and other aspects of customers' intangibles (such as satisfaction) possess some empirical validity in terms of being associated with market values of companies.[59]

Chandra Seethamraju extended available research on customer-related intangibles by considering trademarks.[60] In contrast with patents,

2000, p. B1) reports that of 245 dot-coms surveyed, 42 had closed operations since the end of 1999.

55. *Innovation sales* refers to a measure indicating the percent of total revenues from products and services introduced in recent years.

56. For a general discussion of brand management, see Aaker (1996).

57. Ittner and Larcker (1998).

58. Barth and others (1998).

59. Similar to the Brynjolfsson and Yang (1999) findings on the valuation of computer capital, it may be that the brand and customer satisfaction measures associated with market values serve as proxies for other company attributes valued by investors, such as growth or geographical extension; see Seethamraju (2000).

60. Seethamraju (2000).

which have drawn considerable research attention, trademarks still suffer from research neglect. A trademark includes any word, name, symbol, device, or combination thereof that a person has a bona fide intention to use in commerce to identify and distinguish goods or products from those manufactured by others.

Trademarks lack the citations record of patents, which allow the measurement of various patent attributes, such as technological strength. Nevertheless, Seethamraju provides useful findings. For a sample of companies that acquired trademarks from other companies, he finds a positive and statistically significant investor reaction to the acquisition announcement, indicating that investors expect, on average, value added from the trademarks beyond the price paid (from, for example, synergies, or increased market control).[61] More important, for internally developed trademarks, Seethamraju develops a methodology to value trademarks based on their contribution to future sales. He estimates that the mean value of trademarks in his sample is $580 million. Further tests have established a positive association between the estimated values of firms' trademarks and

> *It appears that useful quantitative measures of customer-related intangibles can be defined and estimated.*

their capital market values, lending support to the valuation methodology. This preliminary research into the valuation of customer-related intangibles suggests that useful output measures of these assets can be defined and estimated.

Internet Traffic Measures

The advent of the Internet provides a rich set of new indicators reflecting various important aspects of customer-related intangibles. I refer here to what is generally known as traffic measures of Internet companies. These measures, generally collected by specialized companies, such as Media Metrix and Nielsen/Netrating, indicate important attributes of customers of Internet companies.

----

61. An example of trademark acquisition: in July 1998 Sara Lee Corporation acquired the domestic trademarks of the Lovable Company for $9.5 million; see Seethamraju (2000).

Common traffic measures reflect three attributes of web users:[62]

—*Reach* indicates the percent of unique visitors (not repeat visits) to the company site during a given period (generally a week or a month), relative to all web users. For example, during April 2000, Amazon.com had close to 11 million unique visitors (according to Nielsen/Netrating), constituting 13.68 percent of reach of all U.S. web users.

—*Stickiness* specifies the extent or depth of the firms' web use. This important aspect of customers is often indicated by the average number of web pages viewed by a person and the average time a person spends at the site. Stickiness measures are particularly important to advertisers, since advertising on a site is obviously more valuable when site visits are of an extended duration. For Amazon, in April 2000 visitors to the site viewed a total of 254 million pages, which amounts to 23 pages, on average, per person (Amazon ranked thirteenth among all sites covered by Nielsen, according to this measure). The mean Amazon visit lasted 11.6 minutes.

—*Loyalty* is a measure of propensity for repeat visits. In April 2000 Amazon had just over two visits per person, on average. This measure reflects an important characteristic of the firms' brand value: the higher the number of repeat visits, the higher the brand value, in general.

Several empirical studies on the valuation of Internet companies report that the three traffic indicators outlined above were positively associated with market values of Internet companies (price-to-sales value and market-to-book value), during 1999 and early 2000 suggesting that these measures reflect important attributes (profit potential, growth) of Internet companies. Some traffic measures were relevant even after the Internet shakeout in April 2000.[63] Further, they can be used to improve the prediction of future revenues of Internet companies. It can be concluded that for Internet companies, where users access is recorded, various output measures of customer-related intangibles are publicly available. The usefulness of such measures will be improved when they reflect the actual purchase behavior of customers rather than just visits and time spent on the site. Such value measures, however, are not yet publicly available.

62. For elaboration on Internet traffic measures and the following examples for Amazon.com, see Demers and Lev (2000).
63. See Trueman, Wong, and Zhang (1999); Hand (2000); Demers and Lev (2000).

Summary

Research into customer-related intangibles is in its infancy, relative to work on discovery intangibles. Nevertheless, the available evidence reveals the existence and usefulness of both input (such as customer acquisition costs) and output (trademarks, Internet traffic measures) indicators, reflecting various aspects of these intangibles.

What about Human Resources? Amazon.com's 1999 annual report provides the following information about its employees.

As of December 31, 1999, the Company employed approximately 7,600 full-time and part-time employees. The Company also employs independent contractors and temporary personnel. None of the Company's employees is represented by a labor union, and the Company considers its employee relations to be good. Competition for qualified personnel in the Company's industry is intense, particularly for software development and other technical staff. The Company believes that its future success will depend in part on its continued ability to attract, hire and retain qualified personnel.[64]

This is essentially the full extent of employee-related information provided by Amazon to its shareholders and other constituents.[65] In this arena, Amazon is not an aberration but an exemplar. Indeed, an examination of the financial reports of forty large public companies indicates that, without exception, there were no disclosures of relevant, quantitative information concerning human resources except for the frequent platitude: "Our employees are our most important asset."[66] No wonder then that, in contrast to the two intangibles nexuses discussed above— discovery and organizational assets—systematic research on the measurement and valuation of human resource intangibles is extremely lean.

---

64. From Amazon.com 1999 annual report, Form 10-K.

65. Public companies have to provide information in the financial report on obligations for pensions and other postretirement benefits, as well as information on the value of assets covering these obligations. Public companies have also to provide information on employee incentive plans and stock options. These disclosures, however, do not convey direct information relevant to the value of human resource intangibles.

66. Bassi and others (1999).

What Are Human Resource Intangibles?

Clearly, in a nonslave society business enterprises do not own their employees. Nevertheless, such enterprises invest considerable resources in their labor force. On- and off-the-job training, specific compensation plans (such as employee stock options) aimed at increasing work incentives and reducing employee turnover, systems aimed at sharing information among employees (like Intranet systems), and coding tacit knowledge and experience residing in employees' brains are examples of corporate expenditures on human resources. Expenditures, however, do not necessarily create assets. Only when the benefits from such expenditures—in the form of increased employee productivity—exceed costs is an asset created.

The empirical determination of whether human resource practices, such as employee training, incentive-based compensation, and evaluation methods, create intangible assets—namely, contribute to profitability and market values—is seriously hampered by the absence of publicly disclosed information on such practices. For example, a recent publication on the knowledge-based economy includes extensive data on R&D and information technology but no enterprise-based data on investment in human resources.[67] Accordingly, large-scale econometric studies like those conducted on the impact of R&D on productivity or market values (see above) are infrequent in the human resource area.

Some Research Findings

Various cross-sectional (multifirm) statistical analyses focusing on human resource investments and practices and controlling for other factors (firm size, industry factors, risk) have been conducted. Such studies examine the effect of specific work practices and human resource policies on employee productivity and firm value. Human resource policies and practices, such as total quality management programs, teamwork training, and pay-for-skill and profit-sharing systems, can create intangible assets, providing that they generate sustained benefits that exceed the costs of such programs. A recent study yields tentative results concerning such benefits.

> The results of our analysis suggest that the effects of these work practices on productivity appear to be positive, consistent with other recent research, although in our data little or none of this

67. OECD (1999).

evidence is statistically significant. At the same time, there are benefits to employees from innovative work practices based on employee involvement in the form of higher labor cost/higher compensation . . . there is no evidence of net benefits to employers associated with these practices, as labor cost increases tend to offset any productivity increases. . . . Indeed, it is possible that "high performance" work practices have other beneficial consequences (higher morale, greater adaptability, lower waste, etc.) that either do not affect firm performance measurably or do so in ways not captured by our performance measures.[68]

An examination of human resources practices focusing on a single company and practice, using real data in contrast to surveys, provides sharper results regarding the benefits of such practices. Edward Lazear, for example, examines the effects on the productivity of employees in the Safelite Glass Corporation (a large automobile glass company) of changing the compensation method from hourly wages to piece-rate pay.[69] Using detailed data on compensation, productivity, quality of employees, and turnover, Lazear documents that the productivity gains from switching compensation practices were substantial and that the company attracted a higher-quality work force. The impact of the compensation switch on company profitability, however, was left open, since the higher productivity was accompanied with higher wages paid to employees. The cost-benefit analysis is complicated. "The benefit is a productivity gain. Costs may be associated with measurement difficulties, undesirable risk transfers, or quality [of product] declines."[70]

Thus in contrast to discovery and organizational intangibles, for which systematic evidence indicates the existence of significant links between investment and value created, the research on human resource expenditures is in its infancy and is seriously hampered by the absence of publicly disclosed corporate data on human resources. The consequent reliance of researchers on survey data adds noise and uncertainty to their findings. I conclude, therefore, that with a few exceptions the jury is still out concerning the existence and value of human resource intangibles.

68. Cappelli and Neumark (1999, pp. 39–40). However, Huselid (1995) and Becker and Huselid (1998) provide survey-based evidence of a positive link between human resource practices and market values.
69. Lazear (2000).
70. Lazear (2000, p. 1359).

In closing this empirically oriented section, I briefly mention two research strands related to the valuation aspects of human resources. Several attempts have been made to measure the quality of scientific and R&D personnel by the number of their scientific publications and the status of their co-authors and to relate such quality measures to firm value. One study measured biotechnology firms' intellectual human capital by counting the number of scientific articles the firms' employees co-authored with "star scientists" (for example, Nobel laureates), including of course cases in which the firms' scientists were themselves stars.[71] The authors report that these human resource measures are associated with biotechnology companies' future economic success and market values.[72]

Another study, using a measure of firm-specific human capital based on the present value of expected costs of compensating employees, reports that the estimated human capital values are positively associated with enterprise risk as perceived by the capital market (beta values).[73] Human capital values are missing from the assets section of the balance sheet and so have an associated liability in the form of an obligation for future employee compensation, which is also missing from the balance sheet. This off-balance-sheet liability, the study argues, increases the firm's financial leverage (debt-equity ratio) relative to that reported on the balance sheet; hence the finding that the inherent risk of the enterprise increases with the value of its human capital.

Summary

Of the various intangible assets considered above, we have the least systematic information on human resources. It is not even clear at this stage which expenditures on human resources (training? incentive-based compensation?) create assets. It appears that research on human resource intangibles will significantly advance only with the disclosure of meaningful data by the corporate sector.

71. Darby, Liu, and Zucker (1999).

72. See Stephan (1996) for discussion of additional research linking human capital measures to productivity and growth.

73. Rosett (2000). This study used a methodology proposed by Lev and Schwartz (1971) for the estimation of a firm's human capital value. Interestingly, while the Lev-Schwartz methodology was, to the best of my knowledge, not adopted by U.S. companies, it has been adopted by several Indian companies. Infosys Technologies (a software company), in its 1999–2000 annual report, estimates the "value" of its employees, using the Lev-Schwartz approach, as Rs. 2,23,741 lakhs.

Synopsis Extensive empirical research, particularly on discovery intangibles (R&D, patents, innovations) and organizational intangibles (information technology, brands, customer acquisition costs), has established the existence of strong links between these investments and corporate value and performance. This record corroborates the considerable value creation potential of intangibles resulting from their nonrivalry, increasing returns, and network effects (see chapter 2).

The research provides the foundation for the measurement and management of these all-important productive inputs. Various quantifiable input and output measures of specific intangible assets—such as renewal investment (R&D, technology, information technology), patent and trademark values, customer acquisition costs, Internet companies' traffic measures, network effects, and scientific human capital values—can be used by both managers and investors to assess corporate performance and value. Quantitative indicators of intangibles are also useful to policymakers in forming and evaluating public policy concerning intangibles.

Various quantifiable input and output measures of specific intangible assets can be used by both managers and investors to assess corporate performance and value.

The reliance of research on corporate-disclosed data is crucial. Occasionally, surveys and interviews provide some useful information. Yet by and large significant research advances are predicated on systematic and credible (audited) information disclosed by business enterprises or public agencies (such as the patent office). The wealth of information gained from research on R&D and patents, relative to human resources, for example, attests to the centrality of corporate information on intangibles to the advancement of knowledge and policymaking. This highlights the importance of enriching the information environment concerning intangible investments (addressed in chapters 4 and 5).

CHAPTER FOUR

Intangibles in the Dark

M
ost people who write and comment about intangible (intellectual) assets, as well as many pundits of the new economy, elaborate on the sharp distinction between the accounting treatment of physical and intangible investments: While the former are considered assets and are reported (along with financial investments like stocks and bonds) on firms' balance sheets, the latter are by and large written off in the income statement, along with regular expenses such as wages, rents, and interest.[1] This difference between the accounting treatment of tangible and intangible assets, it is generally argued, has dire consequences for managers, investors, and policymakers relying on financial information (such as corporate financial reports and prospectuses). Proposed remedies range from encouraging firms to voluntarily disclose more information about intangibles (the majority of commentators) to suggesting changes in the regulated accounting and reporting system (a minority view).

On the whole, while agreeing with some of the recommendations for improved disclosure, I find the arguments about information deficiencies—and particularly the proposed remedies—unconvincing and lacking solid foundation. Missing from the debate are the following elements:

1. The major exception in the United States to the immediate expensing of intangibles is the requirement to capitalize (recognize as asset) software development costs beyond the attainment of project feasibility; see Aboody and Lev (1998). See appendix A for a detailed description of generally accepted accounting principles (GAAP) concerning intangibles.

—A thorough analysis of the economic reasons for the differences in the accounting treatment of physical and intangible investments. Current practices are not just the result of accountants' conservatism, or resistance to change.

—An awareness of the politics of intangibles, namely the motives and incentives of managers, public accountants, and financial analysts concerning the disclosure of meaningful information about intangibles. More information about intangibles will not fall like manna from heaven just because writers or committees call for it. The incentives of the major players in the information arena will have to be changed substantively to improve the information environment concerning intangibles.

Substantive improvements in the disclosure of information about intangibles can be brought about by policy changes— and these can be triggered only in the face of documented significant social and private harms.

—An examination of the empirical evidence concerning the current state of information availability and the social harms caused by information deficiencies concerning intangibles. Substantive improvements in the disclosure of information about intangibles can be brought about, in my opinion, by policy changes (otherwise, the information would have been voluntarily disclosed by now). These policy changes can be triggered only in the face of documented significant social and private harms.

—A realization that many of the information challenges facing corporate outsiders (investors and policymakers) also beset insiders (managers and board members). The belief that managers have sophisticated internal systems to measure and value intangibles is a myth. Certainly, managers often use some nonfinancial measures internally—such as customer satisfaction, employee turnover, or a fine partition of research and development (R&D) by project. Nevertheless, the managerial usefulness of such measures is restricted due to lack of standardization and public availability; hence these measures cannot be used for benchmarking. Furthermore, beyond simple indicators, such as employee turnover, most companies do not have the capacity to conduct an in-depth analysis, such as an evaluation of the return on investment in intangibles, which is essential for optimal resource allocation.

—A comprehensive plan for improvement in the measurement and disclosure of intangibles and for a change in the current incentives for managers and accountants to elicit such information. The suggestions generally advanced, such as a disclosure of more nonfinancial measures, are haphazard and lack consistency, and the calls for a period of experimentation with improved measures are, in my opinion, vacuous. If there is insufficient experimentation now, what will motivate more of it in the future?

The following discussion is organized according to three of the elements outlined above: reasons for current deficiencies, the politics of intangibles, and social harms.[2]

The Tangibles-Intangibles Accounting Asymmetry

"To know the past, one must first know the future." This counterintuitive yet profound statement by the mathematician Raymond Smullyan, though not referring to accounting, reflects the essence of accounting measurements, their objectives, and limitations better than any textbook discussion I have encountered.[3] A simple, accounting-based example can clarify Smullyan's statement.

Despite widely held beliefs that corporate financial statements convey historical, objective facts, practically every material item on the balance sheet and income statement, with the exception of cash, is based on subjective estimates about future events. A few examples are as follows:

—The net value of accounts receivable (or loans of banks) depends on managers' estimates concerning future customers' defaults (loan loss reserves).

—The relevance of the stated (cost) value of fixed-income securities (bonds) held to maturity depends on managers' intent and ability to hold the securities until maturity, irrespective of future economic conditions and financial needs.

—The net value of property, plant, and equipment depends on the validity of managers' depreciation estimates.

—Obligations for pensions and postretirement benefits rely on heroic, long-term assumptions concerning future wage increases and the rate of return on pension assets.

---

2. The last two elements—managerial information needs and a proposal for an information system (including incentives for changes in information disclosure)—are addressed in chapter 5.

3. Smullyan's statement is quoted in Yuji Ijiri's (1989) important, though not widely read, study on momentum accounting.

—The firm's contingent liabilities for product warranties or insurance claims are based on estimates of future payments to fulfill these obligations, often stretching over several years.[4]

Obviously, to know the past—to report accurately on last quarter's or last year's earnings and asset and liability values—one must have a pretty good knowledge of the future (assets' useful life, customers' rate of default, or future wage increases). Stated differently, a financial statement for, say, fiscal 2000 prepared in 2010, when much of the uncertainty concerning the firm's activities and economic condition in the post-2000 period is resolved (for example, the actual default record of the credit sales of 2000 will be perfectly known by 2010), will be much more accurate (though less relevant) than a fiscal 2000 financial statement prepared in February 2001, when considerable uncertainty concerning events beyond 2000 still prevails. Thus the quality and relevance of accounting-based information depends crucially on the extent of uncertainty surrounding future outcomes and the ability to pierce this uncertainty (that is, to know the future).

The crux of the accounting problem with intangibles is that to know the past, one must know the future.

Herein lies the crux of the accounting problems with intangibles: To know the past—to evaluate the performance and assess the value of intangible assets—one must know the future, namely the outcomes of these investments (for example, the commercial success of a drug or software program under development). But as the discussion in chapter 2 makes clear, the future of intangibles is generally murky. The uncertainty associated with most intangible assets is inherently higher than that of physical and financial assets.

—Motorola's (and partners') $5 billion investment in the Iridium project (telecommunication satellites) is currently in chapter 11 bankruptcy protection.

—Monsanto's far-reaching transition from a chemical to an agribusiness company, initially hailed as a great success, hit a wall of consumer

---

4. A dramatic example of the uncertainty associated with customer warranties was the predicament of Bridgestone/Firestone and Ford Motor Company concerning the massive Ford Explorer tire recall in mid to late 2000.

resistance to genetically modified products and led a battered Monsanto to be acquired by Pharmacia.[5]

—The massive investments of many Internet e-tailers during the late 1990s in intangibles (product development and customer acquisition costs) were essentially lost as the business models of many of these companies were found in 2000 to be unsustainable.[6]

On the positive end of the intangibles' risk spectrum—risk entails both unexpected losses and unexpected successes—is Cisco Systems, which created a powerhouse worth $115 billion (in March 31, 2001) from smart investments in technology, and America Online, with its dominant Internet position gained by shrewd investment in customer acquisition and product development.[7]

Tangible and intangible assets receive differing accounting treatments (the former are considered assets, while the latter are expensed), primarily because of the high uncertainty regarding future outcomes of intangible investments. Further motivation for the expensing of intangibles rests on the unique characteristics of this type of asset: partial excludability (lack of full control) and nontradability (see chapter 2). What is not controlled by the enterprise (inability to exclude nonowners from enjoying some benefits), goes the accounting argument, cannot be considered an asset, and the value of what cannot be compared with similar assets (due to absence of markets) is inherently subjective and its estimation unreliable.

Any serious proposal for improvement in the measurement and reporting of intangibles has, therefore, to deal with the root causes of high uncertainty, partial excludability, and the nontradability attributes of intangibles. I demonstrate briefly here (and at greater length in chapter 5)

5. For the Monsanto story, see "Biotechnology Food: From the Lab to a Debacle," *New York Times*, January 25, 2001, p. 1.

6. The *Wall Street Journal* (November 15, 2000, p. B1) reports that of 245 dotcoms surveyed, 42 had closed operations since the end of 1999.

7. Clearly indicating the uncertainty of intangible investments is the attitude of financial analysts toward AOL's customer acquisition costs. When AOL capitalized some of these costs in 1995–96, claiming that these are investments rather than expenses, it was blamed by analysts as manipulating earnings, since, they argued, these costs would in all likelihood not generate future benefits. Continuously harassed by analysts and the Securities and Exchange Commission (SEC), AOL gave up in 1997 and wrote off all the previously capitalized acquisition costs, to the tune of $385 million. For details of the write-off, see AOL's 10-K report for fiscal 1998.

how an appreciation of these attributes of intangibles and the foundations of accounting measurements can guide useful proposals for change.

The high uncertainty of intangibles highlights the importance of information on risk reduction of these assets as they move along the value chain from ideas through technological feasibility to commercialization. For example, systematic information on the results of clinical tests of drugs under development and beta tests for software programs falls into this category of important risk-related information.[8] Obviously, the commercialization prospects of technologically feasible products are substantially better than prefeasibility products and services. The high uncertainty of intangibles also highlights the importance of information concerning risk sharing. R&D alliances and joint ventures, the securitization of intangibles, and cross-licensing of patents are among the primary means used by firms to manage the risk of intangibles. Therefore, detailed information on these risk management activities and their consequences possess high relevance to both investors and managers (including board members).

The partial excludability and nontradability attributes of intangibles point at the importance of information on the firm's ability and success in appropriating maximum benefits from intangible investments. The extent of patenting and trademarking of discoveries, the volume of revenues from licensing patents and know-how, and the success of the firm in litigating patent infringements are important indicators of the firm's ability to exclude others from reaping the benefits of its innovations. Similarly, information about trading knowledge assets in the traditional and virtual (Internet) markets for intellectual capital is highly relevant to both managers and investors. These indicators also have important accounting implications. Effective exclusion of outsiders implies control over assets, an essential condition for asset recognition in financial statements. Thus reliance on the economic framework for intangibles allows one to specify information relevant to decisionmakers.

An appreciation of the structure and limitations of accounting as it relates to intangibles also allows for a critical assessment of current proposals for information disclosure. Consider, for example, the suggestions for continuous (daily, weekly) financial reporting instead of the current quarterly and annual financial reports. No doubt, frequent releases of information on key items—such as software sales last month, airplane

---

8. Aboody and Lev (1998) empirically demonstrate that information on the technological feasibility of software programs is relevant to investors' decisions.

occupancy last week, or even daily retail store revenue—may provide relevant information to investors. For example, on November 27, 2000, three days after Thanksgiving, the *Wall Street Journal* reported that Wal-Mart "said same-store sales on Friday rose 4% to 6% over the same day last year, while total sales for the day increased to more than $1.1 billion, up slightly from last year."[9]

Lost in the discussion about continuous reporting, however, is the crucial factor of reliability of the estimates underlying earnings and asset measurements. In general, the shorter the reporting period (a quarter, say, compared with a year), the less reliable are the estimates underlying the computation of earnings and asset values. Consider, for example, the estimate of the provision for customers' defaults (loan loss reserve). A default estimate based on past experience with annual sales may provide a reasonable estimate of future default, since many transitory events and factors are smoothed out over the course of a year. In contrast, an estimate of customers' default related to last week's or yesterday's sales (continuous reporting) will be subject to enormous random errors and hence highly unreliable, adversely impacting the quality of reported earnings and asset values. Indeed, empirical studies show that the longer the accounting period (a quarter, a year, five years), the more reliable earnings are as measures of corporate performance.[10] Thus a clear distinction has to be made between continuous reporting of some key measures (sales, for example) that may be beneficial, and frequent reporting of earnings (say, weekly income), which will probably enhance the already considerable noise and uncertainty in capital markets.

The Politics of Intangibles

Why are task forces calling for the disclosure of more information about intangibles and policymakers (the U.S. Senate, the SEC) conducting hearings about the presumed inadequacy of information on intangibles?[11] Are market forces not supposed to ensure that a demand for information on intangibles will be met by adequate supply? Is there a market failure for information on intangibles? And why?

9. *Wall Street Journal*, November 27, 2000, p. B1.
10. Lev (1989); Easton, Harris, and Ohlson (1992).
11. For an example task force, see FASB (2000).

The Information Revelation Principle

Economic theory and sheer common sense suggest that when there is demand for certain information items there will generally be sufficient incentives to supply the information. Consider a simple hypothetical scenario of a capital market in which investors have no information about the companies traded in that market. In such a state of complete ignorance, the market value of all the traded companies will be identical, since investors will assign the same probabilities of success and failure to all the traded companies. A uniform valuation of all securities will prevail.

Most likely, there will be at least one company in the market whose executives strongly believe that its intrinsic (true) value is higher than the uniform value prevailing in the market. At least one company must have above-average worth. The executives of this above-average company obviously have an incentive to provide information to investors about the "true worth" of their company (sales growth, earnings, asset values). Upon disclosure of such information, investors will increase demand for the stocks and upgrade the prices of the disclosing company (if the information is credible, of course), and downgrade—this is key—the prices of those who keep silent. The reason: investors are getting increasingly suspicious (concerned) about companies that keep silent while others disclose information. In capital markets, no news is bad news.

As the market values of silent companies continue to fall below the initial uniform value, even those that initially had good reasons to keep silent, namely companies with intrinsic value below the initial average market price, now have incentives to disclose information, since the recently reduced prices are now below their intrinsic value. This information revelation process will evolve until all companies disclose their information—the full-revelation principle, in economic parlance.[12] Full revelation will prevail, of course, if the costs of disclosure (benefiting competitors, for example) are not significant.

The Failure of Full Revelation for Intangibles

Why does the full revelation principle fail to operate in the intangibles context? Why did a recent extensive study by the Financial Accounting Stan-

---

12. Of course, in what economists call a rational expectations environment, in which people base decisions on optimal expectations, the full-revelation process will evolve instantaneously, as those with bad news know that the market will ultimately force them to disclose. So why wait?

dards Board (FASB) of voluntary information disclosure by public corporations conclude that "the Steering Committee was pleasantly surprised to discover that companies presently are voluntarily disclosing an extensive amount of useful business information. . . . The results of the over-all study included some disappointments. One was the general lack of meaningful and useful disclosures about intangible assets."[13] The FASB's findings of "an extensive amount of useful business information" currently disclosed voluntarily are consistent with the full-revelation scenario outlined above. But why the information failure when it comes to intangibles? Clearly, prescriptions concerning improved information disclosure have to address this question.

The main reason for the intangibles' information failure lies, in my opinion, in the complex web of motives of the major players in the information arena: managers, auditors, and well-connected financial analysts. I refer to this web of motives as the politics of intangibles' disclosure. A specific example can highlight my argument.

The term *in-process R&D* refers to research and technology projects in the development process that are acquired by business enterprises, often with other tangible and intangible assets. The data in table 4-1 provide an example of in-process R&D included in IBM's acquisition of Lotus Development Corporation. IBM estimated $1.84 billion as the value of in-process R&D (essentially software programs and products under development) included in the Lotus acquisition (that is, 57 percent of the acquisition price of $3.24 billion).

U.S. accounting regulations (generally accepted accounting principles, or GAAP) prescribe that in-process R&D, once identified and valued, should be immediately and fully expensed in the acquiring company's financial report. This expensing caused IBM to report a whopping loss of $538 million in the third quarter of 1995, compared with a profit of $710 million in the same quarter a year earlier. IBM is not an aberration. The acquisition of R&D and technology has been mushrooming in recent years as companies attempt to shore up their technological capabilities, with many companies having multiple acquisitions a year and staggering in-process R&D write-offs.[14] For example, during 1997–99, Cisco Systems conducted fourteen acquisitions accounted for by the purchase

13. FASB (2000).
14. See Deng and Lev (1998) for an empirical analysis of the in-process R&D phenomenon.

TABLE 4-1. In-process R&D data for IBM's acquisition of
Lotus Development Corp., 1995

Millions of dollars

Asset/Liability	Fair Value
Tangible net assets	305
Identifiable intangible assets	542
Current software products	290
Software technology under development	1,840
Goodwill	564
Deferred tax liabilities	(305)
Total acquisition price	3,236

Source: IBM's third quarter (September 30) 1995 report.

method.[15] The total price paid for these acquisitions was $1.77 billion, of which $1.36 billion (77 percent) was expensed as in-process R&D.[16]

One would expect corporate executives to rebel against an accounting rule that forces them to declare a major part of the value of corporate acquisitions a current expense (akin to sunk costs), in the process depressing reported earnings and asset values. In fact, however, when the FASB announced in 1999 its intention to change the in-process R&D expensing rule, it encountered such strong opposition by managers that it backtracked. Why the opposition to a change of a clearly inappropriate procedure—expensing asset values acquired in arm's length transactions? Enter the politics of intangibles' disclosure.

The GAAP-mandated expensing of practically all investments in intangibles is a recipe for inflating future reported profitability and growth (and also protects managers against embarrassments).

The GAAP-mandated expensing of practically all investments in intangibles—both internally developed (R&D, customer acquisition costs) and acquired from others—is a recipe for inflating future reported prof-

15. During that period, Cisco had additional acquisitions that were accounted for by the pooling method, including the $6.9 billion Cerent acquisition. Under pooling, however, there is no in-process R&D.
16. Data derived from Cisco System's 1999 annual report, p. 42.

itability and growth and, in addition, serves to protect managers against embarrassments. When IBM expenses almost 60 percent of the Lotus acquisition and when Cisco writes off almost 80 percent of the value of its acquisitions, they guarantee that future revenues and earnings derived from these acquisitions will be reported unencumbered by the major expense item: the amortization of the acquisition costs.[17] Hence the inflation in future profitability and growth. The expensing of intangibles also causes commonly used profitability measures, such as the return on equity and return on assets—often among the drivers of management compensation—to be inflated, since the denominators of these ratios (equity and total assets, respectively) are missing the expensed part of the acquisitions. Even when acquisitions fail to yield the expected return, the low (after in-process R&D expensing) equity base in the denominator will obscure the failure from outsiders.

And what about the depressed earnings due to the expensing of in-process R&D? Not to worry. Investors generally consider these write-offs as one-time items, of no consequence for valuation.[18] Thus companies get the best of all worlds from in-process R&D expensing: no price hit at the time of expensing and a significant boost to future reported profitability.[19]

This is not the end of the in-process R&D story. Given the high risk of intangibles, the probability of acquired R&D or technology under development to disappoint expectations is not insignificant. If the acquisitions were considered assets, such failure would have required a public write-off of the investment in the financial report, triggering questions about the reasonableness of the acquisition and, possibly, lawsuits. An immediate expensing obviates the need to provide explanations in case of failure.

The in-process R&D case generalizes to other intangible investments. The immediate expensing of these investments and virtually no information disclosure about the progress of products under development or of return on investments suit managers well, particularly given the generally high level of uncertainty associated with intangibles. Failures generally

17. If those acquisitions were considered an asset, as it should be for an arm's length transaction, this asset would have been amortized against future revenues.

18. Indeed, when IBM announced its third-quarter 1995 loss of $538 million (on October 18, 1995), its stock price increased from $586.78 (October 17, 1995) to $590.65 (October 19, 1995).

19. See Deng and Lev (1998) for evidence on investors' positive reaction to in-process R&D.

draw attention more than do successes, and immediate expensing upon acquisition or investment, as well as minimal information disclosure about project development, obscures most failures.[20]

What about the benefits from disclosure, which drive the full-revelation principle discussed above? Economic theory postulates that the disclosure of relevant information is rewarded by lower cost of capital (relative to no disclosure). In reality, there is still only scant evidence of a link between improved disclosure and cost of capital, and the estimated reduction in cost of capital is very modest.[21] In my opinion, this evidence is too fragile to counter the strong incentives to inflate future profitability and avoid embarrassments.

Finally, what about public accountants and financial analysts? Aren't they interested in improved disclosure about intangibles? The former, mainly concerned with shareholder lawsuits, are comfortable with accounting rules that eliminate risky assets from the balance sheet that, in the occurrence of company failure, may draw lawsuits by irate shareholders. The latter (analysts), particularly well-connected ones, believe that they obtain from managers (via conference calls, background briefings, and so on) sufficient information about firms' innovation activities. In fact, public disclosure in financial reports of such information may strip them of privileged information.[22]

The politics of intangibles' disclosure is not a diabolical scheme to obscure relevant information. Rather, it reflects expected attitudes, given the economic characteristics of intangible investments: high risk and difficulties to fully secure benefits. What is important is not to place the blame for the scarcity of information but rather to understand the motives (crucial for the design of effective remedies) and, particularly, the conse-

---

20. Except, of course, for major failures, such as Motorola's investment in the Iridium project, AT&T's acquisition of National Cash Register (NCR) Company, and sale by Mattel of the Learning Company, acquired sixteen months earlier for $3.5 billion and sold for virtually nothing. This latter failure was a major factor in the resignation of Mattel's chief executive officer Jill Barad.

21. The two studies linking disclosure to cost of capital that I am familiar with are Botosan (1997); and Sengupta (1998). The latter, for example, reports that the cost of capital difference between firms with the best and worst disclosure is only 1.1 percentage points.

22. This analysts' attitude may change with the enactment of Regulation FD (Selective Disclosure and Insider Trading, Securities and Exchange Commission, 17 CFR pts. 240, 243, and 249, August 2000), which prohibits the disclosure of material corporate information to individuals.

quences of nondisclosure. I, therefore, turn next to an empirical analysis of the consequences of information deficiencies concerning intangibles.

Intangibles Darkly: So what if the accounting system fails to
The Consequences reflect important attributes of intangibles?
Perhaps managers, investors, and policy-makers obtain the missing information from other sources (such as conference calls with executives). Are there really serious social and private harms caused by the scarcity of information on intangible investments? Here is the evidence.

The Current Disclosure Environment

With but one important exception—software development costs—practically all intangible investments are expensed as incurred in financial reports.[23] The costs of developing software products beyond the stage of technological feasibility (usually determined by the existence of a working model; that is, successful alpha or beta tests) have to be capitalized—namely, considered an asset—and amortized according to the expected useful life of the software products.[24] In 1998 the American Institute of Certified Public Accountants issued a statement of position extending the capitalization of software development costs (beyond technological feasibility) to products intended for internal use.[25] The justification for the software exception to the general rule of expensing intangibles appears to be that software projects are generally well defined (separable), they are of relatively short duration (compared, say, with drug development), and their benefits can in most cases be directly attributed to the investments. Such separability of projects and identifiability of benefits is missing, argue accountants, from most other intangibles.

In reality, however, even this limited requirement to capitalize software development costs is ignored by many software companies, including the industry leaders, Microsoft and Oracle. These and other firms routinely

23. Some relatively minor intangibles, such as movie rights and commissions paid for life insurance and mortgages, can be capitalized; see appendix A. Also capitalized is goodwill, which is the difference between the price paid for a business enterprise in an acquisition (accounted for by the "purchase method") and the fair value of the acquired assets net of liabilities.
24. The capitalization of software development costs is required; see FASB (1985b).
25. AICPA (1998).

expense all software development costs.[26] Undoubtedly, financial analysts' skepticism of the capitalization of intangibles strongly drives the expensing decision of many successful software companies.[27] The drag on future earnings due to the amortization of capitalized software and, in extreme cases, the need to write off software capital that is no longer commercially viable are additional deterrents to following the FASB's software capitalization requirement.

Whether capitalized (infrequently) or expensed (the general rule), R&D expenditures are at least reported separately (a line item) in companies' financial statements.[28] This is not the case for most other intangible investments. In general, no information is provided in financial reports on firms' expenditures regarding employee training, brand enhancement, information technology investment, or other intangibles. Thus companies provide the general public with detailed information on investment in tangible and financial assets but no information on intangible investment (except for R&D). This results in an almost complete lack of transparency concerning intangibles. With few exceptions this situation prevails worldwide.

Companies provide the general public with detailed information on investment in tangible and financial assets but no information on intangible investment, apart from R&D.

The distinction between the measurement issues concerning intangibles (for example, whether they should be recognized as assets or

---

26. See Aboody and Lev (1998) for a description of the software development costs capitalization requirements and for data on the characteristics of companies following and ignoring the accounting standard. For a comprehensive annual survey of the accounting practices of software companies, see Deloitte & Touche (1998).

27. "We are not enamored of recording self-developed intangible assets unless their values are readily apparent. We consider the cost of creating them to be so often unrelated to their actual value as to be irrelevant in the investment valuation process." AIMR (1993, p. 50).

28. In many developed countries, even this is not required (see appendix A for details). The requirement in the United States to separately report R&D expenditures leaves open the question of what should be defined as R&D. This is largely left to managers' discretion, adding to the uncertainty surrounding information about intangibles. There has been an attempt to define and classify R&D expenditures, but it is not binding in the United States and clearly requires updating, given the technological changes that have occurred since its formulation; see OECD (1993).

expensed) and the disclosure of substantive information about intangibles is often lost in the public debate. Too often one hears that it is impossible to value intangibles and that, therefore, no change should be made in current corporate disclosures. This argument reflects the confusion of the measurement and disclosure issues. The difficulties in valuing intangibles—a measurement issue—should not preclude the disclosure in footnotes to financial reports or by other means of factual, important information, such as on investment in information technology, employee training, customer acquisitions costs, and Internet activities. I return to this issue in chapter 5, but I first ask, here, what economic theory says about the consequences of information deficiencies.

The Consequences of Information Asymmetry

Economic theory postulates that information asymmetry—differences in the information available to parties to a contract or to a social arrangement (such as a stock exchange)—leads to adverse private and social consequences. Such consequences were thoroughly investigated in the capital markets context, where some participants (managers, well-connected financial analysts) are generally better informed than others about firms' activities and future prospects. Here are some salient conclusions from the voluminous economic literature on information asymmetry that are of particular relevance to intangibles.

—*Abnormal gains to informed investors.* Albert Kyle, among others, established that informed persons (such as managers having information about the success of a drug under development in human clinical tests) would gainfully trade to exploit their private information.[29] Given human nature, this is of course far from surprising, but Kyle also established that active information search by investors (financial analysts, for example) will not eliminate the edge of insiders. Thus contrary to widespread beliefs, the extensive information gathering and analysis by financial analysts and institutional investors, aided by the Internet, will not level the

29. Kyle (1985, 1989). A case from 2000: "The Securities and Exchange Commission has ordered an investigation into possible insider trading of Bristol–Myers Squibb Company shares, the pharmaceutical giant confirmed. The SEC is focusing on trades made between Nov. 8, 1999, and April 19, 2000, when the New York–based company disclosed that it was withdrawing its application to the FDA for its experimental blood pressure drug, Vanlev. The news sent its shares plummeting 23%." See *Wall Street Journal*, October 12, 2000, p. B5.

playing field. Ways will have to be found to motivate insiders to disclose in a timely manner at least some of their private information.

—*Intangibles' contribution to information asymmetry.* Particularly relevant to this analysis is the conclusion from Kyle's model that the gains of informed investors will be a function of the variability of the value of the firm. We know that intangibles increase the variability (volatility) of firms' values, and we can, therefore, expect the extent of information asymmetry and insider gains to increase with the intensity of intangibles.[30] The adverse social consequences of substantial gains to informed investors are the corresponding losses to other investors and the deterioration in investors' confidence in the integrity of capital markets. This, of course, is the reason for the strict securities regulation of insider trading.

—*Increasing bid-ask securities spread.* Lawrence Glosten and Paul Milgrom established that information asymmetry is the major determinant of securities' bid-ask spread (namely, the price differential that traders or market makers quote for buying or selling a security).[31] Bid-ask spreads widen, for example, when the market maker faces better informed investors, as a self-protecting mechanism against excessive losses to these investors. An important implication of the Glosten-Milgrom model is as follows:

> There can be occasions on which the market shuts down. Indeed, if the insiders are too numerous or their information is too good relative to the elasticity of liquidity traders' [uninformed investors] supplies and demands, there will be no bid and ask prices at which trading can occur and the specialist can break even . . . a market, once closed, will stay closed, until the insiders go away or their information is at least partly disseminated to market participants from some other information source. . . . The problem of matching buyers with sellers is most acute in trading shares of small companies.[32]

Thus severe information asymmetries will lead to decreases in volume of trade and in the social gains from trade.[33]

---

30. See, for example, Kothari, Laguesse, and Leone (1998) on intangibles and volatility. The theoretical prediction about insiders' gains is strongly corroborated by Aboody and Lev (2000).

31. Glosten and Milgrom (1985).

32. Glosten and Milgrom (1985, pp. 71, 74).

33. A similar result in the real markets was derived by Akerlof (1970) in the famous lemons (defective used cars) case.

—Increasing cost of capital. Yakov Amihud and Haim Mendelson established the important linkages between information asymmetry, bid–ask spreads, and firms' cost of capital.[34] Large spreads imply high transaction costs to investors (the spread is the cost of a round trip: buying and then selling the security). Investors will demand a compensation for high transaction costs in terms of a higher return, which in turn implies a higher cost of capital to the company. A high cost of capital impedes investment and growth. Hence the adverse private and social consequences of information asymmetry.

Economic theory thus establishes the fundamental cycle of business enterprises and capital markets (depicted in figure 4-1), which can have virtuous or vicious implications for firms and their employees. Serious information deficiencies (upper link in the figure) lead to excessive cost of capital, low employee compensation (for example, out-of-the-money stock options), and in extreme cases takeover of the entire enterprise, triggered by low market values (lower link). This scenario is particularly relevant to intangibles-intensive enterprises, given the deficient public information about these assets, which are, as theory postulates, mostly serious for small, early-stage enterprises. Are these theoretical predictions borne out by the evidence?

Evidence of Harms

I elaborate in the following on specific cases of documented harms from information deficiencies about intangibles.

The High Cost of Capital

Jeff Boone and K. K. Raman examine the impact of changes in R&D expenditures on the bid-ask spread of stocks.[35] Relating R&D changes to bid-ask spreads is an effective way to examine the harmful consequences of the information asymmetries created by R&D (and, by implication, by other intangibles), since the bid-ask spread reflects investors' transaction costs, which in turn affect companies' cost of capital. Boone and Raman report a statistically significant association between increases in R&D expenditures and the widening of securities' spreads.[36] R&D changes are

34. Amihud and Mendelson (1986).
35. Boone and Raman (1999).
36. The authors control, of course, for other factors known to affect spreads, like company size.

FIGURE 4-1. The Virtuous-Vicious Cycle

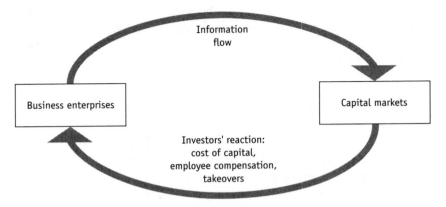

also found to be negatively associated with the depth of trade: the quantity of securities the market maker is willing to commit for a given quoted spread.

The above relates to the cost of equity. There is also evidence that increases in R&D expenditures are associated with increases in the cost of debt of public companies.[37] In addition to these findings, consider the studies reporting a positive link between the quality of financial information (not necessarily on intangibles) and firms' cost of capital.[38] The conclusion is clear: deficiencies in information disclosure to capital markets, particularly pronounced for intangibles-intensive companies, result in excessive cost of capital, which in turn hinders business investment and growth. Hard evidence on the amount of savings in capital costs by improving disclosure—a necessary condition to convince managers to enhance disclosure—is still sparse, however.

The Systematic Undervaluation of Intangibles

Attempts to empirically identify systematic mispricing of securities or anomalous behavior of investors (such as overreaction to certain types of information) follow a widely accepted research methodology: portfolios of securities are formed on the basis of the hypothesized trigger of mispricing (for example, a negative earnings surprise), followed by an exam-

37. Shi (1999).
38. For instance, see Botosan (1997); Sengupta (1998).

ination of the pattern of risk-adjusted returns on these portfolios subsequent to their formation. If the examined securities are properly priced, subsequent risk-adjusted returns should randomly wander around a zero mean. If, on the other hand, the examined securities are systematically mispriced, and if investors recognize the mispricing over time, then the portfolio returns will systematically drift upward or downward, as investors correct the mispricing.[39]

With coauthors, I examined more than 1,500 R&D-intensive companies, paying particular attention to financial reporting biases related to R&D.[40] Bias is defined as the difference between reported earnings (R&D fully expensed) and earnings under R&D capitalization. We found that companies with a high growth rate of R&D expenditures—but relatively low growth rate of earnings, typical to young, intangibles-intensive enterprises—are systematically undervalued by investors. This is indicated by the high positive risk-adjusted portfolio returns that are generated during the five years after formation. This finding makes sense, since companies with high growth of R&D, but low earnings growth, portray the worst performance to capital markets, due to the full expensing of R&D. Given the low reported profitability of these companies, investors apparently heavily discount the prospects of their R&D, hence the undervaluation. When the R&D ultimately bears fruit, investors correct the undervaluation.

In corroboration, returns on portfolios of companies with high R&D expenditures relative to their market values were found to be systematically positive and large, consistent with the undervaluation of such companies.[41] This evidence is closely related to that discussed above (information deficiencies leading to high cost of capital); undervaluation of securities implies an excessively high cost of capital to the issuing companies. The harmful social consequences are obvious: companies that invest consistently in intangibles (technology, knowledge), yet are still not

---

39. Examples of research in the securities mispricing area are De Bondt and Thaler's (1985) study documenting investors' overreaction to good/bad news; Bernard and Thomas's (1990) study recording systematic underreaction to earnings surprises. Lakonishok, Shleifer, and Vishny (1994) document systematic positive return differential for value stocks (stock with low market value relative to such fundamentals as book value or earnings) relative to glamor stocks. They ascribe this finding to a systematic overpricing of glamor (growth) stocks, which is reversed by contrarians.

40. Lev, Sarath, and Sougiannis (2000).

41. Chan, Lakonishok, and Sougiannis (1998).

stellar performers, tend to have an inflation-related high cost of capital imposed on them by capital markets, impeding their investment and growth.[42]

A Level Playing Field?

The most direct evidence on the existence of a unique, intangibles-related information asymmetry between managers and investors, and the exploitation of such asymmetry by some executives, comes from a study of insider gains in R&D companies.[43] Corporate executives' compensation packages are heavily weighted with stocks and stock options, particularly in technology and science-based companies (software, computers, biotech). These executives are, of course, allowed to trade in the shares of their companies, but they are prohibited from trading on material inside information, loosely defined as information that would affect investors' decisions, once disclosed. Corporate executives, along with other insiders, are required to report their trades to the Securities and Exchange Commission no later than the tenth day of the month following the trade. This publicly available information about insider trades allows researchers to examine important issues, such as the extent of insider profits, the relevance of inside information to investors, and the adequacy of regulations concerning insider gains.[44]

David Aboody and I examined all trades by corporate officers in the stocks of their companies over the 1985–98 period and conclude the following:

—Gains to insiders in companies with R&D activities are, on average, three to four times larger than insider gains in companies without R&D.

—When insider trades in R&D companies are publicly disclosed through the SEC filings—on average, one month after the trades are exe-

---

42. Some readers may find the evidence of undervaluation of certain R&D-intensive companies counterintuitive. Weren't all technology stocks overpriced through mid-2000? The answer is that only the profitable ones (the Microsofts, Intels, and Ciscos) may have been overvalued. Many other companies struggle in the capital markets. During 1999, for example, while stock indexes soared to new heights, most stock prices of individual companies actually fell. Of the S&P 500 companies, the stock prices of 256 companies declined during 1999. See "Heard on the Street," *Wall Street Journal*, January 18, 2000.

43. Aboody and Lev (2000).

44. The estimates of insider gains based on information filed with the SEC are, of course, downward biased. Egregious violations of trading on inside information are likely not reported to the SEC, such as trades made through friends or relatives.

cuted—investors react to the information by buying shares when insider purchases are reported and by selling shares when informed that insiders have unloaded shares (approximately one month previously).[45]

This evidence indicates that intangibles create significant information asymmetries (managers knowing well before investors about a drug failing clinical tests, about a software program successfully passing a beta test, or about an acquired technology that failed to live up to expectations) and that much of this information is kept from investors until the disclosure of insider trade (hence investors' reaction to such disclosure).

> *Evidence indicates that intangibles create significant information asymmetries. The private and social harms of such information deficiencies are obvious: insider gains come at the expense of outside investors.*

The private and social harms of such information deficiencies are obvious: insider gains come at the expense of outside investors. Furthermore, excessive insider gains erode investors' confidence in the integrity of capital markets, leading to thin trades and a decrease in the social benefits from large, transparent capital markets (such as in optimally allocating investors' capital). The prospects of gains from inside information may also distort the incentives of some managers, leading to decisions and actions that are not in the best interest of shareholders and society.

The Deteriorating Usefulness of Financial Reports

The strength of correlation between a message (an earnings report, for example) and receivers' reaction to the message (stock price changes around the earnings release) is an effective measure of the information content or usefulness of the message. Low correlation, indicating that the message did not trigger significant action by receivers, suggests that the message was not very informative; whereas high correlation—strong receivers' action—indicates informative messages. Figure 4-2 portrays the

45. Aboody and Lev (2000). Here, as elsewhere in intangibles' empirical research, the focus on R&D is due to the fact that it is the only significant intangible investment disclosed by public companies.

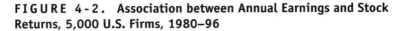

FIGURE 4-2. Association between Annual Earnings and Stock Returns, 5,000 U.S. Firms, 1980–96

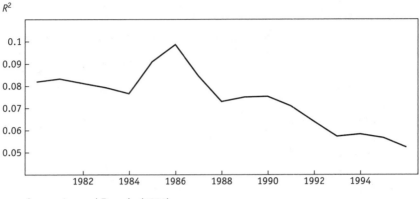

Source: Lev and Zarowin (1999).

pattern of the association between corporate earnings (of approximately 5,000 U.S. enterprises) and stock price changes (returns) over the period 1980–96. The message is unmistakable: reported earnings are playing a decreasing role in the total information affecting investors' decisions.

What about other information items? Various researchers document a decreasing pattern of association between stock prices and returns and key financial variables, such as earnings, cash flow, and book (equity) values.[46] And what about nonaccounting information? Eli Amir and colleagues added to the set of financial (accounting) variables the present value of five-year forecasts of earnings made by financial analysts.[47] Presumably, analysts are privy to considerable information beyond the financial reports, and they reflect this information in their earnings forecasts. Hence combining the information in financial reports with that in analysts' forecasts, and correlating the combined information with stock returns (reflecting the consequences of investors' decisions) will indicate the usefulness of much of the information available to investors (from financial reports and other sources). Estimates by Amir and colleagues clearly indicate that the decreasing pattern of usefulness portrayed in figure 4-2 holds also for the wide information set, combining financial and

46. Lev and Zarowin (1999); Brown, Lo, and Lys (1998); Chang (1998). For contradictory evidence, see Francis and Schipper (1999).
47. Amir, Lev, and Sougiannis (2000).

other information. Interestingly, where financial information fails the most—intangibles-intensive enterprises—the contribution of financial analysts is the largest. Yet even with this differential contribution of analysts, the decreasing trend of usefulness of publicly available information over the period 1980–2000 is unmistakable.

Why the deterioration in the usefulness of information available to investors? The following two culprits surface: the fast increase in the proportion and importance of knowledge-based, intangibles-intensive companies in capital markets; and the deficiency of information concerning the assets and activities of these companies. Herein lies the main social harm: the current economic environment is characterized by a fast pace of change and high uncertainty. In this environment, relevant and reliable information is a crucial guide to the decisions of managers, investors, and policy-makers. In this economic environment, a failure in the major information system—corporate financial reports—is particularly damaging.

> *In the current economic environment, characterized by rapid change and high uncertainty, a failure in the major information system—corporate financial reports—is particularly damaging.*

Manipulation through Intangibles

Since R&D and most other intangible investments are immediately expensed in financial reports, changes in these expenditures affect the bottom line—earnings—dollar for dollar. The temptation to change the level of investment in intangibles in order to manage reported earnings to meet and exceed analysts' expectations is therefore large. In contrast, if R&D were capitalized, changes in periodic R&D expenditures would have a protracted effect on earnings, reducing the potency of intangibles as earnings management tools.

Evidence indicates that, in the year of initial public offering, firms tend to have decreased R&D levels and, consequently, higher reported earnings, apparently in an attempt to improve investors' perceptions about the company's prospects.[48] Similar evidence has been gathered on the use of

---

48. Darrough and Rangan (2001).

R&D to manage routinely reported earnings.[49] Surprisingly, some companies even publicly announce the use of R&D as an earnings booster. For example, in a report on Eastman Kodak's warning to investors of weak sales and earnings, Kodak's chief financial officer declared, according to the *Wall Street Journal*, that Kodak was considering "belt-tightening measures, including a cut in digital [cameras] R&D."[50] The broader concern, of course, is that some managers may harm the long-term prospects of their companies to meet short-term earnings targets by cutting or postponing intangible investments.

Summary

Economic theory attributes seriously harmful private and social consequences to information asymmetry: decreased social gains from trade, high cost of capital (and the consequent impediments to corporate growth), and abnormally large gains to insiders at the expense of outside investors. Dated accounting and reporting rules concerning intangibles contribute to information asymmetry. The empirical evidence discussed above, though sparse in certain areas, indeed indicates that this information asymmetry leads to the predicted undesirable consequences, namely, systematic mispricing of securities, high cost of capital, and excessive gains from insider trading.

Synopsis

The distinction between the accounting treatment of tangible and intangible assets originates from substantive differences between the two types of capital: the partial excludability, high uncertainty, and nontradability attributes of intangibles. While these attributes may provide some justification for applying specific accounting measurement rules (like the expensing of employee training costs),

Measurement and valuation difficulties concerning intangibles should not provide an excuse for nondisclosure of relevant information about intangibles.

they do not provide any justification for denying investors fundamental information about intangibles (like the disclosure of employee training

---

49. Bushee (1998).
50. *Wall Street Journal*, September 27, 2000, p. B8.

costs in footnotes). Measurement and valuation difficulties concerning intangibles should not provide an excuse for nondisclosure of relevant information about intangibles.

The major players in the information arena—managers, auditors, financial analysts—are generally comfortable with the current disclosure (rather nondisclosure) environment concerning intangibles. The immediate expensing of internal and acquired R&D, for example, is a recipe for boosting future growth of reported earnings. It also decreases managerial embarrassment and litigation exposure. In such a comfortable arrangement, it will take more than the frequently heard calls for voluntary information disclosure and a period of experimentation to generate a significant change in the information environment.

Hard evidence regarding the harmful private and social consequences of the disclosure environment of intangibles (both within business organizations and in capital markets) is fast accumulating. From excessive cost of capital, through manipulation of financial information, to abnormally high insider gains, the evidence indicates that significant information asymmetries lead to serious private and social harms. There is thus a scientific base for the call for a substantial improvement in information disclosure concerning intangibles.

CHAPTER FIVE

What Then Must We Do?

Investors, and often managers too, are deprived of intangibles-related information on essential business capabilities and performance characteristics.[1] Examples of important, yet not disclosed, performance indicators follow.

—*The utilization of intellectual property.* Firms generally develop only a small fraction of the patents and know-how they possess into products or services, resulting in an underutilization of intellectual property. Effective managers license unused patents or develop know-how in collaboration with others. Information on the extent of the utilization of intellectual property—in the form of a breakdown of patents into three categories (under development, licensed, and in collaboration) as well as the volume of licensing revenues—provides an important indication of the effectiveness of the firm's management of knowledge.

> *Investors, and often managers too, are deprived of intangibles-related information on such essential business capabilities and performance as*
>
> *—the utilization of intellectual property*
>
> *—bringing new products to the market*
>
> *—Internet involvement*

1. The title of this chapter follows that of a 1902 essay by Leo Tolstoy on poverty (material, not informational).

—*Bringing new products to the market.* The ability to commercialize innovations (such as convincing physicians to use a new drug or medical instrument) is often as important as the scientific or technological ability to generate the innovation. However, reliable indicators of innovation and commercialization capabilities are rarely available to investors. The highly aggregated sales figures publicly disclosed are too coarse to indicate these capabilities. "Innovation revenues" (a measure indicating the percent of total revenues from recently introduced products or services) is an effective indicator of the firm's innovation capacity and ability to bring products expeditiously to the market. This measure, however, is not widely disclosed.

—*Internet involvement.* Early experience indicates that Internet-based supply and distribution channels lead to considerable benefits and cost savings.[2] The extent and rate of increase of the firms' Internet activities is thus an important leading indicator of future revenue growth and efficiency gains. However, rarely if ever do investors receive systematic information on firms' Internet activities (percent of online sales of total revenues, cost of online activities), despite the fact that such information is readily available and its disclosure not competitively harmful.

The above are but a few examples of crucial intangibles-related managerial capabilities and performance measures—managing knowledge, commercializing new products, utilizing the Internet—that are not disclosed to investors and often are not even utilized effectively by managers and board members. True, ultimately managerial capabilities and the quality of corporate assets will be reflected by sales and earnings figures—but only ultimately and in a highly aggregated manner. An effective information system provides early indications of things to come and enables decisionmakers to identify specific performance drivers.

Given that information (particularly on the disclosure-challenged intangibles) is essential to managers, investors, and policymakers, I devote this chapter to proposing a comprehensive information system highlighting the performance and capabilities of modern business enterprises. Since some of the proposed information is not transaction based

2. For example, "the companies that have gone furthest" in the use of the Internet for business-to-business transactions "claim to save astonishing amounts. GE plans to cut 15% from its cost base of $100 billion in both 2001 and 2002." See *Economist*, November 11, 2000, p. 6 of e-management survey. See also Garicano and Kaplan (2000).

and is of a nonfinancial nature (regarding quality of patents, products in the pipeline, and so on), the system extends well beyond the confines of traditional accounting and can be considered a satellite information system to the current one. In regard to accounting, I briefly outline my views of the changes required to enhance the usefulness of this 500-year-old system to reflect the performance and potential of modern business enterprises.

The Objectives of the Proposed System

Current proposals for improving the information available on knowledge-intensive enterprises are either silent about the objectives of the proposed information or set general and vague targets such as the improvement of resource allocation or the leveling of the playing field (between investors and information-privileged analysts or managers). Such objectives, while desirable, are too general and nebulous to guide the construction of a complex information system aimed at reflecting the value and contribution of elusive assets, such as intangibles. We need an operational objective for designing an improved information system.

The objective of the information system proposed below is the facilitation of two of the major forces characterizing modern economies: the democratization and the externalization of decisionmaking processes both within organizations and in capital markets. By democratization and externalization I mean, respectively, the growing participation of individuals in capital markets and the increasing need to engage external entities in the management of businesses. Let me elaborate.

The democratization of capital markets is reflected in the increasing role of individual investors in these markets. No longer content with holding indexed funds, individual investors increasingly wish to perform their own investment analyses and structure built-to-order portfolios. Thus while professional financial analysts and investment advisers still play a central role in capital markets, millions of individual investors are becoming their own analysts. A large number of financial websites attempt to cater to the needs of these new "analysts," but what the sites provide are mainly voluminous data with very little relevant information. Particularly missing is information on intangibles (such as investment in and productivity of alliances), because these sites basically compile and manipulate publicly available information such as financial statement data, analysts' earnings forecasts, and so on, which are devoid of meaningful information about intangible or knowledge assets. While analysts may obtain some such information from management, individual investors cannot.[3]

The externalization of managerial decisionmaking processes may be more subtle but not less real and fundamental than the democratization of capital markets. In the industrial-era vertically integrated corporation, decisionmaking authority was largely centralized and confined within the boundaries of the organization. Managers had in house most of the information they needed. In contrast, in the modern corporation an increasing number of important decisions are shared with entities residing outside the legal confines of the corporation: customers, alliance partners, suppliers of outsourced services, and so on.

Merck, for example, is currently a partner in more than a hundred R&D alliances and joint ventures. Thus important R&D decisions that were previously made exclusively and privately inside Merck are now being made jointly with a large number of outsiders. Cisco Systems outsources most of its production and assembly activities, leading to crucial production and delivery decisions being shared with outsiders. Dell's computer configuration decisions (product design) are largely being made by its customers (the built-to-order concept), Wal-Mart's suppliers make most of its inventory and supply decisions, and the design of open-source software programs (like Linux) is constantly improved by an informal association of code writers (with a final decision authority given to a committee). Such externalization of decisionmaking, of course, fundamentally differs from the intrafirm decentralization of decisionmaking, common to the industrial-era corporations, and increases significantly the scope of information required by managers and investors.

The democratization-externalization (a mouthful) process—evolving both in capital markets and in "the real economy" (business enterprises)—creates new constituencies and enhanced demand for relevant information. Individual investors now need access to the detailed and nuanced information that has thus far been the exclusive domain of financial analysts and investment advisers. Filling this need would level the playing field. But more important, it would make capital markets more competi-

---

3. The ability of analysts to obtain proprietary information from management may be curtailed by Regulation FD (Selective Disclosure and Insider Trading, Securities and Exchange Commission, 17 CFR pts. 240, 243, and 249, August 2000), which prohibits the disclosure of material corporate information to individuals.

tive and enhance the ability of investors to monitor managers' activities—both important economic objectives of public policy. The networked corporation, with its alliance members, suppliers and customers, subcontractors, and public institutions (for example, universities cross-licensing patents with business enterprises), needs timely information about its partners and is called to provide information about itself to network partners (for example, on its scientific and commercialization capabilities).

This then is the major objective of the information system proposed below: to provide the needs of the emerging constituencies—primarily individual investors and the myriad partners to the networked corporations—enabling these constituencies to make and execute decisions at the level of professional investors and managers. This objective is analogous to the disruptive innovation concept advanced by Clayton Christensen.[4] Here is the role of disruptive (to the status quo, but socially desirable) innovation, in Christensen's words:

> Disruptive innovations typically enable a larger population of less skilled people to do things previously performed by specialists in less convenient, centralized settings. It has been one of the fundamental causal mechanisms through which our lives have improved. So, take the computer, for example. Remember when you had to take your punch cards to somebody else in a central office? Then along comes the PC. It couldn't do nearly the sophisticated problems that you can solve on a mainframe—but it brought the masses into the computing business. And from that disruptive root, it has gotten so good that we can now do in the convenience of our homes and offices so much more. . . . You can tell the same story about photocopying—or equity investing. . . . We still need healthcare innovations that enable individuals to do for themselves what historically nurses had to provide, that enable nurses to do what you needed a family-practice physicians to provide, and enable family-practice physicians to do what you needed a specialist to do. . . . In cases where that's already happened, we've actually received the Holy Grail of lower cost, higher quality and more convenient healthcare. . . . Again, it's those kinds of innovations that enable a larger population of less skilled people to do things that historically you needed specialists to do.[5]

4. Christensen (1997).
5. Christensen (2000, pp. 10–11).

In an increasingly democratized and externalized decisionmaking environment, an important role of information should be (paraphrasing Christensen's last sentence, quoted above) to enable a larger population of investors to do things that until now only highly qualified financial analysts could do. Similarly, to provide a constantly increasing number of partners to the networked corporation with sufficient information for optimal decision making. This is the major objective of the information system outlined below.

> *In an increasingly democratized and externalized decisionmaking environment, an important role of information should be to enable a larger population of investors to do things that until now only highly qualified financial analysts could do.*

The Fundamentals of the Proposed Information System

An analysis of frequently asked questions in conference calls between managers and financial analysts, of surveys of voluntary disclosures by corporations, and polls of decisionmakers indicates that the information most relevant to decisionmakers in the current economic environment concerns the enterprise's value chain (*business model,* in analysts' parlance).[6] This is also the information that the accounting system by and large does not convey in a timely manner. By *value chain,* I mean the fundamental economic process of innovation—vital to the survival and success of business enterprises—that starts with the discovery of new products or services or processes, proceeds through the development phase of these discoveries and the establishment of technological feasibility, and culminates in the commercialization of the new products or services. This value chain—the lifeline of innovative and successful business enterprises—is depicted in figure 5-1.

Note that the nine detailed information boxes of the figure represent a broad cross section of economic sectors and technologies. The intention is to provide a comprehensive representation of relevant information items. Specific companies are represented by a subset of items. For example,

6. For conference calls see, for example, Tasker (1998); for voluntary disclosures see FASB (2000); for polls see, for example, Eccles and others (2001, chap. 7).

FIGURE 5-1. The Value Chain Scoreboard

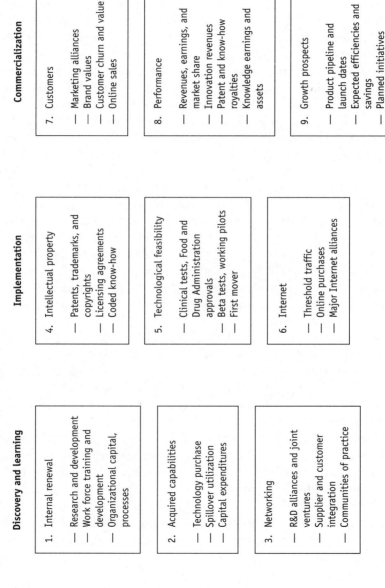

Discovery and learning

1. Internal renewal
   — Research and development
   — Work force training and development
   — Organizational capital, processes

2. Acquired capabilities
   — Technology purchase
   — Spillover utilization
   — Capital expenditures

3. Networking
   — R&D alliances and joint ventures
   — Supplier and customer integration
   — Communities of practice

Implementation

4. Intellectual property
   — Patents, trademarks, and copyrights
   — Licensing agreements
   — Coded know-how

5. Technological feasibility
   — Clinical tests, Food and Drug Administration approvals
   — Beta tests, working pilots
   — First mover

6. Internet
   — Threshold traffic
   — Online purchases
   — Major Internet alliances

Commercialization

7. Customers
   — Marketing alliances
   — Brand values
   — Customer churn and value
   — Online sales

8. Performance
   — Revenues, earnings, and market share
   — Innovation revenues
   — Patent and know-how royalties
   — Knowledge earnings and assets

9. Growth prospects
   — Product pipeline and launch dates
   — Expected efficiencies and savings
   — Planned initiatives
   — Expected breakeven and cash burn rate

information box 4 is irrelevant for companies without patents, and the Internet-related information in boxes 6 and 7 will be missing for companies without online activities.

The value chain of businesses generally starts with the discovery of new ideas for products, services, or processes (consider Cisco's online product installation and maintenance system, discussed earlier as an example of a business process). Such ideas can emanate from the firm's internal R&D operation or from employees' networks (communities of practice), such as Xerox's Eureka system—which shares information and experience among its technicians—or from R&D intranet systems (box 1). Increasingly, knowledge and ideas are obtained from the outside, embedded in acquired assets. For many companies, the acquisition of technology and in-process R&D now matches or surpasses in value internal R&D.[7]

Knowledge is also acquired by learning from and imitation of (reverse engineering) others' innovations. This process—termed by economists *R&D spillovers*—refers to the benefits to organizations (or nations) from the innovative activities of others. Effective and systematic organizational learning requires specific capacity to learn (adaptive capacity), as operationalized by a specially designated and staffed corporate function, with qualified personnel actively engaged in learning (for example, scientists liaising with universities and research institutes). These activities are detailed in box 2.

The third major source of new ideas and knowledge, particularly prominent in the modern corporation, is active and formal networking (box 3). Research alliances and joint ventures, and the integration of suppliers and customers into the firm's operations (such as Wal-Mart's integration of its suppliers), provide valuable information for the design and improvement of new products, services, or processes.[8]

These internal, external, and networking sources of information and ideas constitute the discovery phase, initiating the corporate value chain. This phase generally requires significant and consistent allocation of resources and is the most intangibles-intensive phase of the value chain.

The next phase of the value chain represents the crucial stage of implementation—achieving technological feasibility of the products, services, or processes under development. In a sense, this marks the transformation

---

7. Deng and Lev (1998).
8. For more on Internet alliances, see Elfenbein and Lerner (2000).

of ideas into working products. Given the large variety of products and services developed by business enterprises, technological feasibility is marked by numerous milestones. In some cases, patents and trademarks (box 4) signal a feasible product (although quite often patents are issued at a very early stage of the development phase). In other cases, the successful passing of formal feasibility hurdles, such as a clinical test for drugs, or a beta test for software programs, is the mark of feasibility (box 5). Technological feasibility and readiness for commercialization requires, of course, an adequate labor force, in terms of both quantity and quality, and appropriate work practices, such as incentive-based pay.

Increasingly, Internet and intranet technologies offer quantitative measures to indicate technological feasibility (box 6). For example, online operations that gain a reasonable number of visitors (indicated by such frequently used traffic measures as "reach")—and even more important, repeat visitors—clearly exhibit a degree of technological feasibility of network operations.[9] J. C. Penney, for example, recently had 1.3 million unique visitors a month (repeat visitors are counted only once) to its website—more than any other retailer of apparel and home furnishings.[10] This is clearly an indication of a successful website.[11]

Technological feasibility marks a particularly important phase of the value chain, bringing with it a substantial reduction in the risk associated with products and services under development (recall the discussion of the risk of intangibles in chapter 2). Thus information on technological feasibility provides investors and managers important risk gauges.

The final phase of the value chain, commercialization, signifies the successful realization of the innovation process. Ideas, transformed into workable products and services, are in turn brought expeditiously to the market to generate sales and earnings. When such earnings exceed the cost of capital, value is created. That is what a business enterprise is all about.

Customers are naturally the focal point of the commercialization phase of the value chain (box 7). Brand value, manifested by a large market share or the ability to charge premium price (for example, the difference between the price of Bayer aspirin and a generic product) is an

9. For a discussion of traffic measures, see Demers and Lev (2000).
10. "Penney Wise," *Forbes*, September 4, 2000, p. 72.
11. The ultimate test, of course, is the extent of purchases by website visitors, an aspect of its commercial success.

important commercialization indicator. Successful marketing alliances with leading companies (a small biotechnology company marketing a drug with Pfizer, for example) are indicators of potential sales growth. For Internet operations, repeat and satisfied buyers, as well as high volume per online customer, bode well for the operation. These and other matters are valuable customer-related indicators of the commercial viability of the innovative process.

Box 8 provides important performance indicators, which are currently outside obligatory disclosure by generally accepted accounting principles (GAAP). Foremost among such measures is "innovation revenues," indicating the share of revenue from recently introduced (within three to five years) products. This important indicator of innovation capabilities, and particularly of the firm's success at bringing products quickly to the market, is a reliable predictor of operational success and shareholder value creation.[12] Also reflecting top-line success are indicators of market share for the firm's products and the effectiveness of the firm's online distribution activities and marketing alliances.

Bottom-line (profitability) measures (box 8) not routinely disclosed include indicators highlighting the economic profitability of the enterprise, such as the value added of operations (earnings minus a charge for the cost of equity capital) and the recently introduced measure of knowledge earnings, indicating the contribution of intangible assets to productivity.[13]

Finally, box 9 provides essential forward-looking information. This is the only component of the proposed value chain scoreboard that is not factually based. It informs on the product pipeline, crucial for estimating the growth prospects of pharmaceutical and software companies, among others. It provides managers' estimates about the expected efficiencies from restructuring activities and expected growth of market share. For money-losing enterprises (frequent in Internet, biotechnology), it also provides an estimate of time to break even and the cash burn rate (months of operations supported by current liquid assets). All of these information items are frequently and persistently sought from management in conference calls.[14]

12. Crepon, Duguet, and Mairesse (1998).
13. Regarding value added, FASB (2000) indicates that some companies already provide information on economic value contributed by operations. Regarding knowledge earnings, see annual ranking of companies by this measure published in *CFO* magazine (most recently, April 2001) and *Fortune* (April 2001).
14. Tasker (1998).

This is then an outline of the proposed information system—the value chain scoreboard—which is aimed at providing a comprehensive and in-depth portrayal of the enterprise's capabilities and success in creating economic value. The focus is on innovation, and information on intangibles (R&D, patents, brands, alliances, networking) obviously plays a prominent role in this information system.

The value chain scoreboard provides a comprehensive portrayal of the firm's capabilities and success in creating economic value. Scoreboard indicators should be

—Quantitative

—Standardized

—Empirically linked to value

The Scoreboard Criteria

The value chain scoreboard provides an information system for use in both internal decisionmaking and disclosure to investors. Specific scoreboard indicators should satisfy three criteria to ensure maximal usefulness. First, they should be quantitative. Qualitative aspects of the value chain (such as employee work practices, patent cross-licensing) may be provided in an annex to the scoreboard. Second, they should be standardized (or easily standardizable), meaning that they can be compared across firms for valuation and benchmarking purposes. Third and most important, they should be confirmed by empirical evidence as relevant to users (generally by establishing a significant statistical association between the measures and indicators of corporate value such as stock return and productivity improvement).

These three criteria for choice of the specific scorecard indicators ensure that the proposed information system satisfies current needs of users (for example, comparability within an industry) and is scientifically robust (empirical research support). For concreteness sake, I thus provide several examples of operationalizing the scoreboard criteria.

Voluminous empirical evidence (surveyed in chapter 3) indicates that, on average, investment in R&D, information technology, and customers pays off in terms of increased productivity and enhancement of market values of companies. This supports the disclosure (box 1, figure 5-1) of periodic R&D expenditures, meaningfully classified (for example, R&D

aimed at new products, the improvement or maintenance of existing products, and process R&D).[15] Data relating to customer acquisition costs (particularly relevant for Internet companies) should be disclosed separately from advertising and marketing expenses, given that empirical evidence has established a statistical association between customer acquisition costs and market values.[16]

Box 4 of the scoreboard conveys information on the firm's intellectual property—intangibles secured by legal rights. The number of patents, trademarks, and copyrights registered during the period, as well as patent renewals, provides the rudimentary information. Empirical research indicates that various attributes of patents, such as the number of citations to the firm's patent portfolio contained in subsequent patents (forward citations), are important indicators of the quality of the firm's science and technology.[17] These quality measures are in turn linked to market values of corporations. Data on patents and their attributes thus meet the three scoreboard criteria: they are quantifiable, they are standardized (available from various vendors),[18] and they are supported by research as value drivers.

Of particular importance are data on royalties (box 8) received from the licensing of patents and know-how. Investors place higher value on such royalties than on most other components of income, probably due to the long-term nature of licensing agreements. Furthermore, royalties assist investors in valuing the prospects of the R&D expenditures of companies. Evidence indicates that the R&D expenditures of firms with substantial royalty income are accorded higher market valuations than R&D of companies lacking royalties, probably because the existence of customers for the firm's patents attests to the superior value of its R&D.[19]

For online (Internet) operations, the state of technological feasibility can be communicated (box 6) by traffic (eyeball) measures, such as unique visitors to the site, or by reach (percent of unique visitors of total web users). Such measures—collected by specialized companies (Nielsen/Netrating, Media Metrix)—can be used for benchmarking and have been

15. Currently, most companies disclose just total R&D expenditures.
16. See, for example, Demers and Lev (2000).
17. See, for example, Deng, Lev, and Narin (1999); Hall, Jaffe, and Trajtenberg (2000).
18. Investors can purchase the patent data on their own, but obviously, if the reporting company will acquire the patent data and disclose it to investors, considerable costs will be saved relative to individual investors acquiring the information.
19. Gu and Lev (2000).

shown to be statistically associated with market values.[20] Of particular importance is information on customers' "stickiness"—that is, the extent of web usage (time spent, on average, in the firm's site, number of pages read, and so on)—as well as information on customer loyalty (repeat buyers). Here, too, the company can provide this information at substantially lower cost, compared with its purchase by individual investors.

The above examples demonstrate the key attributes of the scoreboard component indicators: quantifiability, standardizability, and scientifically based linkage to value.

The Scoreboard: An Example

The proposed information system covers the relevant information for a wide variety of enterprises, but a typical company generally will have a parsimonious set of ten to twelve key value chain indicators. For example, I would expect a biotechnology company to report the following twelve items in its value chain scoreboard.

For the *discovery and learning* phase:

—Investment in internal and acquired R&D, classified by type of R&D (basic, applied), reported for the past three to five years

—Investment in alliances and joint ventures; total number of such alliances; classification into active and dormant ventures (including data on the volume of investments of alliance partners)

—Investment in information technology, both internal and acquired

Informing on the *implementation* stage:

—Number of new patents granted and the various attributes of (such as citations to) the company's patent portfolio; trademarks and copyrights granted, if any

—Cross-licensing of patents and royalty income from patent licensing

—Results of clinical tests and U.S. Food and Drug Administration (FDA) approvals

—Employee retention data and work force structure (such as ratio of scientists and R&D personnel to total employees); "hot skills"—employees who are star scientists (prestigious award winners)[21]

And finally, the biotechnology company will have five categories related to *commercialization*:

20. See, for example, Demers and Lev (2000).
21. Darby, Liu, and Zucker (1999) have established a statistical association between star scientists and the value of biotechnology companies.

—Innovation revenues (percent of revenue from recent products)

—Revenues from alliances, joint ventures, patent licensing

—Cash burn rate (length of operations on current resources)

—Product pipeline; expected launch dates of new products; products off patents

—Expected market potential for major new products

As noted earlier, the proposed value chain scoreboard is aimed at internal (managers, board members) as well as external (investors, suppliers, policymakers) purposes. The difference—and the devil—lies in the details. At the internal (managerial) level, for example, data on the investment in and productivity of alliances would be provided at the individual alliance or joint venture level. For external reporting purposes, aggregate data on the number of alliances and the total investment in them, along with a breakdown of alliances into operating (including revenues from alliances) and dormant ventures, will suffice.

What about Accounting?

It is widely recognized that the current accounting system does not convey relevant and timely information about the value chain (business model).[22] Investment in discovery and learning, both internal and acquired, is usually expensed immediately in financial reports, with most expenditures (on employee training, software acquisitions, and web-based distribution systems, for example) not even separately disclosed to investors. The transaction-based accounting system all but ignores the implementation stage of the value chain (an FDA drug approval, a patent granted, or a successful beta test of a software product), although considerable value creation or destruction, as well as risk reduction, generally occurs during this stage. And even the commercialization stage of the value chain, which generates recordable costs and revenues, is reported in a highly aggregated manner, defying attempts to evaluate the efficiency of the firm's innovation process (the assessment of return on R&D or technology acquisition, the success of collaborative efforts, or the firm's ability to expeditiously bring products to the market).

Some of the limitations of accounting-based information are rooted in the structure of accounting, which essentially reflects legally binding

22. Evidence the Senate hearings on this issue, the public committee set up in 2000 by the Securities and Exchange Commission to examine the adequacy of reported information to investors, FASB (2000), and such research findings as Lev and Zarowin (1999).

transactions with third parties (sales, purchases, borrowing funds, stock issues). In the industrial and agricultural economies, most of the value of business enterprises was created by transactions—the legal transfer of property rights. In the current, knowledge-based economy, much of value creation or destruction precedes, sometime by years, the occurrence of transactions. The successful development of a drug, for example, creates considerable value, but actual transactions (sales) may take years to materialize. This is, by the way, the major reason for the growing disconnect between market values and financial information.[23]

> *In the current, knowledge-based economy, much of value creation or destruction precedes, sometimes by years, the occurrence of recordable transactions. This is the major reason for the growing disconnect between market values and financial information.*

Viewed from this perspective, the proposed information system, which focuses on the fundamental phases of the value chain (the business proposition of the enterprise), precedes and complements accounting-based information. The special emphasis of the proposed value chain scoreboard on intangible investments clearly distinguishes it from current financial reports. Accounting, in a sense, provides a final reality check on the proposed system of value creation or destruction as products, services, or processes move along the value chain.

Eliciting Disclosure

The proposed value chain scoreboard is aimed at informing both managers and investors—at different levels of detail and frequency, of course—about the company's innovation activities, with special emphasis on investment in intangibles and their transformation to tangible results. Corporate decisionmakers will presumably secure value chain information as needs arise. But how will investors obtain such information? What will motivate managers to publicly disclose this information in a systematic and consistent manner?

---

23. Lev and Zarowin (1999).

Some believe that it is a matter of time until managers realize that a need exists for extensive, intangibles-related information and that they will then provide the information. In the meantime, it is argued, a period of experimentation with new information modes should be encouraged. This approach, however, flies in the face of reality: if after ten or fifteen years of unprecedented growth in the value and economic impact of intangibles the Financial Accounting Standards Board (FASB) still concludes that there is "lack of meaningful and useful disclosures about intangible assets," one must ask whether this experimentation process is working—and how long it might last.[24]

The second approach at eliciting information from managers centers on the creation of the right incentives for information disclosure. By *right incentives* the advocates of this approach generally mean the strengthening of safe harbor rules shielding managers from shareholder litigation. There are two major problems with this approach. First, there are already reasonably strong safe harbor rules for forward-looking managerial disclosures. Any considerable strengthening of these rules will come close to completely immunizing managers from shareholder litigation. Is this in the public's interest? Moreover, economic theory (optimal signaling) postulates that, for a message to be credible and effective, there must be a considerable penalty for misinformation. Clearly, the more effective the safe harbor rule, the lower the expected penalty, and the less credible the disclosed information will be. The second problem with the proposal to enhance safe harbor rules in order to motivate the disclosure of intangibles-related information is that most of this information is historically based (factual), rather than forward looking. For example, of the nine links in the proposed value chain scoreboard, the first eight deal with factual information. Safe harbor rules, intended to shield forward-looking disclosures, are largely immaterial for such information.

The Dual Role of Accounting Policy

Accounting policymakers such as the FASB, the Securities and Exchange Commission (SEC), and the American Institute of Certified Public Accountants (and corresponding bodies in other countries) have dual roles: they prescribe (mandate) information structures (such as a cash flow statement) and individual items (employee stock option information) that

---

24. FASB (2000).

have to be disclosed in financial reports; and they attempt to establish standards (a common language of disclosure). The first—the regulatory role of policymakers—is widely known and often contested by corporate managers. The latter—the standardization role—is much less appreciated. An example of the standardization role of accounting policymaking is the FASB's conceptual framework, which consists of six extensive statements, published during 1978–85, outlining the nature and measurement of financial information items, such as assets, liabilities, revenues, and expenses; as well as the fundamental postulates underlying accounting principles, such as relevance, reliability, and materiality.

Notably, there is no regulation (required disclosure) in the conceptual framework; rather, it is an attempt to create a uniform standard of measurement and reporting. The discussion of assets, for example, outlines the characteristics required for an asset to be recognized in financial reports (the future economic benefits, the control the enterprise has over these benefits, and so on), as well as valuation criteria for assets (such as write-off in case of impairment).[25] Such standardization creates a useful language; it enables users of financial reports to understand the meaning of the numbers in financial statements (for example, that asset values on the balance sheet refer to historical costs, not current values) and to compare this information across companies. Such standardization through common language creation is, I believe, required to elicit wide disclosure of intangibles-related information to investors, given the considerable uncertainty about the definition and measurement of intangibles.

I propose that an appropriate accounting policymaking body, preferably the FASB, with strong encouragement from and oversight by the SEC, take up the major task of standardizing intangibles-related information.

Standardizing Information on Intangibles

I propose that an appropriate accounting policymaking body, preferably the FASB with strong encouragement and oversight by the SEC, take upon itself the major task of standardizing intangibles-related information.

25. FASB (1985a, paras. 25–34).

By *standardization* I mean creating a coherent structure of information and defining the individual information items composing the information structure. By *information structure* I mean a comprehensive set of interrelated reports on value chain (business model) development, with special emphasis on intangible investments and assets. This reporting construct would complement the conventional one (balance sheet, income statement) by providing systematic and standardized information on innovation and intangible investments.

The individual items that make up the information structure— expenditures on customer acquisition, Internet traffic measures, or innovation revenues—require careful definition (such as what goes into customer acquisition costs). Valuation criteria must be clearly specified (Should customer acquisition costs be amortized? And how?).[26]

I strongly believe that if a coherent, well-defined, and decision-relevant system is developed to reflect the major attributes of intangible assets and their role (along with other assets) in the overall value creation process of the enterprise, most managers will respond by disclosing voluntarily some or all of the information. The reason for my optimism is that the availability of a new disclosure structure, endorsed by the major accounting policy-making institutions—and perhaps by other influential bodies (the large accounting firms)—will initiate the information revelation process discussed in chapter 4. Enterprises with good news (high innovation revenues, successful alliances) will start disclosing—in effect, motivating others to join ranks. No news is bad news in capital markets; silence is penalized.

The Big Bang The reader must be asking, What about overhauling the current accounting system? In recent extensive interviews, I called for substantive changes in GAAP.[27] Yet here I propose a voluntary information structure that complements financial reports. What about an overhaul?

I still strongly believe that a significant change in the current accounting system is called for, and I briefly outline the change below. Such a change, however, will require regulatory intervention—changing current accounting rules and regulations—which is bound to raise sig-

26. This is obviously not the place to delve into the details of the standard-setting task, but given the extent and pervasiveness of intangibles, it clearly is a major endeavor. However, the extensive experience of accounting policymakers in setting standards for financial information will come in handy.

27. *Fast Company*, January–February 2000; *Barron's*, November 20, 2000.

nificant managerial antagonism.[28] I therefore altered the priorities of my plan to enhance the likelihood of success: start with a voluntary yet well-defined and structured reporting system (the value chain scoreboard) and proceed later with changing the accounting system. Antagonism to the latter will be reduced, I believe, when managers and accountants gain experience with the disclosure of intangibles-related information and observe its successful dissemination in capital markets.

> *Start with a voluntary yet well-defined and structured reporting system—the value chain scoreboard—and proceed later with changing the accounting system.*

The most significant and urgent change required in the present accounting system relates to the recognition of assets. Current GAAP essentially rules out practically all intangibles from being recognized as assets.[29] This includes both internally generated intangibles and most acquired intangibles (in-process R&D, for example). Such a broad denial of intangibles as assets detracts from the quality of information provided in the balance sheet. Even more serious is its adverse effect on the measurement of earnings. The matching of revenues with expenses—the fundamental process underlying earnings measurement—is distorted by front-loading costs (the immediate expensing of intangibles) and recording revenues in subsequent periods unencumbered by those costs.[30]

What is required, then, is a significant broadening of the recognition of assets in financial reports, relaxing to some extent the requirements of reliability (that expected benefits of the asset should be subject to highly reliable estimation) and control (that the benefits of the asset will be under the complete control of the enterprise). As the discussion of the attributes of intangibles in chapter 2 makes clear, the benefits of intangibles are in general riskier (less amenable to reliable estimation) than those of physi-

28. Recall the chapter 4 discussion of the politics of intangibles.
29. The major exception is software development costs (see appendix A), yet many software companies immediately expense such costs; see Aboody and Lev (1998).
30. The immediate expensing of intangibles distorts both current and future earnings, sometimes understating earnings (conservative reporting), while under certain circumstances, typical of mature companies, overstating earnings (aggressive reporting); see Lev, Sarath, and Sougiannis (2000) for elaboration and empirical evidence.

cal assets, and full control of benefits of intangibles (excludability of nonowners) is in most cases impossible to achieve.

In principle, the FASB has not ruled out recognition of intangibles as assets: "Assets . . . may be intangible, and although not exchangeable they may be usable by the entity in producing or distributing other goods or services."[31] "Anything that is commonly used to produce goods or services, whether tangible or intangible and whether or not it has a market price or is otherwise exchangeable, also has future economic benefit."[32] Objections to the practical recognition of intangibles as assets emanate from the uncertainty associated with the benefits of intangibles (possibly leading to unreliable estimates) and the fact that in some cases (such as nonpatented know-how, customer acquisition costs) the enterprise does not exercise full control over the benefits of intangibles.

Given the heightened uncertainty, it makes sense to recognize intangible investments as assets when the uncertainty about benefits is considerably resolved. As projects under development advance from formulation of the initial idea through increasingly demanding feasibility tests (alpha and beta tests for software products, for example) to the final product, the notorious uncertainty about technological feasibility and commercial success continually decreases. Accordingly, a reasonable balance between relevance of asset reporting (to investors) and reliability of information would suggest the recognition of an intangible investment as an asset when the project successfully passes a significant technological feasibility test, such as a working model for software products or a clinical test for a drug. Surely, uncertainty about the future benefits of a clinically proven drug is not larger than the uncertainty associated with the expected benefits of commercial property in a newly developed area or of a loan granted to an enterprise operating in a developing country, which are both recognized as assets by GAAP. This suggested approach to asset recognition underlies U.S. software-for-sale standards (the major exception in the United States to intangibles expensing) and the recently enacted international standard for intangibles.[33]

Accordingly, I propose the recognition as assets of all intangible investments with attributable benefits that have passed certain prespecified tech-

31. FASB (1985b, para. 26).
32. FASB (1985b, para. 173).
33. For U.S. software, see FASB (1995); for international intangibles, see IASC (1998).

nological feasibility tests. I depart from the software capitalization standard by proposing that, once asset recognition commences (postfeasibility test), all the project-related previously expensed R&D should also be recognized as assets.[34] Given that uncertainty about the project's viability has been substantially reduced, I see no reason for a different accounting treatment of pre- and postfeasibility R&D.

Note that my intangibles recognition proposal, which is conditioned on the achievement of technological feasibility, differs substantially from a mechanical capitalization (accumulation) of all expenditures on intangibles. A major advantage of the proposed asset recognition is its allowance of managers to convey important information about the progress and success of the development program. Indiscriminate capitalization of all expenditures on intangibles does not provide such information.

Empirical evidence supports the proposed broadening of asset recognition. For example, capitalized values of R&D are significantly associated with stock prices (controlling for reported book values).[35] Similarly, reported asset values of internally developed software are positively and significantly associated with companies' market values.[36] Furthermore, the annual values of software development costs recognized as assets are associated with subsequent changes in earnings, suggesting that such asset recognition provides relevant information for the prediction of future earnings—an important objective of financial information.[37] A study of U.S. companies indicates that investors implicitly recognize customer acquisition costs as assets rather than expenses, whereas revaluations of intangibles by Australian companies are associated with market values.[38] Finally, a simulation-based analysis demonstrates the general

> *Empirical evidence supports the proposed broadening of asset recognition.*

---

34. See FASB (1995) for current software capitalization standard.
35. Lev and Sougiannis (1996).
36. Aboody and Lev (1998).
37. The predictive ability of annual software costs recognized as assets with respect to future earnings is expected, since the capitalization of software development costs is predicated on the success of the development program (for example, passing feasibility tests or developing a working pilot). Such developmental success should be associated with increases in subsequent sales and earnings.
38. For the United States, see Amir and Lev (1996); for Australia, see Barth and Clinch (1998).

superiority of intangibles' recognition as assets versus immediate expensing in providing meaningful performance data to investors.[39]

As with tangible assets, the amortization of intangibles would be based on management's estimates of productive lives, guided by industry norms and research findings. The amortization rates may be revised as the actual benefits of intangibles materialize. A strict periodic impairment test, along the lines of the current requirement for fixed assets, should be applied as a safeguard against overvaluation.[40]

How will the reporting deficiencies (discussed in chapter 4) be alleviated by the proposed asset recognition of intangibles? First and foremost, such recognition will improve the periodic matching of costs and benefits, particularly for firms with high growth rates of intangible investment. Specifically, when intangible inputs (R&D expenditures, brand enhancement) are expensed up front, and their benefits recorded in later periods, the reported earnings of both the early and subsequent periods are distorted. The same truth prevails when all restructuring (reorganization) costs are immediately expensed. Recognition of intangibles as assets will lead to reported earnings that more meaningfully reflect enterprise performance. Growth (momentum) measures—a focal point of investors— are currently inflated by intangibles' expensing (of in-process R&D, for example). Asset recognition will lead to more realistic earnings growth patterns.

The recognized intangibles will be reported on corporate balance sheets, thereby placing intangible assets on a common footing with physical assets. The amortization and write-offs of intangibles will convey valuable information about managers' assessment of the expected benefits of intangibles.[41] Thus broadening current asset recognition rules to include intangibles is indeed a major overhaul of accounting.

The recognition of intangibles as assets obviously increases the possibilities of earnings management and manipulation. However, in contrast to other means of managerial manipulation, such as the early recognition of revenues or exaggerated restructuring charges, intangibles' recognition

39. Healy, Myers, and Howe (1997).
40. FASB (1995). This is consistent with the recent FASB suggestion to require an impairment test for goodwill, a major intangible.
41. Indeed, Aboody and Lev (1998) find that the amortization of capitalized software is negatively and significantly associated with stock returns, implying that the amortization provides relevant information to investors. Intangibles' write-offs are also found value relevant by Healy, Myers, and Howe (1997).

is clearly and separately disclosed in the financial reports, allowing skeptical investors to easily reverse (undo) the procedure. At best, intangibles' asset recognition is a vehicle for managers to share with investors valuable information about the progress and success of innovation-producing activities. At worst, such recognition can be reversed, thereby restoring the financial reports to their current (full-expensing) status. This seems like a win-win situation.

Synopsis The key to achieving substantial improvement in the disclosure of information about intangibles, both within businesses and to capital markets, is the construction of a comprehensive and coherent information structure that focuses on the essential—the value creation (innovation) process of the enterprise—and places intangible assets in their proper role within this structure.

While focusing on what information yields functionality through disclosure, it is equally important to clarify what does not. In particular, managers should not be expected to disclose *values* of intangibles (the market value of a patent or the worth of key employees, for example). The determination of asset and enterprise value is better left to outsiders, such as financial analysts.

> The way to induce the release of meaningful information about intangibles is for policymakers to establish an information standard.

In my opinion, the way to induce the release of meaningful information about intangibles is for policymakers to establish a comprehensive information standard. Standards have previously worked wonders toward enhancing production and widespread participation in networks.[42] A standard scoreboard, such as the one outlined above, portraying the innovation process of businesses and focusing on the intangible investments generating the process, will drive a larger number of companies to provide new and useful information, internally and externally.

Along with the disclosure of voluntary information about intangibles, there is an urgent need to change current accounting and reporting systems. The change I propose focuses on a considerable broadening of the current rules of asset recognition to include technologically feasible intangibles with attributable benefits.

42. See Shapiro and Varian (1999) on the importance of standards (for example, a computer operating system) in the development of markets and technologies.

CHAPTER SIX

The Road Ahead

A s I conclude writing this book, in early 2001, Nasdaq companies have lost, on average, more than half their value of a year earlier. Internet companies lost more than 80 percent of the year-earlier value. Profit warnings by companies, including erstwhile technology powerhouses such as Cisco, Sun Microsystems, and Intel, abound, and the major question at the top of everyone's mind—from Federal Reserve chairman Alan Greenspan to the factory shop worker threatened with a layoff—is whether the U.S. economy is just slowing down, halting to a grind, or, God forbid, sliding into a serious, protracted recession.[1]

It is too early to tell how serious the downturn will be. True, labor productivity growth in the last three quarters of 2000 has "turned south": 6.1 percent, 3.0 percent, and 2.4 percent, respectively. Yet the 2.4 percent productivity growth in the last quarter of 2000 is just a tad below the total productivity growth in 1999 (2.6 percent) and substantially higher than the 1.4 percent mean

---

1. Perhaps the clearest sign of an economic slowdown is the return of formal dress to corporate America. As noted by the *Economist* ("Dressing for the Downturn," February 17, 2001, p. 26): "Only a year ago, the suit and tie seemed headed for extinction—along with other old-economy anomalies like profits, proven products and payment in cash. Now, it turns out, the vision of an open-neck future was but a mirage. Suits are back. Sales of suits and dress shirts bottomed in the third quarter of last year, and have since rebounded sharply. The suit is the perfect attire for hard economic times. It speaks of seriousness of purpose and self-discipline. It speaks of dullness, too, which is a welcome contrast with the anarchic creativity of the dotcoms."

annual productivity growth during 1974–90.[2] However, a whiff of inflation is in the air,[3] and consumer confidence plunged to a four-and-a-half-
year low. On the bright side, unemployment is still low in early 2001, and
the index of leading economic indicators jumped 0.8 percent in January—
its first increase in four months. Confusing signs indeed.

While the jury is still out concerning the severity of the slowdown, as
well as its long-term implications, some are quick to eulogize—even
ridicule—the "new economy:" "The downturn that is already gripping
America has removed the last shreds of credibility from the ultra-optimistic
'new economy' theories once espoused by Wall Street's and Silicon Valley's
most gung-ho believers. Thanks to wondrous new technology, the business cycle was supposedly consigned to the history books, and productivity would grow forever at a miraculous rate. So much for that."[4] Many of
the heroes of the late 1990s (technology entrepreneurs, venture capitalists,
and technology stock financial analysts and fund managers) are now portrayed as incompetent at best and villains—deceiving unwary investors—
at worst.[5]

Since I never joined the new economy–information revolution fan
club, I do not feel compelled to participate in the current anguish, flagel-
lation, and soul searching around the bursting of the technology bubble.
I am concerned, however, that intangibles—to which I have devoted this
book and much of my research and professional activities in recent
years—will be swept by the tide of disillusionment and ridicule surrounding the new economy. That people will lump together the permanent phenomenon of intangible investments as the major source of corporate
growth and value with transitory economic downturns, stock market
volatility, and the financial difficulties currently encountered by certain
technology sectors. That the exaggerated, often unfounded claims about
technological revolutions and new business models, now in disrepute, will

2. Productivity data published by the Bureau of Labor Statistics, Department of
Labor, February 7, 2001.

3. On February 16, 2001, the Labor Department announced a big jump of
1.1 percent in January in the producer price index. The "core" PPI, which excludes the
volatile food and energy sectors, rose 0.7 percent in January, the biggest increase since
December 1998.

4. *Economist*, February 10, 2001, p. 61.

5. See, for example, the *New York Times* front-page report (March 4, 2001) on
Henry Blodget, Merrill Lynch's "celebrated" Internet analyst who predicted in 1999
that Amazon's stock price would reach $400 (it indeed reached $400, but it closed at
$10 on March 2, 2001).

overshadow real and fundamental economic developments in which technological change and innovation, ushered by intangible investments, play such a major role.

And what are these fundamental economic developments present during both economic expansions and recessions? In the words of Paul Krugman, MIT's prominent economist and *New York Times* columnist:

> In the past, businesses primarily invested in the tangible means of production, things like buildings and machines. The value of a company was at least somewhat related to the value of its physical capital; to grow bigger a business had to build new factories roughly in proportion to the increase in its sales. But now businesses increasingly invest in intangibles. And once you have designed a chip, or written the code for a new operating system, no further investment is needed to ship the product to yet another customer. . . . The intangibility of a company's most important assets makes it extremely hard to figure out what that company is really worth. That may partly explain the nauseating volatility of stock prices.[6]

Similarly, observes Stanford University's Paul Romer, a major contributor to modern economic growth theory: "The most interesting positive implication of the [economic growth] model is that an economy with a larger total stock of human capital [capable of creating new knowledge] will experience faster growth."[7] And, adds the innovation strategist Gary Hamel: "In our hypertransparent world, competitive advantage will increasingly rest on an ability to create products, services and business models that are unique and utterly compelling."[8]

These, then, are the permanents: the central economic role of investment in intangible assets in general, and in human capital in particular, aimed at meeting the constantly increasing demand to innovate in order to gain competitive edge. While the rate of intangible investment may be affected, to some extent, by economic circumstances and capital market conditions, its centrality in corporate success, economic growth, and the enhancement of social welfare is unchallenged.

6. *New York Times*, October 22, 2000, p. 15.
7. Romer (1990, p. S99).
8. Gary Hamel, "Edison's Curse," *Fortune*, March 5, 2001, p. 176.

Current economic circumstances and capital market conditions notwithstanding, pharmaceutical and biotech companies will continue to direct most of their resources toward intangible investment in scientific discoveries and drug development; chemical companies will continue to devote significant capital to research and development (R&D) targeted at new products and economizing on the production of chemicals and fertilizers; retailers with their razor-thin margins and transparent prices will create value by expanding online operations and instituting improved supply chain processes; the growth of financial institutions and insurance companies will come mainly from new products and improved customer relations; the machine tool industry will continue to create value for the entire manufacturing sector with smarter, computer-laden tools that can speak electronically to each other; and the key to the health care sector's financial success will rest on the judicious use of improved technologies and on enhancing relations between professionals and patients. Whether perceived as the old or the new economy, an enterprise's competitive survival and success will primarily depend on smart intangible investments leading to innovation and effective commercialization. Economic slowdowns and capital market declines do not change these fundamentals.

> *Economic slowdowns and capital market declines do not change these fundamentals: that an enterprise's competitive survival and success will primarily depend on smart intangible investments leading to innovation and effective commercialization.*

What is changing, though, is the *urgent need* to gain a thorough understanding of the role of intangible capital—along with tangible and financial assets—in the process of value creation by business enterprises (the economics of intangibles); to improve managerial processes for coping with the idiosyncratic challenges posed by intangibles—spillovers of benefits (partial excludability), high risk, and no tradability; and to develop measurement and valuation tools for both managers and investors capable of rising to the major challenge articulated by Paul Krugman: "The intangibility of a company's most important assets makes it extremely hard to figure out what that company is really worth."[9]

9. *New York Times*, October 22, 2000, p. 15.

In the booming economy and roaring capital markets of the 1990s, crude measurement and valuation models, rules of thumb, and me-too policies ("we should also invest in dotcoms") could be tolerated, at least for a while. Speed and agility (first-to-market by corporations, day trading by investors) carried the day. In today's slow-growth economy and stagnant capital markets, on the other hand, meticulous attention to corporate resource allocation is required from managers, along with a thorough, fundamental analysis of securities from investors.[10]

In particular, managers should develop the capability to assess the expected return on investment in R&D, employee training, information technology, brand enhancement, online activities, and other intangibles and compare these returns with those of physical investment in an effort to achieve optimal allocation of corporate resources. Managers should also continuously monitor the efficiency of intangible asset deployment. While licensing patents and know-how, for example, may not be a top priority when earnings are ample and speed to market crucial, it is an important source of income during periods of slow growth. Similarly with human resource practices, such as incentive-based compensation, closely monitored training, and personally targeted employee benefits, which require careful planning and assessment of consequent benefits particularly when the going is tough. At this time, most business enterprises do not have the information and monitoring tools required for the effective management of intangibles.

In a challenging business environment with unforgiving capital markets, it is now time to move on from low-hanging fruit, such as patent licensing, to the full incorporation of intangible capital in managerial strategic and control processes and the full recognition of the role of key intangibles in corporate value creation.

In capital markets, superficial investment analysis with a focus on short-term corporate earnings will no longer suffice in a volatile but

10. On February 19, 2001, CNNfn reported that "Peter Bonfield, British Telecom's chief executive, said the firm had spent more than it should have on new mobile phone licenses, giving it the right to broadcast video, data and web services to cellular handsets. British Telecom paid $14B more than it should have." That is what I have in mind when I speak of the need for meticulous attention to corporate resource allocation.

generally flat stock market. The crude valuation models currently used by most analysts lack the capability to provide early warning signals of impending problems and will have to be replaced by an in-depth analysis of the enterprise's business model (recall the value chain scoreboard of chapter 5), with a focus on the capacity of the firm to learn, innovate, and secure maximum benefits from products and services.[11] A continuous assessment of managers' deployment of intangible and tangible resources will have to precede and underlie the current prediction of next quarter's earnings.

In short, in a challenging business environment and unforgiving capital markets, I foresee a need for increased, rather than decreased, attention to intangibles—the major drivers of corporate value and growth—by both managers and investors. The emphasis, however, should shift from superficial clichés like information revolution, the new economy, knowledge workers' or mental capital and half-baked knowledge management recipes to a serious analysis of the economics of intangible assets and their role in corporate value creation and the enhancement of social welfare. It is now time to move from exclusively dealing with "low-hanging fruit," such as patent licensing and intranet systems, to the full incorporation of intangible capital in the managerial strategic and control processes; and from essentially ignoring key intangibles (human resources, in particular) in the analysis and valuation of investments to fully recognizing their role in corporate value creation.

This book, which sets forth a systematic analysis of the economics of intangible assets, draws attention to rigorous research findings, and emphasizes the urgency of improving both internal and external information systems and disclosure about intangibles, will, I hope, pave the way for a comprehensive integration of intangible assets in managerial strategy and execution processes as well as in investors' analysis of securities and portfolio performance.

11. The very limited usefulness of analysts' valuation models is demonstrated by the preponderance of *after-the-fact* revisions of forecasts and recommendations. A case in point: On February 16, 2001, CNNfn reported that Nortel Networks warned Wall Street that it would post a first-quarter loss instead of anticipated profit and announced that it would lay off 10,000 employees. Shares of Nortel fell 32.8 percent in the day. After the warning, Credit Suisse First Boston pronounced a "dramatic sales disappointment," leading to downgraded Nortel shares; Goldman Sachs lowered its 2001 earnings estimate for Nortel, as did Salomon Smith Barney.

Accounting Rules and Regulations for Intangibles

Shyam Vallabhajosyula

T he accounting methods concerning intangible assets practiced in the United States and those prescribed by international standards are reviewed below.[1]

Generally Accepted Accounting Principles in the United States

The generally accepted accounting principles (GAAP) governing intangibles in the United States can be divided into general principles and specific practices.

General Principles

The broad principles governing accounting for intangible assets are laid out in APB (Accounting Principles Board) 17, paragraph 9, which directs a company to record as assets the costs of intangible assets acquired from others, including goodwill.[2] All costs incurred to develop intangible assets that are not specifically identifiable should be recorded as expenses. When an intangible asset has been recorded, its cost should be amortized by systematic charges to income over the estimated period of benefit of the asset. The amortization period should not exceed forty years in any case.

---

1. Shyam Vallabhajosyula is a Ph.D. candidate at the Stern School of Business, New York University.
2. FASB (1970b).

The provisions of APB 17 apply to intangible assets recorded on the acquisition of some or all of the stock held by minority stockholders of a subsidiary company. APB 17 is also applicable to the costs of developing goodwill and other unidentifiable intangible assets with indeterminate lives, provided that a company records such expenditure as assets. APB 17 itself does not mandate as to what type of expenditures should be deferred as assets.

Acquired Intangible Assets

Intangible assets acquired singly should be recorded at cost at date of acquisition. Cost is measured by one of the following: the amount of cash disbursed, the fair value of other assets distributed, the present value of amounts to be paid for liabilities incurred, or the fair value of consideration received for stock issued as described in APB 16.[3]

Intangible assets acquired as part of a group of assets or as part of an acquired company should also be recorded at cost at date of acquisition. Cost is measured differently for specifically identifiable intangible assets and those lacking specific identification. The cost of identifiable intangible assets is an assigned part of the total cost of the group of assets or enterprise acquired, normally based on the fair values of the individual assets. The cost of unidentifiable intangible assets is measured by the difference between the cost of the group of assets or enterprise acquired and the sum of the assigned costs of individual tangible and identifiable intangible assets acquired less liability assumed. Cost should be assigned to all

---

3. FASB (1970a). According to APB 16, paragraph 67, the general principles to apply the historical cost basis of accounting to an acquisition of an asset depend on the nature of the transaction:

—An asset acquired by exchanging cash or other assets is recorded at cost (at the amount of cash disbursed or the fair value of other assets distributed).

—An asset acquired by incurring liabilities is recorded at cost (at the present value of the amounts to be paid).

—An asset acquired by issuing shares of stock of the acquiring corporation is recorded at the fair value of the asset (shares of stock issued are recorded at the fair value of the consideration received for the stock).

The general principles must be supplemented to apply them in certain transactions. For example, the fair value of an asset received for stock issued may not be reliably determinable, or the fair value of an asset acquired in an exchange may be more reliably determinable than the fair value of a noncash asset given up. Restraints on measurement have led to the practical rule that assets acquired for other than cash, including shares of stock issued, should be stated at cost when they are acquired. In this case, cost may be determined either by the fair value of the consideration given or by the fair value of the property acquired, whichever is the more clearly evident.

specifically identifiable intangible assets; cost of identifiable assets should not be included in goodwill.

Acquired Intangible Assets for a Banking or Thrift Institution

Statement of Financial Accounting Standards (SFAS) 72 contains the rules for accounting for intangible assets arising during the acquisition of a commercial bank, a savings and loan association, a mutual savings bank, a credit union, or any other depository institution.[4] For proper accounting it is important to recognize whether the acquired intangible assets are identifiable or unidentifiable. Acquired intangible assets that can be separately identified should be assigned a portion of the total cost of the acquired enterprise if the fair values of those assets can be reliably determined. The fair values of assets that relate to depositor or borrower relationships should be based on the estimated benefits attributable to the relationships that exist at the date of acquisition. Hence new depositors or borrowers who may replace existing relationships should be ignored while allocating the fair value. Identified intangible assets have to be amortized over the estimated lives of the existing relationships.

If the fair value of liabilities assumed exceeds the fair value of tangible and identified intangible assets acquired, the excess constitutes an unidentifiable intangible asset. The intangible unidentified asset should be amortized to expense over a period that does not exceed the estimated remaining life of the long-term interest-bearing assets acquired. The amortization period should not exceed forty years in any case. The amortization rate is applied to the carrying amount of the interest-bearing assets that, based on their terms, are expected to be outstanding at the beginning of each subsequent period.

Goodwill

Goodwill is defined as the excess of the cost of an acquired company over the sum of identifiable net assets. It is the most common unidentifiable intangible asset. While identifiable intangible assets may be acquired singly, as a part of a group of assets or as part of an entire enterprise, unidentifiable assets cannot be acquired singly.

APB 17 requires that goodwill be amortized using the straight-line method unless a company can demonstrate that another systematic method is more appropriate. To use an accelerated method to amortize

4. FASB (1983).

goodwill, a company has to demonstrate that the amount assigned to goodwill represents an amount paid for factors such as those listed in paragraph 27[5] but that there is not a satisfactory basis for determining appraised values for the individual factors; and that the benefits expected to be received from the factors decline over the expected life of those factors. APB 17, paragraph 31, also specifies that a company has to continuously evaluate the period of amortization of intangibles to determine whether later events and circumstances warrant revised estimates of useful lives. However, the useful life of the unidentifiable intangible asset cannot be revised upward in any case.

Subsequent Costs

The costs of developing, maintaining, or restoring intangible assets should be deducted from income when incurred provided any of the following conditions are satisfied:

—The asset is not specifically identifiable.

—The asset has an indeterminate life.

—The asset is inherent in a continuing business and is related to an enterprise as a whole.

Specific Practices

Below, the current treatment of a variety of accounting items is listed, by industry.

Customer Acquisitions and Retention

In general, costs associated with collection, storage, and repeated access of information relating to customers are treated as operating expenditure.

5. Factors that should be considered in estimating the useful lives of intangible assets include:

—Legal, regulatory, or contractual provisions may limit the maximum useful life.

—Provisions for renewal or extension may alter a specified limit on useful life.

—The effects of obsolescence, demand, competition, and other economic factors may reduce a useful life.

—A useful life may parallel the service life expectancies of individuals or groups of employees.

—Expected actions of competitors and others may restrict present competitive advantages.

—An apparently unlimited useful life may in fact be indefinite, and benefits cannot be reasonably projected.

—An intangible asset may be a composite of many individual factors with varying effective lives.

The accounting rules do not require the recognition, valuation, and disclosure of such expenditure as assets.[6]

Credit information records. In the banking and thrift industry, SFAS 105 requires the following footnote disclosures, which are useful in estimating the nature of customer credit quality:

—All significant concentrations of credit risk arising from all financial instruments, whether from an individual counter party or groups of counter parties

—Group concentrations of credit risk if a number of counter parties are either engaged in similar activities or activities in the same region or have similar economic characteristics, such that their ability to meet contractual obligations would be similarly affected by changes in economic or other conditions

—For each significant concentration, information about the shared activity, region, or economic characteristic that identifies the concentration; and the amount of the accounting loss due to credit risk the entity would incur if parties to the financial instruments that make up the concentration fail completely to perform according to the terms of the contracts and the collateral or other security, if any, for the amount due proved to be of no value to the entity

—Collateral or other security to support financial instruments subject to credit risk, information about access to that collateral or other security, and the nature and a brief description of the collateral or other security supporting those financial instruments

Customer relations. In all customer-oriented industries, self-generated goodwill and customer relations are not explicitly recognized in the income statement or the balance sheet. Amounts spent on acquisition of customer relations and goodwill are treated as selling, advertisement, and sales promotion expenditure and expensed in the period incurred. Emerging Issues Task Force 88-20 deals with the issue when an enterprise purchases for cash the credit card portfolio, including the cardholder relationships, of a financial institution and the amount paid exceeds the sum of the amounts due under credit card receivables.[7] The difference between the amount paid and the sum of the balances of the credit card

6. FASB (1990a, para. 20).
7. FASB (1988).

loans at the date of purchase should be allocated between the intangible relationship assets and the loans acquired. The premium allocated to the loans should be amortized over the life of the loans, in accordance with SFAS 91.[8]

Customer support costs. The accounting for these costs is explicitly discussed only in SFAS 86.[9] According to paragraph 6, customer maintenance and support costs for computer software should be charged to expense when related revenue is recognized or when those costs are incurred, whichever occurs first. Maintenance is defined as activities undertaken after the product is available for general release to customers to correct errors or to keep the product updated with current information. Such activities include routine changes and additions. When the sales price of a product includes customer support for several periods and the price of that support is not separately stated, the estimated related costs should be accrued in the same period that the sales price is recognized.

Subscriber acquisition and maintenance. The treatment of such costs in relation to cable television companies is specified under SFAS 51.[10] The standard deals with accounting for subscriber-related costs, which are defined as costs incurred to obtain and retain subscribers to the cable television system. It includes costs of billing and collection, bad debts, mailings, repairs and maintenance of taps and connections, franchise fees related to revenues or number of subscribers, general and administrative system costs, programming costs for additional channels used in the marketing effort, and direct selling costs.

In the prematurity period, subscriber-related costs are expensed as period costs. Prematurity is the period during which the cable television system is partially under construction and partially in service. The period begins with the first earned subscriber revenue; its end varies with the circumstances of the system. The end is usually determined based on plans for completion of the first major construction period or achievement of a specified predetermined subscriber level at which no additional investment will be required for other than the cable television plant. The length of the prematurity period also varies with the franchise development and construction plans. It is usually not more than two years.

8. FASB (1986).
9. FASB (1985b).
10. FASB (1959)

For a continuing cable operation, initial hookup revenue is recognized as revenue only to the extent of direct selling costs incurred. The remainder of costs is deferred and amortized to income over the estimated average period that subscribers are expected to remain connected to the system. Direct selling costs include commissions, salespersons' compensation (other than commissions) for obtaining new subscribers, local advertising targeted for acquisition of new subscribers, and costs of processing documents related to new subscribers acquired. Direct selling costs do not include supervisory and administrative expenses or indirect expenses, such as rent and costs of facilities.

Initial subscriber installation costs, including material, labor, and overhead costs of the drop, are capitalized and depreciated over a period no longer than the depreciation period used for cable television plants.[11] The cost of subsequently disconnecting and reconnecting is charged to expense.

Customer lists and databases. SFAS 131 deals with accounting for such expenses in cases of health maintenance organizations, the hospitality industry, and publications. According to paragraph 39, footnote disclosure is required in certain cases.[12] Information about major customers is required to provide information about the extent of reliance on major customers if revenues from transactions with a single external customer amounts to 10 percent or more of an enterprise's revenues. Disclosures required are the total amount of revenues from each such customer and the identity of the segment or segments reporting the revenues (disclosure of the identity of a major customer or the amount of revenues that each segment reports from that customer is not required). A group of entities under common control is considered to be a single customer, and the federal government, a state government, a local government (for example, a county or municipality), or a foreign government each is considered to be a single customer.

Innovations
All expenditure on intangible assets related to blueprints, drawings, designs, patterns, documentation, laboratory notebooks, and recipes,

11. *Drops* is the hardware that provides access to the main cable. It comprises the short length of cable that brings the signal from the main cable to the subscriber's television set and other associated hardware, which may include a trap to block particular channels.
12. FASB (1997).

including chemical formulations, should be expensed following APB 17.[13] The cost of internally developing computer software is specifically not required to be capitalized. SFAS 86 deals with accounting for software, refers only to accounting for software that is developed for sale or lease.[14] According to the discussion in SFAS 86, the Financial Accounting Standards Board was "not persuaded" that the predominant practice of expensing cost of internally developed software was improper.

Media Creative Assets

Books, publications, libraries, music, and master recordings for the publishing, record, and music industries. According to SFAS 50, the cost incurred by the record company on a record master should be reported as an asset if the past performance and current popularity of the artist provides a sound basis for estimating that the cost will be recovered from future sales.[15] Otherwise, such costs should be expensed. Where an asset is recognized, it should be amortized over the estimated life of the recorded performance using a method that reasonably relates the amount to the net revenue expected to be realized.

Motion picture libraries of motion picture, television, and media companies. According to SFAS 53, motion pictures produced by a company should be capitalized as "inventory of films produced" and valued at production cost.[16] The cost of a film is amortized using the individual film forecast computation method. An alternative amortization method, the periodic table computation method, can be used if the result would approximate the result achieved by the first method. Amortization of film costs begins when a film is released, revenues on that film are recognized, and the amortization procedure relates the film costs to gross revenues reported, to yield a constant rate of gross profit before period expenses. Under the individual film forecast computation method, film costs are amortized in the ratio that current gross revenues bear to anticipated total gross revenues. Hence the method requires the determina-

13. FASB (1970b).
14. FASB (1985b).
15. FASB (1958, para. 11).
16. FASB (1981).

tion of total gross revenues during the entire useful life from exploitation in all markets.

Production costs for an individual film are accumulated in four chronological steps: acquisition of the story rights, preproduction (script development, costume design, set design and construction), principal photography (shooting the film), and postproduction (activities culminating in a completed master negative).

Motion picture companies are required to present either a classified or an unclassified balance sheet. In a classified balance sheet, film costs are segregated between current and noncurrent assets. Costs classified as current assets are unamortized costs of film inventory released and allocated to the primary market; completed films not released (reduced by the portion allocated to secondary markets); and television films in production that are under contract of sale. All other capitalized film costs are classified as noncurrent assets.

The allocated portion of film costs expected to be realized from secondary television or other exploitation should be reported as a noncurrent asset and amortized as revenues are recorded.

Since anticipated total gross revenues vary from actual total gross revenues, estimates of anticipated total gross revenues should be reviewed periodically and revised when necessary to reflect more current information. When anticipated total gross revenues are revised, a new denominator is determined to include only the anticipated total gross revenues from the beginning of the current year; the numerator (actual gross revenues for the current period) is not affected. The revised fraction is applied to the unrecovered film costs (production and other capitalized film costs) as of the beginning of the current year.

The periodic table computation method uses tables prepared from the historical revenue patterns of a large group of films. That revenue pattern is assumed to provide a reasonable guide to the experience of succeeding groups of films produced and distributed under similar conditions. The periodic table computation method ordinarily is used only to amortize that portion of film costs relating to film rights licensed to movie theaters, and film costs are accordingly allocated between those markets for which the table is used and other markets. The periodic tables should be reviewed regularly and updated whenever revenue patterns change significantly. Such tables should not be used for a film whose distribution pattern differs significantly from those used in compiling the table, for example, a film released for reserved seat theater exhibition.

Assets Arising from Contractual Arrangements

Cooperative agreements, patents, and trademarks. No specific regulation could be identified for these arrangements. In the absence of any other specific standard, the costs of developing these intangible assets should be expensed following APB 17.[17]

Franchise agreements and joint ventures. SFAS 45 deals with accounting for franchise fees by the franchiser.[18] The intangible asset represented by the contractual relationship on the part of the franchisee is not accounted for at all.

Favorable lease agreements and leasehold rights. No specific regulation could be identified. In the absence of any other specific standard, the costs of developing these intangible assets should be expensed following APB 17.

Environmental rights, including exemptions. No specific regulation could be identified. In the absence of any other specific standard, the costs of developing these intangible assets should be expensed following APB 17. However, general environmental contamination treatment costs, according to Emerging Issues Task Force 90-8, should be charged to expense.[19] The costs may be capitalized only if any one of the following criteria is met:

—The costs extend the life, increase the capacity, or improve the safety or efficiency of the property owned by the company. For the purposes of this criterion, the condition of that property after the costs are incurred must be improved compared with the condition of that property when originally constructed or acquired, if later.

—The costs mitigate or prevent environmental contamination that has yet to occur and that otherwise may result from future operations or activities. In addition, the costs improve the property compared with its condition when constructed or acquired, if later.

17. FASB (1970b).
18. FASB (1955).
19. FASB (1990b).

—The costs are incurred in preparing for sale that property currently held for sale.

Distribution rights and development rights.   No specific regulation could be identified. In the absence of any other specific standard, the costs of developing these intangible assets should be expensed following APB 17.

Insurance claims.   Under SFAS 5, claims payable are treated as contingencies, but claims receivable are not recognized.[20] Insurance claims receivable are not recognized until realized under the currently prevailing revenue recognition principles.

Take-or-pay, throughput, and project financing contracts.[21]   SFAS 47 does not require recognition of such contracts from the viewpoint of capitalizing the value of the intangible asset, if any. According to SFAS 47, the purchaser (or the receiving party) should disclose the following information with respect to purchase obligations (provided they meet the specified criteria):

—The nature and term of the obligation

—The amount of the fixed and determinable portion of the obligation as of the date of the latest balance sheet presented and for each of the five succeeding fiscal years

—The nature of any variable components of the obligation

—The amounts purchased under the obligation for each period for which an income statement is presented

---

20. FASB (1975).

21. According to SFAS 47, a *take-or-pay contract* is an agreement between a purchaser and a seller that provides for the purchaser to pay specified amounts periodically in return for products or services (FASB [1956]). The purchaser must make specified minimum payments even if not taking delivery of the contracted products or services. A *throughput contract* is an agreement between a shipper (processor) and the owner of a transportation facility (such as an oil or natural gas pipeline or a ship) or a manufacturing facility. The contract provides for the shipper (processor) to pay specified amounts periodically in return for the transportation (processing) of a product. The shipper (processor) is obligated to provide specified minimum quantities to be transported (processed) in each period and is required to make cash payments even if not providing the contracted quantities. A *project financing arrangement* relates to the financing of a major capital project in which the lender looks upon the cash flows and earnings of the project as the source of funds for repayment. The assets of the project serve as collateral for the loan.

Disclosure of the amount of imputed interest necessary to reduce the unconditional purchase obligation to present value is encouraged but not required.

Specific Industry-Related Intangibles

Airport landing rights for airlines. No specific regulation could be identified. In the absence of any other specific standard, the costs of developing these intangible assets should be expensed following APB 17.[22]

Federal Communications Commission (FCC) licenses for the broadcasting industry. No specific regulation could be identified. In the absence of any other specific standard, the costs of developing these intangible assets should be expensed following APB 17.

Network affiliation agreement for the broadcasting industry. SFAS 63 deals with accounting for agreements under which a broadcaster may be affiliated with a network of other television or radio broadcasters (network affiliation agreements).[23] Usually, under the agreement, the station receives compensation for the network programming that it carries based on a formula designed to compensate the station for advertising sold on a network basis and included in network programming. A network affiliate would generally have a lower programming cost than an independent station because an affiliate does not incur such costs for network programs. Network affiliation agreements are presented in the balance sheet of a broadcaster as intangible assets. If a network affiliation is terminated and not immediately replaced or under agreement to be replaced, the unamortized balance of the amount originally allocated to the network affiliation agreement is charged to expense. If a network affiliation is terminated and immediately replaced or under agreement to be replaced, a loss is recognized to the extent that the unamortized cost of the terminated affiliation exceeds the fair value of the new affiliation. However, a gain is not recognized if the fair value of the new network affiliation exceeds the unamortized cost of the terminated affiliation.

License agreements for programs in the broadcasting industry. SFAS 63 deals with the accounting for such license agreements. A typical license

22. FASB (1970b).
23. FASB (1982).

agreement for program material (features, specials, series, cartoons) covers several programs (a package). The agreement grants a broadcasting station, group of stations, network, pay television, or cable television system (licensee) the right to broadcast either a specified number or an unlimited number of showings over a maximum period of time (license period) for a specified fee. Ordinarily, the fee is paid in installments over a period generally shorter than the license period. The agreement usually contains a separate license for each program in the package. The license expires at the earlier of the last allowed broadcast or the end of the license period. The licensee pays the required fee whether or not the rights are exercised. If the licensee does not exercise the contractual rights, the rights revert to the licensor with no refund to the licensee. The license period is not intended to provide continued use of the program material throughout that period but rather to define a reasonable period of time within which the licensee can exercise the limited rights to use the program material.

The licensee reports an asset and a liability for the rights acquired and obligations incurred under a license agreement when the license period begins (and certain conditions are met). The asset is segregated on the balance sheet between current and noncurrent based on estimated time of usage. The liability is segregated between current and noncurrent based on the payment terms. The rights capitalized are amortized based on the estimated number of future showings, except that licenses providing for unlimited showings of cartoons and programs with similar characteristics may be amortized over the period of the agreement because the estimated number of future showings may not be determinable. If the first showing is more valuable to a station than reruns, an accelerated method of amortization is to be used. Otherwise, the straight-line amortization method is used.

The capitalized costs of rights to program materials are reported in the balance sheet at the lower of unamortized cost or estimated net realizable value on a program-by-program, series, package, or day part basis, as appropriate.[24] If management's expectations of the programming usefulness of a program, series, package, or day part are revised downward, the unamortized cost is revised downward to the estimated net realizable

24. A *day part* is an aggregation of programs broadcast during a particular time of day (daytime, evening, late night) or programs of a similar type (sports, news, children's shows). Broadcasters generally sell access to viewing audiences to advertisers on a day part basis.

value. The management is not permitted to revise the value upward if the program is more successful than originally anticipated.

FCC radio band licenses. No specific regulation could be identified. In the absence of any other specific standard, the costs of developing these intangible assets should be expensed following APB 17.

Drilling and mineral rights for the extractive industries. SFAS 19 deals with mineral interests in properties for oil and gas companies.[25] Mineral rights cover a fee ownership or a lease, concession, or other interest representing the right to extract oil or gas subject to such terms as may be imposed by the conveyance of that interest. It includes royalty interests, production payments payable in oil or gas, other nonoperating interests in properties operated by others, and agreements with foreign governments or authorities under which the company participates in the operation or serves as producer of the underlying reserves. Mineral rights do not include any supply agreements or contracts that represent the right to purchase (as opposed to extract) oil and gas. Mineral rights are classified as proved or unproved, as either unproved properties (properties with no proved reserves) or proved properties (properties with proved reserves). Properties with unproved reserves are expensed whenever it is established that no recovery is possible.

Interstate operating rights in the transportation industry. SAFS 44 deals with the accounting for intangible assets as represented by operating rights.[26] An operating right (also known as an operating authority) is defined as a franchise or permit issued by the Interstate Commerce Commission or a similar state agency to a motor carrier to transport specified commodities over specified routes with limited competition. These rights are either granted directly by the Interstate Commerce Commission or a state agency, purchased from other motor carriers, or acquired through business combinations. The statement requires that the cost of acquiring operating rights be charged to income and, if material, reported as an extraordinary item. In the case of a business combination of motor carrier companies, the costs of intangible assets should be assigned to interstate operating rights, other identifiable intangible assets (including intrastate operating rights), and goodwill.

25. FASB (1977).
26. FASB (1980).

The cost of identifiable intangible assets (including operating rights) should not be included in goodwill. Costs assigned to intangible assets should not reflect costs of developing, maintaining, or restoring those intangibles after they were acquired. Costs assigned to identifiable intangibles, including operating rights, should not be merged with or replaced by amounts relating to other identifiable intangibles or goodwill. If a company cannot separately identify its interstate operating rights, other identifiable intangible assets, and goodwill and cannot assign costs to them as specified by this statement or finds that it is impracticable to do so, it will be presumed that all of those costs relate to interstate operating rights.

Mortgage servicing rights in the banking industry. According to SFAS 125, the servicer of financial assets commonly receives the benefits of servicing (revenues from servicing fees, late charges, and other ancillary sources, including a "float") when it performs the servicing and incurs the costs of servicing the assets.[27] If the benefits of servicing are not expected to adequately compensate the servicer for performing the servicing, the contract results in a servicing liability. A company that undertakes the servicing obligation should recognize an asset or a liability. However, if the transferor secures the assets, retains all of the resulting securities, and classifies them as debt securities held to maturity in accordance with SFAS 115, then the servicing asset or liability should be reported together with the asset being serviced.[28] A servicing asset or liability that was purchased or assumed rather than undertaken in a sale or a securement of the financial assets being serviced should be measured at the price paid (considered the fair value). The servicing asset or liability should be amortized in proportion to and over the period of estimated net servicing income (when servicing revenues exceed servicing costs) or net servicing loss (when servicing costs exceed servicing revenues). The servicing asset

27. FASB (1996). Servicing of mortgage loans, credit card receivables, or other financial assets includes, but is not limited to, collecting principal, interest, and escrow payments from borrowers; paying taxes and insurance from escrowed funds; monitoring delinquencies; executing foreclosure if necessary; temporarily investing funds pending distribution; remitting fees to guarantors, trustees, and others providing services; and accounting for and remitting principal and interest payments to the holders of beneficial interests in the financial assets. While servicing is inherent in all financial assets, it becomes a distinct asset or liability only when contractually separated from the underlying assets by sale or securitization of the assets with servicing retained or separate purchase or assumption of the servicing.

28. See FASB (1993).

or liability should be assessed for impairment or increased obligation based on its fair value.

Motion picture exhibition rights for motion picture theaters. According to SFAS 53, motion picture exhibition rights are generally sold (licensed) to theaters on the basis of a percentage of the box office receipts or, in some markets, for a flat fee.[29] In some markets guarantees may be received that are essentially outright sales because the licenser has no reasonable expectations of receiving additional revenues based on percentages of box office receipts, particularly where there is a lack of control over distribution. The licenser recognizes revenues on the dates of exhibition for both percentage and flat-fee engagements. Nonrefundable guarantees should be deferred and recognized as revenues on the dates of exhibition. Guarantees that are, in substance, outright sales, are recognized as revenue (provided certain conditions are met).

For films licensed to television, the license agreement for television program material is a sale of a right or a group of rights. Revenue from a license agreement is recognized when the license period begins and all of the following conditions have been met: the license fee for each film is known, the cost of each film is known or is reasonably determinable, the collectibility of the full license fee is reasonably assured, the film has been accepted by the licensee, and the film is available for its first showing or telecast. The license fee for each film ordinarily is specified in the contract; the present value of that amount should be used as the sales price for each film.

According to paragraph 20 of SFAS 53, a license agreement for sale of film rights for television exhibition should not be reported on the balance sheet until the time of revenue recognition. Amounts received on such agreements before revenue recognition are reported as advance payments and are included in current liabilities, if those advance payments relate to film cost inventory classified as current assets.

International Accounting Standards

International Accounting Standard (IAS) 38 deals with the accounting of intangible assets.[30]

29. FASB (1981).
30. IASC (1998).

General Principles

According to IAS 38, an intangible asset is recognized on the balance sheet if the asset's cost can be reliably measured and all future economic benefits specifically attributable to the asset will flow to the enterprise. All other costs incurred for nonmonetary intangible items should be expensed. The intangible asset is reported in the balance sheet at its cost less any accumulated amortization and any accumulated impairment costs.

Definitions

Intangible assets are defined as nonmonetary assets without physical substance held for use in production or supply of goods or services, for rental to others, or for administrative purposes and that are identifiable, that are controlled by an enterprise as a result of past events, and from which future economic benefits are expected to flow to the enterprise. The definition of intangible assets requires that the asset be identifiable in order to distinguish it from goodwill.

Goodwill represents future economic benefits from synergy between identifiable assets or from intangible assets that do not meet the criteria for recognition as an intangible asset.

Cost is the amount of cash or cash equivalents paid or the fair value of the other consideration given to acquire an asset at the time of its acquisition or production.

Recognition and Measurement of Intangible Assets

According to the standard, an intangible asset should be recognized as an asset if and only if it is probable that future economic benefits specifically attributable to the asset will flow to the enterprise and if the cost of the asset can be measured reliably. The asset that is recognized should be initially measured at cost. The future economic benefits flowing from an intangible asset may include revenue from sale of products or services, cost savings, or other benefits arising from use of the asset by the enterprise itself.

The standard lays down rules for an enterprise to demonstrate that future economic benefits specifically attributable to an intangible asset will flow back to an enterprise. The enterprise is required to show that the intangible asset will enhance the enterprise's net inflow of future economic benefits; that it has the intention and ability to use the intangible asset; and that it has the adequate technical, financial, and other resources available to obtain the expected future economic benefits.

Internally Generated Goodwill

Under no circumstances should internally generated goodwill be recognized as an asset. Internally generated goodwill is not recognized as an asset because no resource is created that is controlled by the enterprise, which will generate specific future economic benefits and that can be reliably measured at cost.

Subsequent Costs

Subsequent costs on an intangible asset should be recognized as an expense when they are incurred, unless it is probable that these costs will enable the asset to generate specifically attributable future economic benefits in excess of the originally assessed standards of performance and unless these costs can be reliably measured and attributed to the asset. In the absence of these conditions, the subsequent costs incurred on the intangible asset should be expensed.

Amortization

IAS 38 requires that costs of the intangible asset be amortized over the estimated useful life of the asset. In the absence of any other information to the contrary, the useful life of an intangible asset is presumed to be twenty years.

Specific Intangibles

In the absence of any other specific provisions, IAS 38 treatment applies to the following assets.

Customer Acquisition and Retention
—Credit information records for the banking and thrift industries
—Customer relations and goodwill for customer-oriented industries
—Customer support costs for consumer services industries (including computer software)
—Subscriber acquisition and maintenance for the cable television industry
—Customer lists and databases for health maintenance organizations and the hospitality and publication industries

Innovations
—Blueprints, drawings, designs, patterns, documentation, laboratory notebooks, and recipes for the engineering, pharmaceutical, and hospitality industries
—Chemical formulations for the chemical and pharmaceutical industries
—Internally developed computer software for the technology, manufacturing, retail, and transportation industries

Assets Not Specifically Recognized
—Books, publications, libraries, music, and master recordings of the publishing, record, and music industries
—Distribution networks of the consumer and industrial products industries
—Motion picture libraries for the motion picture, television, and media industries

Assets Arising from Contractual Arrangements
—Cooperative agreements
—Patents and trademarks
—Open-to-ship customer orders
—Franchise agreements and joint ventures
—Favorable lease agreements
—Environmental rights (including exemptions)
—Leasehold interest
—Distribution and development rights
—Insurance claims
—Project financing arrangements, take-or-pay contracts
—Throughput contracts, other unconditional purchase commitments, and open-to-ship purchase orders

Specific Industry-Related Intangibles
—Airport landing rights for the airlines industry
—FCC licenses for the broadcasting industry
—Network affiliation agreements for the broadcasting industry
—License agreements for programs in the broadcasting industry

—FCC radio band licenses for the broadcasting and communications industries
  —Drilling and mineral rights for the extractive industries
  —Interstate operating rights for the transportation industry
  —Mortgage servicing rights for the banking industry
  —Motion picture exhibition rights for the motion picture industry

Intellectual Capital Management Best Practices

Suzanne Harrison, Patrick H. Sullivan Sr., and
Michael J. Castagna of ICMG

T he quest to understand how best to extract value from intellectual capital has been ongoing for a number of years. In an effort to learn more about what companies were doing in this area, a meeting was held in January 1995 to convene all of the companies actively managing their intellectual capital.

At this first meeting of what was to become the ICM Gathering, participants determined that they needed to agree on a definition of the term *intellectual capital* as well as to understand its major elements. The ICM Gathering defined intellectual capital as "knowledge that can be converted into profits." The ICM Gathering now consists of approximately thirty companies. The materials in this appendix were derived from this group.

Roles for Intellectual Capital

Companies ascribe a range of roles for value extraction from their intellectual capital. While most people tend to think quickly of the revenue-generating role, there is a range of others that are employed. The following represent some of those most often mentioned.

Defensive Roles

—Protecting the products and services resulting from the innovations of the company's information capital
—Protecting freedom of design
—Avoiding litigation

Offensive Roles

—Generating revenue from the products and services resulting from the firm's innovations; from the intellectual properties of the firm; from the intellectual assets of the firm; and from the knowledge and know-how of the firm
—Creating standards in new markets or for new products and services
—Obtaining access to the technology of others
—Obtaining access to new markets
—Supporting the business activities of the firm's strategic business units
—Creating barriers to entry for new competitors

A Decision System for Optimizing the Value of a Firm's Intellectual Capital

Over the course of several years of meetings, the ICM Gathering companies came to learn that there was a generic set of activities and decisions involved with extracting the optimum value from their firms' intellectual capital. When organized into a commonsense flow or process, these activities (decisions, decision processes, information gathering, and work processes) allow companies to systematically evaluate and extract value from their intellectual assets. This generic system has come to be called the intellectual asset management system. Because the system reflects the collective learning from more than thirty companies, there is no one company that uses the system exactly as defined. Yet if they were able to begin all over again, each would likely choose a system with the following components (see figure B-1):

—*The innovation process.* All firms have their own approach and method for developing new or innovative ideas that create value. For many technology companies the innovation process is a research and development (R&D) activity. Service companies, on the other hand, often have a creativity department. Still others rely on their employees in the field to produce innovative ideas. Whatever the firm's source of innovations, the generic system calls this the *innovation process.*

—*Portfolio inclusion.* The go/no-go decision. Most firms have a method for evaluating the innovative ideas that emerge from the innovation process. Innovations that pass the screening—those that are deemed likely to be useful to the company in pursuit of its strategy—are selected

FIGURE B-1 The Intellectual Asset Management System

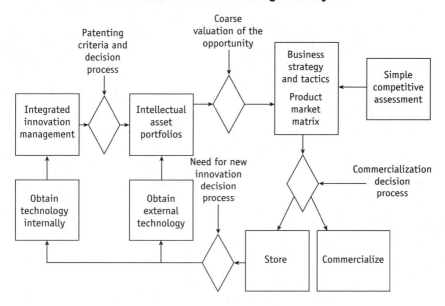

for inclusion in the company's portfolio of intellectual assets. Some companies use the screening process to determine which innovations will be patented; the decision to patent requires an investment of up to $200,000 to obtain and maintain legal protection for an innovation for its twenty-year life. This decision is important for all companies because it separates ideas that are of particular interest to the firm from ideas that, though they may be good and interesting, are not aligned with the firm's strategy. (When a firm decides to not patent, it often maintains an innovation in the know-how of its employees, sometimes formally protecting this knowledge as a trade secret.)

—*The intellectual asset portfolio.* The portfolio is in fact a series of portfolios containing the firm's different kinds of intellectual assets. Some of the portfolios may contain intellectual properties, others may contain documents of potential business interest (such as customer lists, price lists, business practices, and internal processes), and others may contain ideas or innovations that are in the portfolio because of their potential to create profits.

—*Coarse valuation of opportunity.* Each innovation of potential interest should be valued before it is reviewed for use. Valuation, in this sense, is a bifurcated process. The first part of the valuation process is to narratively describe how the intellectual asset is expected to bring value to the firm. Following this qualitative valuation, and where it is possible to do so, the firm should attempt to quantify the amount of value it expects the innovation to provide.

—*A simple competitive assessment.* While competitive assessments in business are commonplace, the competitive assessment contemplated here is one that is focused on the intellectual assets of the competition. In the case of technology companies, that focus might be on a competitor's technology as well as on its portfolio of patents.

—*The business-strategy-tactics-product-market mix.* This portion of the intellectual asset management system involves a review of intellectual assets of interest matched with the firm's business strategy, tactics, and product market mix. The outcome of this review is an assessment of the fit between this asset, the organization's strategy, and a decision about how to use or dispose of the intellectual asset under review.

—*The disposition decision process.* The decision concerning the disposition of reviewed intellectual assets may have several possible outcomes. The intellectual asset may be commercialized or stored until another innovation is developed that makes the first one more marketable.

—*The commercialization decision process.* This process results in a decision about which mechanism or mechanisms will be used to convert the innovation to cash.

—*Deciding where to seek innovation.* This decision process is invoked when it has been decided that a new innovation should be sought to add to an existing innovation to make the first more marketable. In this case, the question is whether to seek the second innovation from inside or outside the company (through, for example, in-licensing or acquisition of a company).

Each firm involved in extracting value from its intangible assets inevitably uses a set of activities and decisions similar to that described above. Each such firm tailors the activities and decisions to suit its individual context. In addition to tailoring the activities and decisions involved in the management of the firm's intangible assets, there are also significant issues surrounding how a firm will organize itself to operate and manage this set of decisions and activities.

Below are profiles of three companies, all of which are considered by ICMG to be best-practice leaders in the management of their intellectual capital. As is obvious from the profiles, they each have different purposes for their intellectual capital, different areas of focus, and different management mechanisms in place. Despite these superficial differences, each of these firms has designed its intellectual capital management function using the principles and concepts outlined above.

Neste Oy

In today's competitive environment, the frequency of mergers and acquisitions (M&A) has increased dramatically. Much M&A activity may be attributed to the ascendancy of knowledge in the new economy. In high-technology industries, the practice of paying well in excess of book value for companies with cutting edge technologies has become the norm. In such an environment, it is vitally important to accurately assess the value of one's company—and this value is more and more determined by a firm's intellectual capital. One company that realized this early on and was able to use its knowledge to great advantage in a merger situation is Neste. Faced with a requirement to merge its petrochemical business with Statoil's petrochemical business, Neste conceptualized and conducted a technology audit to ensure it could obtain the most favorable terms for the impending merger.

Although the merger was the impetus for the technology audit, Neste seized the opportunity to comprehensively identify and categorize all of its intellectual capital. The technology audit was given a broad mandate to assess the value and the extraction potential of Neste's existing intellectual capital portfolio, maximizing value extraction while minimizing the necessary costs of the upkeep and maintenance of an intellectual property portfolio.

Neste's vice president of corporate technology described the firm's intent to establish an intellectual property rights management group, which would use corporate intellectual property rights "as a strategic asset" and technology transfer "as a tool to achieve other corporate objectives."[1]

Having to develop a technology audit strategy from scratch while preparing for a merger forced Neste's management to act decisively. Realizing that the technology asset audit was a paradigm shift in business processes for Neste, and that a quick turnaround was required in order to stay on schedule with the upcoming merger, the chief executive officer and

1. Laento (1998, p. 243).

the president became the lead sponsors of the project. Another prescient decision was to centralize control of Neste's technology at the corporate level, which enabled maximum flexibility and decisive decisionmaking.

At the same time, management realized that the project had to be successfully sold to Neste's employees. They embarked on a painstaking effort to develop a common language around intellectual capital. Once this was accomplished, they developed a clear, simple message articulating management's intent in initiating the project, a message that could be taken directly to employees. This message also defined the technologies of interest and measurement techniques to be used. Being forthright with Neste's employees avoided much of the apprehension that surrounds similar change processes.

Once the project was understood, questionnaires were circulated to uncover the requisite information for each technology. A standard questionnaire was created to identify technology types, technology stages, legal ownership status, and commercialization options. In addition to describing the technology thoroughly, each technology was categorized as either existing or precommercial. The ownership status identified those technologies owned outright or partly owned by Neste. Finally, each technology was assessed for its commercial viability according to exploitation categories such as key, base, spare, pacing, and emerging technologies.

Each technology was also evaluated against Neste's transfer model. This model weighed the amount of investment in a technology against the level of control Neste exercised over it. The model output showed whether a technology should be abandoned, sold, licensed, spun off, and so on.

A Microsoft Access database was created to store information germane to each technology audited. The database system was found to be highly useful and was quickly adopted by many businesses and divisions for current and future technology planning.

The audit project was an opportunity for all of Neste's employees to learn the importance of intellectual capital and its potential to affect the company's bottom line. Now its employees have a common language to address issues relevant to intellectual capital, and this will make further endeavors in this area much easier.

The project succeeded in identifying all of Neste's technologies, classifying them in terms of ownership structure and commercial potential, and analyzing them via the transfer model. Quite to management's surprise, many of their technologies were not well protected, and considerable resources were devoted to shoring up their assets. Also, over 50 percent of their patents were categorized as excess. Most of these were rapidly slated for abandonment or out-licensing; however, in a few situations, the patents could be used to develop novel business opportunities. These actions enabled immediate cost savings and/or increased revenue streams.

Finally, this effort allowed Neste to hone its intellectual capital processes. Systematic reviews are now conducted of its existing patent portfolio and of any new technology potentially worthy of patent protection. Its innovation compensation system was also revamped to allow a more targeted value creation effort.

Dow Chemical Company

The Dow Chemical Company, arguably one of the most successful corporations in America, was one of the first companies to realize that factors leading to corporate success were changing. Fitness in a hypercompetitive global marketplace was no longer sufficient for success. Prosperity in the new business environment would require companies to integrate themselves seamlessly into profitable value chains and adroitly develop relationship capital. At the same time, Dow's management was inspired by ideas circulating in academia, such as the concept of service value used by Yale professor and Nobel Laureate James Tobin. Tobin applied the term *service value* to the gap between the replacement value of a firm's tangible assets and its market value. Dow took the concept of service value (or what it saw as intellectual assets) and built a management system around it.

The basic premise was that intellectual assets had always been managed but that future success depended on a mastery of intellectual asset management. Mastery would come through refined processes facilitating visualization, measurement, and management. Dow envisaged the role of intellectual asset management as a way to maximize "the business value of Dow's intellectual assets and develop a management process that will help to maximize the creation of new valuable intellectual assets."[2]

Realizing that this new tactic would require a substantial amount of process reengineering, Dow's management elected for an evolutionary rather than revolutionary approach. They began with a well-understood

2. Petrash (1998, p. 207).

portion of their intellectual asset repository: patents. Interdepartmental teams were formed to fastidiously map out existing processes and through analysis describe for each an "is process" and a "should be process." Resources were devoted to the transition of "is processes" to "should processes."[3]

Several steps were taken to facilitate the intellectual asset management initiative. Managers were chosen to lead intellectual asset management teams through process reengineering, following a model with six phases: portfolio, classification, strategy, valuation, competitive assessment, and investment.

In the portfolio phase, all of the active and the inactive patents were identified. Once identified, each patent was analyzed to determine where it fit best within Dow's fifteen major business units. Then the business unit was given ownership and responsibility for the patent. Subsequently, in the classification phase, each patent was further categorized as to whether "the business is using, will use, or will not use" the asset.[4] The strategy phase sought to accomplish two important objectives: to maximize value extraction by integrating the patent portfolio into the business's strategy and to identify any intellectual property shortfalls or gaps necessary to fill in order to realize the company's objectives.

The valuation phase determined the value and contribution of the intangible asset. Dow, along with A. D. Little, developed a valuation technique they termed the tech factor method. It uses the net present value of incremental cash flows along with utility and competitive issues to determine fair market value of the intellectual property. During the competitive assessment phase, patent trees were utilized to determine the relevant competitive factors surrounding a technology. These trees reveal the patents' strength and scope but also depict blocking and opportunity windows. The process culminates in the investment phase, in which it is determined what technology must be acquired in order to carry out the business strategy and what the means of acquiring the technology will be (make, buy, joint venture, and so on).

After successfully applying the intellectual asset management model to patents, Dow applied the model to know-how. The key here was to find a way to visualize and communicate know-how. The intellectual asset

3. Petrash (1998, p. 208).
4. Petrash (1998, p. 209).

management teams narrowed their focus by defining know-how as "key technical know-how."[5] To visualize intangible assets, three questions were posed: What is the key technical know-how of a business unit? Where does it reside? How is it articulated? The communication objective was addressed with a corporatewide network.

The initiative proved to be successful on a grand scale. The hypothesis that improved alignment of intellectual assets to the business strategy would create greater value for the corporation was proven correct. Soon after the completion of its auditing and classification efforts Dow saved $1 million. Over the life of its portfolio, Dow was able to save $40 million in patent tax maintenance fees. Meanwhile, the identification of key patents generated new cash flows from licensing. In 1994 Dow received $25 million in revenues from licensing and estimated that by 2000 they would reach $125 million. In fact, they surpassed that number several years ahead of their target date. Dow even found an innovative way to salvage some value from the 30 percent of its patents slated for abandonment by obtaining tax write-offs for donating the patents to universities.[6]

Overall, the intellectual asset management initiative resulted in a number of novel processes, methods, and tools in both the patent and know-how area.

Hewlett-Packard

Innovation has become the lifeblood of today's successful firms. Carly Fiorina, Hewlett-Packard's chief executive officer, understands the importance of innovation and the visceral role it plays in the viability of the firm. She renewed Hewlett-Packard's commitment to innovation at COMDEX '99 by emphatically stating that they would "drive inventiveness for the new economy."

To many, this would seem overly ambitious; however, it may well be within Hewlett-Packard's ability, since HP has developed a world-class process for intellectual property management. Leading in this area requires a culture honed to cultivate a firm's organizational ideas and an intellectual property staff capable of attaining protection for the most valuable ideas—in short order.

5. Petrash (1998, p. 215).
6. Sharon Oriel, director, Intellectual Asset Management Technology Center.

It was clear that the firm's most valuable knowledge existed in tacit form. This "personal, context-specific knowledge" resides with the firm's human capital; therefore, a system to encourage its inventors to convert their tacit knowledge to explicit knowledge was the goal.

Stephen P. Fox, associate general counsel and director of intellectual property for Hewlett-Packard, realized early on the need to create incentive structures properly aligned with a firm's global objectives. Since these objectives have always revolved around innovation, it became clear that a system to encourage inventors to participate in the intellectual property process was crucial.

However, before the inventor incentive program could be enacted, Hewlett-Packard's inventors had to be shown that their ideas were invaluable in the intellectual property process. Educating the inventors was the first step. Fox notes that "it is important to dispel the notion that there is nothing good left to invent and encourage inventors to give themselves the benefit of the doubt when assessing whether they have invented something."[7] It must be stressed that innovation is rarely achieved by a single "flash of genius" but is more often a lengthy, team-engendered process. Finally, the innovation cycle culminates with some form of legal protection enabling value to be extracted from the idea.

Often, organizational policies are not aligned with an organization's goals. For instance, an organization bent on innovation may pressure its inventors to generate valuable ideas and yet counterproductively offer no incentive to draft a disclosure of the find. With time pressures and impending deadlines inventors are faced with a trade-off between inventing and writing, and invention disclosures are thus often neglected.

Hewlett-Packard's incentive program ensures organizational alignment and encourages inventors to participate in the invention disclosure process. The program has four elements. The first two elements are common and can be found in most incentive programs: recognition of employees in public forums, peer groups, and annual banquets; and administrative issues such as funding and inventor identification and nomination. The other elements of the incentive program differ from extant programs in other companies. Cash incentive payments are apportioned so that the first is received at the submission of the invention disclosure and the second after the patent has been secured. Last, there is an important element of flexibility and responsiveness. The whole program is

---

7. Fox (1998, p. 146).

optional for business units and is implemented on a business-by-business basis, and each program is set up with a sunset provision allowing reassessment after the program's first year, making the program highly flexible and easily adaptable.

The program has been extremely successful. The number of invention disclosures has doubled since the inception of the program

References

Aaker, David. 1996. *Building Strong Brands*. Free Press.

Aboody, David, and Baruch Lev. 1998. "The Value Relevance of Intangibles: The Case of Software Capitalization." *Journal of Accounting Research* (supplement) 36:161–91.

———. 2000. "Information Asymmetry, R&D, and Insider Gains." *Journal of Finance* 55:2747–66.

———. 2001. "The Productivity of Chemical Research and Development." Working Paper. New York University, Stern School of Business.

Acs, Zoltan, David Audretsch, and Maryann Feldman. 1994. "R&D Spillovers and Recipient Firm Size." *Review of Economics and Statistics* 76:336–40.

Aghion, Philippe, and Peter Howitt. 1998. *Endogenous Growth Theory*. MIT Press.

AICPA (American Institute of Certified Public Accountants). 1998. "Accounting for Cost of Computer Software Developed or Obtained for Internal Use." Statement of Position 98-1. New York.

AIMR (Association for Investment Management and Research). 1993. *Financial Reporting in the 1990s and Beyond*. Charlottesville, Va.

Akerlof, George. 1970. "The Market for 'Lemons': Quality Uncertainty and the Market Mechanism." *Quarterly Journal of Economics* 84:488–500.

Amihud, Yakov, and Haim Mendelson. 1986. "Asset Pricing and the Bid-Ask Spread." *Journal of Financial Economics* 17:223–49.

Amir, Eli, and Baruch Lev. 1996. "Value-Relevance of Nonfinancial Information: The Wireless Communications Industry." *Journal of Accounting and Economics* 22:3–30.

Amir, Eli, Baruch Lev, and Theodore Sougiannis. 2000. "What Value Analysts?" Working Paper. New York University, Stern School of Business.

Austin, David. 1993. "An Event Study Approach to Measuring Innovative Output: The Case of Biotechnology." *American Economic Review* 83:253–58.

Barth, Mary, and Greg Clinch. 1998. "Revalued Financial, Tangible, and Intangible Assets: Association with Share Prices and Non-Market-Based Value Estimates." Working Paper. Stanford University, Graduate School of Business.

Barth, Mary, and others. 1998. "Brand Values and Capital Market Valuation." *Review of Accounting Studies* 3:41–68.

Bassi, Laurie, and others. 1999. "Measuring Corporate Investment in Human Capital." In *The New Relationship: Human Capital in the American Corporation*, edited by Margaret Blair and Thomas Kochan, 334–82. Brookings.

Becker, Brian, and Mark Huselid. 1998. "High Performance Work Systems and Firm Performance: A Synthesis of Research and Management Implications." *Research in Personnel and Human Resources* 16:53–101.

Ben Zion, Uri. 1978. "The Investment Aspect of Nonproduction Expenditures: An Empirical Test." *Journal of Economics and Business* 30:224–29.

Berger, Philip, and Eli Ofek. 1995. "Diversification's Effect on Firm Value." *Journal of Financial Economics* 37:39–65.

Bernard, Victor, and Jacob Thomas. 1990. "Evidence that Stock Prices Do Not Fully Reflect the Implications of Current Earnings for Future Earnings." *Journal of Accounting and Economics* 13:305–40.

Berndt, Ernst, Robert Pindyck, and Pierre Azoulay. 1999. "Network Effects and Diffusion in Pharmaceutical Markets: Antiulcer Drugs." Working Paper 7024. Cambridge, Mass.: National Bureau of Economic Research.

Bhide, Amar. 2000. *The Origin and Evolution of New Businesses*. Oxford University Press.

Bobrow, Daniel, Robert Cheslow, and Jack Whalen. 2000. *Community Knowledge Sharing in Practice*. Palo Alto, Calif.: Xerox Research Center.

Bond, Stephen, and Jason Cummins. 2000. "The Stock Market and Investment in the New Economy: Some Tangible Facts and Intangible Fictions." Brookings Panel on Economic Activity, March.

Boone, Jeff, and Kris Raman. 1999. "Off-Balance-Sheet R&D Assets and Market Liquidity." Working Paper. Mississippi State University, School of Business.

Botosan, Christine. 1997. "Disclosure Level and the Cost of Equity Capital." *Accounting Review* 72:323–49.

Boulton, Richard, Barry Libert, and Steve Samek. 2000. *Cracking the Value Code*. Harper Business.

Brown, Stephen, Kin Lo, and Tom Lys. 1998. "Use of R^2 in Accounting Research: Measuring Changes in Value Relevance over the Last Four Decades." *Journal of Accounting and Economics* 28:83–115.

Brynjolfsson, Erik, and Shinkyu Yang. 1999. "The Intangible Costs and Benefits of Computer Investments: Evidence from the Financial Markets." Working Paper. Massachusetts Institute of Technology, Sloan School of Management.

Bublitz, B., and M. Ettredge. 1989. "The Information in Discretionary Outlays: Advertising and Research and Development." *Accounting Review* 64:108–24.

Bushee, Brian. 1998. "The Influence of Institutional Investors on Myopic R&D Investment Behavior." *Accounting Review* 73:305–33.

Cappelli, Peter, and David Newmark. 1999. "Do 'High Performance' Work Practices Improve Establishment-Level Outcomes?" Working Paper 7374. Cambridge, Mass: National Bureau of Economic Research.

Chan, Louis, Josef Lakonishok, and Theodore Sougiannis. 1998. "The Stock Market Valuation of Research and Development Expenditures." Working Paper. University of Illinois, School of Business.

Chan, Su, John Kesinger, and John Martin. 1992. "The Market Rewards Promising R&D—and Punishes the Rest." *Journal of Applied Corporate Finance* 5:59–66.

Chandler, Alfred. 1977. *The Visible Hand.* Bellknap.

———. 1990. *Scale and Scope.* Bellknap.

Chang, James. 1998. "The Decline in Value Relevance of Earnings and Book Values." Working Paper. Harvard University, School of Business.

Chauvin, Keith, and Mark Hirschey. 1993. "Advertising, R&D Expenditures and the Market Value of the Firm." *Financial Management* 22:128–40.

Christensen, Clayton. 1997. *The Innovator's Dilemma: When New Technologies Cause Great Firms to Fail.* Harvard Business School Press.

———. 2000. "Innovation in the Connected Economy." *Perspectives on Business Innovation* 5:6–12. Cap Gemini Ernst & Young Center for Business Innovation.

Coase, Ronald. 1937. "The Nature of the Firm." *Economica* 4:386–405.

Cohen, Wesley, Richard Nelson, and John Walsh. 2000. "Protecting Their Intellectual Assets: Appropriability Conditions and Why U.S. Manufacturing Firms Patent (or Not)." Working Paper 7552. Cambridge, Mass.: National Bureau of Economic Research.

Crepon, Bruno, Emmanual Duguet, and Jacques Mairesse. 1998. "Research, Innovation, and Productivity: An Econometric Analysis at the Firm Level." Working Paper 6696. Cambridge, Mass.: National Bureau of Economic Research.

Daley, Lane, Vikas Mehrotra, and Ranjini Sivakumar. 1997. "Corporate Focus and Value Creation: Evidence from Spin-Offs." *Journal of Financial Economics* 45:257–81.

Darby, Michael, Qian Liu, and Lynne Zucker. 1999. "Stakes and Stars: The Effect of Intellectual Human Capital on the Level and Variability of High-Tech Firms' Market Values." Working Paper 7201. Cambridge, Mass.: National Bureau of Economic Research.

Darrough, Masako, and Srinivasan Rangan. 2001. "Do Insiders Manipulate R&D Spending When They Sell Their Shares in an Initial Public Offering?" Working Paper. Baruch College.

De Bondt, Werner, and Richard Thaler. 1985. "Does the Stock Market Overreact?" *Journal of Finance* 40:793–805.

Deloitte & Touche. 1998. *Research and Development Survey of Software Companies*. Boston.

Demers, Elizabeth, and Baruch Lev. 2000. "A Rude Awakening: Internet Shakeout in 2000." Working Paper. University of Rochester, Simon School of Business.

Deng, Zhen, and Baruch Lev. 1998. " 'Flash-then-Flush': The Valuation of Acquired R&D-in-Process." Working Paper. New York University, Stern School of Business.

Deng, Zhen, Baruch Lev, and Francis Narin. 1999. "Science and Technology as Predictors of Stock Performance." *Financial Analysts Journal* 55:20–32.

Easton, Peter, Trevor Harris, and James Ohlson. 1992. "Aggregate Accounting Earnings Can Explain Most of Security Returns: The Case of Long Return Intervals." *Journal of Accounting and Economics* 15:119–42.

Eccles, Robert, and others. 2001. *The Value of Reporting Revolution*. Wiley.

Economides, Nicholas. 1996. "Economics of Networks." *International Journal of Industrial Organization* 14:673–700.

Elfenbein, Dan, and Josh Lerner. 2000. "Links and Hyperlinks: An Empirical Analysis of Internet Portal Alliances." Working Paper. Harvard University, School of Business.

Farrell, Joseph, and Carl Shapiro. 1988. "Dynamic Competition with Switching Costs." *Rand Journal of Economics* 19:123–37.

FASB (Financial Accounting Standards Board). 1955. Statement of Financial Accounting Standards (SFAS) 45. *Long-Term Construction-Type Contracts.* Norwalk, Conn.

———. 1956. SFAS 47. *Accounting for Costs of Pension Plans.*

———. 1958. SFAS 50. *Contingencies.*

———. 1959. SFAS 51. *Consolidated Financial Statements.*

———. 1970a. Accounting Principles Board (APB) Opinion 16. *Business Combinations.*

———. 1970b. APB Opinion 17. *Intangible Assets.*

———. 1975. SFAS 5. *Accounting Contingencies.*

———. 1977. SFAS 19. *Financial Accounting and Reporting by Oil and Gas Producing Companies.*

———. 1980. SFAS 44. *Accounting for Intangible Assets of Motor Carriers.*

———. 1981. SFAS 53. *Financial Reporting by Producers and Distributors of Motion Picture Films.*

———. 1982. SFAS 63. *Financial Reporting by Broadcasters.*

———. 1983. SFAS 72. *Accounting for Certain Acquisitions of Banking or Thrift Institution.*

———. 1985a. Statement of Financial Accounting Concepts 6. *Elements of Financial Statements.*

————. 1985b. SFAS 86. *Accounting for the Costs of Computer Software to Be Sold, Leased, or Otherwise Marketed.*

————. 1986. SFAS 91. *Accounting for Nonrefundable Fees and Costs Associated with Originating or Acquiring Loans and Initial Direct Costs of Leases.*

————. 1988. Emerging Issues Task Force 88-20. *Difference between Initial Investment and Principal Amount of Loans in a Purchased Credit Card Portfolio.*

————. 1990a. SFAS 105. *Disclosure of Information about Financial Instruments with Off-Balance-Sheet Risk and Financial Instruments with Concentrations of Credit Risk.*

————. 1990b. Emerging Issues Task Force 90-8. *Capitalization of Costs to Treat Environmental Contamination.*

————. 1993. SFAS 115. *Accounting for Certain Investments in Debt and Equity Securities.*

————. 1995. SFAS 121. *Accounting for the Impairment of Long-Lived Assets and for Long-Lived Assets to Be Disposed Of.*

————. 1996. SFAS 125. *Accounting for Transfers and Servicing of Financial Assets and Extinguishments of Liabilities.*

————. 1997. SFAS 131. *Disclosures about Segments of an Enterprise and Related Information.*

————. 2000. Business Reporting Research Project, Steering Committee Report, first draft.

Fox, Stephen P. 1998. "Intellectual Property Management: From Theory to Practice." In *Profiting from Intellectual Capital: Extracting Value from Innovation*, edited by Patrick H. Sullivan, 142–56. Wiley.

Francis, Jennifer, and Katherine Schipper. 1999. "Have Financial Statements Lost Their Relevance?" *Journal of Accounting Research* 37:319–52.

Freeman, Chris, and Luc Soete. 1997. *The Economics of Industrial Innovation*, 3d ed. MIT Press.

Garicano, Luis, and Steven Kaplan. 2000. "The Effects of Business-to-Business E-Commerce on Transaction Costs." Working Paper 8017. Cambridge, Mass.: National Bureau of Economic Research.

Glosten, Lawrence, and Paul Milgrom. 1985. "Bid, Ask, and Transaction Prices in a Specialist Market with Heterogeneously Informed Traders." *Journal of Financial Economics* 14:71–100.

Goolsbee, Austan, and Peter Klenow. 1998. "Evidence on Network and Learning Externalities in the Diffusion of Home Computers." Working Paper 7329. Cambridge, Mass.: National Bureau of Economic Research.

Gordon, Robert. 1998. "Interpreting the 'One Big Wave' in U.S. Long-Term Productivity Growth." Working Paper 7752. Cambridge, Mass.: National Bureau of Economic Research.

Griliches, Zvi. 1990. "Patent Statistics as Economic Indicators." *Journal of Economic Literature* 92:630–53.

———. 1995. "R&D and Productivity: Econometric Results and Measurement Issues." In *Handbook of the Economics of Innovation and Technological Change*, edited by Paul Stoneman, 52–89. Oxford, U.K.: Blackwell.

Grossman, Gene, and Elhanan Helpman. 1994. "Endogenous Innovation in the Theory of Growth." *Journal of Economic Perspectives* 8:23–44.

Gu, Feng, and Baruch Lev. 2000. "Markets in Intangibles: Patent Licensing." Working Paper. New York University, Stern School of Business.

Hall, Bronwyn. 1993. "Industrial Research during the 1980s: Did the Rate of Return Fall?" *BPEA: Microeconomics,* 289–393.

Hall, Bronwyn, and Richard Ham. 1999. "The Patent Paradox Revisited: Determinants of Patenting in the U.S. Semiconductor Industry, 1980–94." Working Paper 7062. Cambridge, Mass.: National Bureau of Economic Research.

Hall, Bronwyn, Adam Jaffe, and Manuel Trajtenberg. 2000. "Market Value and Patent Citations: A First Look." Working Paper 7741. Cambridge, Mass.: National Bureau of Economic Research.

Hall, Robert. 1999. "The Stock Market and Capital Accumulation." Working Paper 7180. Cambridge, Mass.: National Bureau of Economic Research.

———. 2000. "E-Capital: The Link between the Stock Market and the Labor Market in the 1990s." Working Paper. Stanford University, Hoover Institution.

Hand, John. 2000. "The Role of Accounting Fundamentals, Web Traffic, and Supply and Demand in the Pricing of U.S. Internet Stocks." Working Paper. University of North Carolina, School of Business.

Healy, Paul, Stewart Myers, and Chris Howe. 1997. "R&D Accounting and the Relevance-Objectivity Trade-Off: A Simulation Using Data from the Pharmaceutical Industry." Working Paper. Harvard Business School.

Hirschey, Mark, Vernon Richardson, and Susan Scholz. 1998. "Value Relevance of Nonfinancial Information: The Case of Patent Data." Working Paper. University of Kansas, School of Business.

Hirschey, Mark, and Jerry Weygandt. 1985. "Amortization Policy for Advertising and Research and Development Expenditure." *Journal of Accounting Research* 23:326–35.

Homer-Dixon, Thomas. 2000. *The Ingenuity Gap.* Knopf.

Huselid, Mark. 1995. "The Impact of Human Resource Management Practices on Turnover, Productivity, and Corporate Financial Performance." *Academy of Management Journal* 38:635–72.

IASC (International Accounting Standards Committee). 1998. International Accounting Standards 38. *Intangible Assets.* London.

Ijiri, Yuji. 1989. "Momentum Accounting and Triple-Entry Bookkeeping: Exploring the Dynamic Structure of Accounting Measurements." Studies in Accounting Research 31. Sarasota, Fla.: American Accounting Association.

Ittner, Christopher, and David Larcker. 1998. "Are Nonfinancial Measures Leading Indicators of Financial Performance? An Analysis of Customer Satisfaction." *Journal of Accounting Research* 36:1–46.

Katz, Michael, and Carl Shapiro. 1986. "Technology Adoption in the Presence of Network Externalities." *Journal of Political Economy* 94:822–41.

Kothari, S. P., Ted Laguesse, and Andrew Leone. 1998. "Capitalization versus Expensing: Evidence on the Uncertainty of Future Earnings from Current Investments in PP&E versus R&D." Working Paper. University of Rochester, Simon Graduate School of Business.

Kyle, Albert. 1985. "Continuous Auctions and Insider Trading." *Econometrica* 6:1315–35.

———. 1989. "Informed Speculation with Imperfect Competition." *Review of Economic Studies* 56:317–56.

Laento, Kari. 1998. "Intellectual Asset Management at Neste." In *Profiting from Intellectual Capital: Extracting Value from Innovation*, edited by Patrick H. Sullivan, 242–52. Wiley.

Lakonishok, Josef, Andrei Shleifer, and Robert Vishny. 1994. "Contrarian Investment, Extrapolation, and Risk." *Journal of Finance* 49:1541–78.

Lamoreaux, Naomi, and Kenneth Sokoloff. 1999. "Inventive Activity and the Market for Technology in the United States." Working Paper 7107. Cambridge, Mass.: National Bureau of Economic Research.

Lanjouw, Jean, and Mark Schankerman. 1997. "Stylized Facts of Patent Litigation: Value, Scope, and Ownership." Working Paper EI/20. London School of Economics.

Lazear, Edward. 2000. "Performance Pay and Productivity." *American Economic Review* 90:1346–61.

Lerner, Josh, and Alexander Tsai. 2000. "Do Equity Financing Cycles Matter? Evidence from Biotechnology Alliances." Working Paper 7464. Cambridge, Mass.: National Bureau of Economic Research.

Lev, Baruch. 1989. "On the Usefulness of Earnings and Earnings Research: Lessons and Directions from Two Decades of Empirical Research." *Journal of Accounting Research* (supplement) 27:153–92.

Lev, Baruch, Bharat Sarath, and Theodore Sougiannis. 2000. "R&D Reporting Biases and Their Consequences." Working Paper. New York University, Stern School of Business.

Lev, Baruch, and Aba Schwartz. 1971. "On the Use of Economic Concepts of Human Capital in Financial Statements." *Accounting Review* 46:103–12.

Lev, Baruch, and Theodore Sougiannis. 1996. "The Capitalization, Amortization, and Value Relevance of R&D." *Journal of Accounting and Economics* 21:107–38.

Lev, Baruch, and Min Wu. 1999. "R&D Financing by SWORDS." Working Paper. New York University, Stern School of Business.

Lev, Baruch, and Paul Zarowin. 1999. "The Boundaries of Financial Reporting and How to Extend Them." *Journal of Accounting Research* (supplement) 37:353–85.

Liebowitz, Stanley, and Stephen Margolis. 1999. *Winners, Losers, and Microsoft: Competition and Antitrust in High Technology.* New York: Independent Institute.

Mansfield, Edwin. 1991. "Academic Research and Industrial Innovation." *Research Policy* 20:1–12.

Mansfield, Edwin, and Samuel Wagner. 1977. *The Production and Application of New Industrial Technology.* Norton.

Megna, Pamela, and Mark Klock. 1993. "The Impact of Intangible Capital on Tobin's Q in the Semiconductor Industry." *American Economic Review* 83:265–69.

Morck, Randall, and Bernard Yeung. 1999. "Why Firms Diversify: Internalization versus Agency Behavior." Working Paper. University of Alberta, Faculty of Business, Institute for Financial Research.

Nadiri, Ishaq. 1993. "Innovation and Technological Spillovers." Working Paper 4423. Cambridge, Mass.: National Bureau of Economic Research.

Nakamura, Leonard. 1999. "Intangibles: What Put the New in the New Economy." *Federal Reserve Bank of Philadelphia, Business Review* (July–August): 3–16.

———. 2000. "Economics and the New Economy: The Invisible Hand Meets Creative Destruction." *Federal Reserve Bank of Philadelphia, Business Review* (July–August): 15–30.

OECD (Organization for Economic Cooperation and Development). 1993. *Main Definitions and Conventions for the Measurement of Research and Experimental Development (R&D).* (The Frascati Manual).

———. 1999. *Science, Technology, and Industry Scoreboard, 1999.*

Patel, Pari, and Keith Pavitt. 1995. "Patterns of Technological Activity: Their Measurement and Interpretation." In *Handbook of the Economics of Innovation and Technological Change,* edited by Paul Stoneman, 14–51. London: Blackwell.

Petrash, Gordon. 1998 "Intellectual Asset Management at Dow Chemical." In *Profiting from Intellectual Capital: Extracting Value from Innovation,* edited by Patrick H. Sullivan, 205–20. Wiley.

Pinches, George, V. Narayanan, and Kathryn Kelm. 1996. "How the Market Values the Different Stages of Corporate R&D—Initiation, Progress, and Commercialization." *Journal of Applied Corporate Finance* 9:60–69.

Rajan, Raghuram, and Luigi Zingales. 2000. "The Governance of the New Enterprise." Working Paper 7958. Cambridge, Mass.: National Bureau of Economic Research.

Rivette, Kevin, and David Kline. 2000a. *Rembrandts in the Attic: Unlocking the Hidden Value of Patents.* Harvard Business School Press.

———. 2000b. "Discovering New Value in Intellectual Property." Harvard Business Review 78 (January-February): 54–66.

Romer, Paul. 1990. "Endogenous Technical Change." *Journal of Political Economy* 98:S71–S102.

———. 1994. "The Origins of Endogenous Growth." *Journal of Economic Perspective* 8 (Winter): 3–22.

———. 1998. "Bank of America Roundtable on the Soft Revolution." *Journal of Applied Corporate Finance* (Summer): 9–14.

Rosett, Joshua. 2000. "Equity Risk and the Labor Stock: The Case of Union Contracts." Working Paper. Tulane University, Freeman School of Business.

Scherer, Frederick, Dietmar Harhoff, and Joerg Kukies. 1998. "Uncertainty and the Size Distribution of Rewards from Technological Innovation." *Journal of Evolutionary Economics* 10:175–200.

Scheutze, Walter. 1993. "What Is an Asset?" *Accounting Horizons* 7:66–70.

Seethamraju, Chandra. 2000. "The Value Relevance of Trademarks." Ph.D. dissertation, New York University.

Sengupta, Partha. 1998. "Corporate Disclosure Quality and the Cost of Debt." *Accounting Review* 73:459–74.

Shane, Hilary. 1993. "Patent Citations as an Indicator of the Value of Intangible Assets in the Semiconductor Industry." Working Paper. University of Pennsylvania, Wharton School.

Shapiro, Carl, and Hal Varian. 1999. *Information Rules.* Harvard Business School Press.

Shi, Charles. 1999. "On the Trade-Off between the Future Benefits and Riskiness of R&D: A Bondholders' Perspective." Working Paper. University of California–Irvine, School of Business.

Solow, Robert. 1956. "A Contribution to the Theory of Economic Growth." *Quarterly Journal of Economics* 70:65–94.

Stephan, Paula. 1996. "The Economics of Science." *Journal of Economic Literature* 34:1199–235.

Stewart, Thomas. 1997. *Intellectual Capital.* Doubleday.

Tasker, Sarah. 1998. "Technology Company Conference Calls: A Small Sample Study." *Journal of Financial Statement Analysis* 4:6–14.

"Technology Licensing Exchanges." 2000. *Research Technology Management* 43 (September–October): 13–15.

Teece, David. 1998. "Technological Change and Nature of the Firm." In *Technical Change and Economic Theory*, edited by G. Dosi, 256—81. London: Printer Publishers.

Trajtenberg, Manuel. 1990. "A Penny for Your Quotes: Patent Citations and the Value of Innovations." *Rand Journal of Economics* 21:172–87.

Trueman, Brett, Franco Wong, and Xiao-Jun Zhang. 1999. "The Eyeballs Have It: Searching for the Value in Internet Companies." Working Paper. University of California–Berkeley, Haas School of Business.

Zingales, Luigi. 2000. "In Search of New Foundations." Working Paper 7706. Cambridge, Mass.: National Bureau of Economic Research.

Comments

F ive of the participants in the symposium on intangibles sponsored by the Brookings Institution Project on Understanding Intangible Sources of Wealth comment below on Baruch Lev's findings.

Comments by Brian Hackett

I am in general agreement with Baruch Lev's assessment of the need to change many accounting, reporting, and governance rules.[1] Some member companies of the Council on Knowledge Management are moving in that direction by adding supplemental annual reports. Some firms are changing and expanding the role of their corporate board committees to review human resource strategies and tactics that impact the investment and use of their intangible assets. However, only a minority of firms are experimenting with linking intangibles to performance measures.

The measurement system becomes the firm's implicit theory of what affects performance. The board has found three general problems with such measurement systems:

—Many measurement systems are too complex and have too many measures. Some "scoreboards" for measuring intellectual capital, for example, have more than a hundred categories.

1. Brian Hackett is program director for the Council on Knowledge Management, a program of the Conference Board. The Conference Board, a nonprofit, nonadvocacy research organization, was founded in 1916 to provide information on current business practices and their implications for society. The board shares that information with a network of senior executives around the world.

—Measurement systems are often highly subjective in implementation.

—Precise metrics often miss important elements of performance that are difficult to quantify but critical to long-term success.

My focus, however, is on how the shift in measuring and disclosing intangible assets can impact operations inside the firm. Measurement processes, even when done with the right intentions, can often lead to distorted or even destructive behaviors inside organizations. Most executives work with inherited measurement systems based on the manufacturing model of work and human behavior. The mantra, "What gets measured gets done," can lead to some unintended consequences. Few accountants worry about measurement systems turning knowledge into action or its effect on the organization's ability to develop long-term strategic capabilities through its people. And few managers are evaluated on their ability to attract and retain people. The employee-to-customer-to-profit model is still rare in most firms. Management accounting is often presumed to be separate and distinct from public accounting; however, when it comes to decisionmaking, at most firms financial measures still trump nonfinancial measures.

In large organizations senior managers are often given more areas in which they are measured than they can manage. Work gets done through projects, most of them with a limited budget and a discrete time frame. Managers need immediate and understandable measures that inform them about how they need to act each day. Long-term intellectual capital measures are not often relevant to that immediate need.

Short-term measures of efficiency, budget targets, and quarterly revenues get senior managers' attention at the expense of long-term investments in human capital. Most leading firms that have made long-term investments in building a learning organization have reduced or eliminated those investments when faced with a new chief executive officer, a merger, or (especially) competitive market conditions. Even firms with strong traditions and cultures of investing in learning quietly decrease those investments when their stock values decline.

Lev asks, What is the cost of a lost idea? Can the process of generating ideas be managed? Such questions lie at the heart of managing intangibles in knowledge-intensive organizations. Knowledge management should be integral to the overall strategy of the firm. A recent study shows that 80 percent of respondent firms were engaged in some form of knowledge management and 60 percent expected knowledge management to be integral to their strategy.[2] However, most firms were not yet making the required systematic resource allocation. One suggestion is to expand the examples of firms that have made strides in their knowledge strategy.

I disagree with Lev's statement that leadership from the top of the organization is required for the successful creation and exploitation of knowledge and that local initiatives are not likely to succeed; many successful knowledge management initiatives start and spread from the bottom up. Only 13 percent of chief executive officers lead their firms' knowledge management efforts.[3] In fact, many firms once held up as models of best practices in knowledge management have faltered, and firms that have not received recognition are slowly and quietly improving their knowledge management practices.

The communities of practice and peer assist approaches to knowledge sharing have proven the most enduring and successful.[4] Unfortunately, communities of practice by their nature are difficult if not impossible to manage or measure. The unit of analysis for measuring the social capital that leads to learning and knowledge sharing is indeed at the local level. Finding measures that link to financial performance may not be worth the effort and cost of tracking them. The most successful cases examined in the study have taken a leap of faith that in a knowledge-based, networked environment you have to change your assumptions about human behavior. Before a firm challenges those assumptions and examines the cultural aspect of knowledge sharing, no measurement system or performance management approach will be useful.

Regarding Lev's remarks on investment in training, I would add that most employers do not track the value of their investments in training. Most large firms spend 2 percent of payroll on training. Senior managers feel that the value of training cannot be isolated from the many variables that affect performance.[5] Investment analysts rarely look at a firm's investment in training when evaluating a company.[6]

Driving performance through compensation measures can also have unintended consequences. The incentive compensation process assumes that performance can be assessed and assigned to individuals. Yet organi-

2. Hackett (2000).
3. Hackett (1997).
4. Hackett (2000).
5. Hackett (1997).
6. Ernst & Young (1994).

zations are systems in which work is accomplished by teams and in which behavior is interdependent. Again, the level of analysis should be the group, but that is very difficult to assign metrics to. Individual performance in an interdependent system will always be difficult if not impossible to measure. A common problem with performance-based pay schemes is that these "best practices" get copied and institutionalized when in fact most firms vary dramatically in their strategies and cultures.

No measurement system is going to perfectly capture all of the important elements of performance or the behaviors that lead to long-term value. Ideally, internal measures should be guides and indicators of progress toward a long-term goal, not a quarterly or even an annual target. At most large firms, the primacy of capital markets has proven to be the real driver of senior management behavior and decisionmaking.

Comments by Stephen Gates

Baruch Lev's research contributes a deep understanding at both the theoretical and policy levels to the debate surrounding disclosure of intangible assets.[7] While he makes the strongest case for reporting intangible assets related to innovation, he also considers carefully the arguments for intangible assets related to organizational practices and human resources. Intangible assets are defined as nonphysical claims to future benefits and are categorized into three major nexuses related to innovation, organizational practices, and human resources. The comments that follow are largely concerned with the latter two categories.

Organizational Practices, Human Resources, and the Value Chain

While it is tempting to place innovation, organizational practices, and human resources under the same umbrella to describe the contribution of intangible assets to a company's value chain, most business models underestimate the latter two categories. Definitional problems seem inevitable. Lev resolves the question "What are these organizational assets?" by presenting concrete examples of customer-related organizational capital, while acknowledging that organizational assets may include such intangibles as business processes built around computer systems. To the question "What are human resource intangibles?" Lev answers that the

---

7. Stephen Gates is principal researcher and project director for the European Council on Investor Relations, a program of the Conference Board.

identification and quantification of benefits from expenditures on human resources pose such problems that the jury is still out.

Although Lev's "value chain scoreboard" is illustrated very well by the biotechnology company example, nearly all the measures relate to innovation, not to organizational practices or human resource intangibles. Presumably, in the value chain scoreboard of a hotel, food, food service, or even an institutional cleaning company, organizational practices and human resource intangibles would contribute significantly in addition to the brand. It would be instructive to see what these companies' value chain scoreboards look like.

Disclosure of Organizational Practices and Human Resources

Lev points out that innovation intangible assets have received the lion's share of research largely because research and development (R&D) expenses must be disclosed. Furthermore, he acknowledges that research on human resource intangibles will advance only with disclosure of meaningful data by the corporate sector. U.S. companies do not reveal meaningful information about organizational practices or human resources. However, an increasing number of Canadian and European companies publish information about their investment in human resources or indicators of human capital (Royal Bank of Canada, Deutsche Bank, BBVA, BSCH, Grand Vision, Celemi, and Skandia, among others).

Lev's policy proposal to encourage standardization in reporting for intangible assets would greatly improve the meaning, comparability, and credibility of organizational practice and human resource intangible assets. Once established, common standards might encourage companies to disclose voluntarily. If this were to happen, it would permit more rigorous research on organizational practices and human resource intangibles, which in turn might generate greater consensus on the contribution of these intangibles to the value chain.

Control over Human Resources

The generally accepted accounting principles (GAAP) of the United States require that to record anything as an asset a company must demonstrate that it has effective control of it. This condition makes it exceedingly difficult to consider a company's employees as its assets.

Nevertheless, many a company's value chain depends critically on teams of key employees.

Companies try to exercise effective control over these key employees through time-related vesting provisions in stock option plans. One empirical question is, "How effective are time-vesting provisions in stock option plans in keeping key employees?"

Disclosure of Intangible Assets

Lev spells out the negative consequences of lack of disclosure of information on intangible assets, pointing out that management's privileged access to information about the intangible asset value chain encourages insider trading, especially in high-technology companies. Although regulators consider insider trading unacceptable, expanding existing disclosure requirements—established for tangible assets—to cover intangible assets would be difficult.

Meanwhile, most managers are engaged in internal measurement mania, as evidenced by Conference Board survey reports.[8] Chief financial officers reported that creating and implementing performance measures would be their number one activity over the three years following the survey. European compensation and benefit directors responded that their top issue would be linking incentive compensation with better performance targets. Furthermore, nearly three-quarters of European companies had, over the previous three years, changed their performance measurement systems at both the company and individual levels, and the majority intended to do so over the following three years. These performance measures are used as targets in the annual and longer-term incentive compensation plans.

Managers are increasingly motivated to focus on measures that increase the value of the company. However, many of these performance measures are not disclosed outside the company. For example, although 74 percent of survey respondents considered that their company's measures of new product development were forward-looking indicators, only 18 percent of firms disclose this performance measure. So while management obtains increasingly fine-tuned information about the progress of intangible value creation inside their companies, investors officially remain in the dark. To overcome the growing information asymmetry, Lev

8. Gates (1999a, 1999b).

makes a considered plea for voluntary disclosure, beginning with standard setting for intangible assets.

Comments by Boyan Jovanovic

Why measure intangibles?[9] The stock of intangibles fluctuates over time. If we do not measure intangibles properly, it will sometimes seem that we are doing poorly when in fact we are simply investing in intangibles. This is especially likely after a new and important technology, like information technology, arrives on the scene. Many now believe that during the productivity slowdown of the 1970s and 1980s the U.S. stock of intangible capital grew rapidly and that it is intangible capital that keeps the stock market high. This is one reason, but not the only one, that I endorse the main idea that Baruch Lev advances in this volume.

Intangibles such as ideas that come from R&D spending, human capital in the work force that results from training, and information and consumer goodwill that stem from advertising raise output and profits as much as do such forms of tangible capital as desks, shovels, and trains. Current accounting practice misses many intangibles, and this causes the market value of capital to drift far from its book value (see Lev's figure 1-1).

Two important intangibles are unmeasured investment in trial start-ups and unmeasured learning in existing companies. In earlier studies my colleagues and I stress that intangible human capital can help us interpret the bad times that the stock market underwent in the 1970s.[10] My aim here is to convey some of these ideas by means of two examples that show precisely how much market values can depart from book values in two specific types of learning.

Intangible 1: Unmeasured Capital in Failed Projects

It takes many failures to get a Microsoft or an Amazon.com, we are told, and the truth of this adage, in fact, lies in unmeasured capital. A large percentage of new ventures fails. Time-series data are hard to find, but it seems that in spite of the great effort that venture capitalists put into screening out proposals that are likely to fail, returns to new ventures are

9. Boyan Jovanovic is professor of economics at the University of Chicago. He specializes in the economics of technological change.
10. Greenwood and Jovanovic (1999); Hobijn and Jovanovic (1999).

highly risky. Blaine Huntsman and James Hoban find that 17 percent of their sample of ventures generated a complete loss (–100 percent) for the investors.[11] Nearly half were losing propositions, and only one-quarter of their sample exceeded the average return of the portfolio. Phillip Horsley and Paul Gompers and Josh Lerner report similar findings.[12] The typical new venture is highly risky; the following example centers on that fact.

Suppose a new venture invests k units of capital at date zero. This could be an up-front investment in a factory and its equipment or a research outlay as in the pharmaceutical industry. Assume that this investment is on the books, so that the firm's book value is just k. The outcome is random and not predictable before the investment is made. Success occurs with probability π, and utter and complete failure occurs with probability $1 - \pi$. Let the value of the profits be

$$y_t = \begin{cases} 0 & \text{forever with probability } 1-\pi. \\ Ak & \text{forever with probability } \pi. \end{cases}$$

In the event of success, the firm is sold to the public. Otherwise the firm never shows up on the stock market. The value of the firm, v, at its initial public offering is the discounted present value of the profits, y/r:

$$v(t) = \begin{cases} 0 & \text{with probability } 1-\pi \text{ — and no public offering.} \\ Ak/r & \text{with probability } 1-\pi \text{ — and an initial public offering.} \end{cases}$$

The point is that we see only the successes in the stock market. This bias originates in the unmeasured intangible: the ks invested in the failed projects.

How high can market-to-book values go? That depends on the values of r, A, and π. One way to pin these parameters down is to realize that the investment must be expected to make money (or else it would never get made). Suppose that, ex ante, the investor expects to break even. That is, that the investor expects the outlay, k, to be more or less offset by the expected revenues from selling the firm off at the initial public offering. The ex ante value is $(\pi/r)(Ak)$. The break-even constraint is just

$$(\pi Ak/r) = k.$$

11. Huntsman and Hoban (1980).
12. Horsley (1997); Gompers and Lerner (1998).

But since the book value of the company is k, the market-book ratio is just A/r, and using the break-even constraint, we find that

$$\text{market-to-book ratio } (A / r) = (1 / \pi).$$

If the class of projects is highly risky, π will be low and, therefore, A/r will need to be high to compensate for this.

Recent technological developments seem to have made the business climate riskier. If true, this means that, for the projects undertaken in equilibrium, A has risen and π has fallen in the last two to three decades. On these grounds, one should not be surprised to find that market-to-book ratios have risen.[13] How far can they rise? The example shows that if Amazon.com's initial chances of success were one in a hundred, $\pi = 0.01$, then Amazon's market-to-book ratio should be one hundred!

Unmeasured Investments of Failed Entrepreneurs
Are investors investing in riskier projects now than they used to? The answer seems to be no. At the turn of the twentieth century, the business climate seems to have been as risky as it is today. Many entrepreneurs and their start-up companies these days make investments that never yield revenue, and the same was true a hundred years ago. A parallel from a hundred years ago is the automobile industry. Glen Carroll and Michael Hannan find that "an astonishing number of hopeful producers populated the early industry" and that "much selection occurred prior to actual production."[14] They identify 3,845 preproduction organizing attempts in the industry. Of these, only 11 percent succeeded in making the transition to the production stage. The automobile evidence parallels some of the pre-initial-public-offering activity of pharmaceutical firms (and probably many other kinds of firms) that build a prototype that they hope the U.S. Food and Drug Administration will approve.

Selection after Entry
Among companies that make it to the production stage, many fail in the early years. When an industry is young, tremendous selection, new listings, and delistings from the stock market occur at a very high rate, just as they did during the early part of the twentieth century—especially between 1915 and 1930—as the nation's businesses and homes were

13. For a recent study that measures the rise in risk, see Comin (1999).
14. Carroll and Hannan (2000, p. 347).

becoming electrified.[15] A technological revolution, therefore, seems to call for an intensified period of selection to determine the fittest firms—which will carry the new technology forward. Schumpeter calls this process creative destruction: new technology destroys everything associated with old technology—old physical capital, old human capital, and old organization capital.

Intangible 2: Human Capital Investment on the Job

Current accounting practice treats the training of workers as an expense, even though training creates human capital. It is not clear how much formal training exists on the job. More likely, much training is informal—that is, learning by doing.[16] This means that output and productivity are smaller while training is going on. Here is a model that captures this fact and that gives a feeling for how large such costs must be in order for market-to-book values to reach five or six, where Lev's figure 1-1 puts them.[17]

Let the production function for output at date t, y_t be

$$y_t = k h_t,$$

where k is physical capital, assumed to be fixed over time and hence carrying no time subscript, and h_t is expertise of the work force. Assume that the firm invests k units at date zero—and never again. On the other hand, it takes time for expertise to build up (learning by doing).

The learning curve is quite simple: learning takes place for T periods, during which the workers' productivity, h_t, is identically zero. After that, productivity rises to $h_t = A$ and remains there forever. That is,

$$h_t = \begin{cases} 0 & \text{for } t < T. \\ A & \text{for } t \ge T. \end{cases}$$

The firm's output therefore is

$$y_t = \begin{cases} 0 & \text{for } t < T. \\ Ak & \text{for } t \ge T. \end{cases}$$

15. Gort and Klepper (1982) extensively document the selection, which is modeled in Jovanovic (1982).
16. Jovanovic and Nyarko (1995).
17. The model is an extension of Yorukoglu (1998).

The firm borrows the funds to finance the initial capital outlays k at $t = 0$, and its wage-cost is w per machine per period. Its output becomes positive at date T, so market value at date t would be

$$v(t, k) = -\left[(w + r)k \,/\, r\right] + \min\left[1,\, e^{-r(T-t)}\right](Ak \,/\, r).$$

The point here is that for $t < T$, the market value of the firm rises steadily:

$$(\partial v \,/\, \partial t) = re^{-r(T-t)}(Ak \,/\, r).$$

How large can the market-to-book ratio become? To answer this question, take $w = 0$ and assume that the capital has been paid out of pocket so that the firm has no debts on the books. Then the expression for $v(.)$ simplifies to

$$v(t, k) = \min\left[1,\, e^{-r(T-t)}\right](Ak \,/\, r).$$

As in the previous example, let us choose the value of A in such a way that at date zero the investor expects to break even. That is, the investor expects the outlay, k, to be more or less offset by the expected revenues from selling the firm off at the initial public offering stage. This is another way of saying that, at the date of investment, Tobin's q is unity. To meet this condition, the ex ante value of the firm must satisfy

$$v(0, k) = k.$$

But

$$v(0, k) = e^{-rT}(Ak \,/\, r),$$

which together with equation 2 implies that $A = re^{rT}$, and that, therefore, when we substitute this value for A into equation 1, we get

$$v(t, k) = \min(e^{rt}, e^{rT})k.$$

Therefore, the market-to-book ratio of this firm rises from unity at date zero to a maximum value of e^{rT}.

Figure 1 (on page 188) plots this maximal value as a function of T, using three separate values of r. The larger r and T are, the larger the market-to-book ratios that such human capital investments can give rise to. Evidence on learning curves at the plant level puts T in the neighborhood of ten years, and so at interest rates of 10–15 percent, we can easily find

FIGURE 1 Maximal Market-to-Book Ratio (e^{rT})

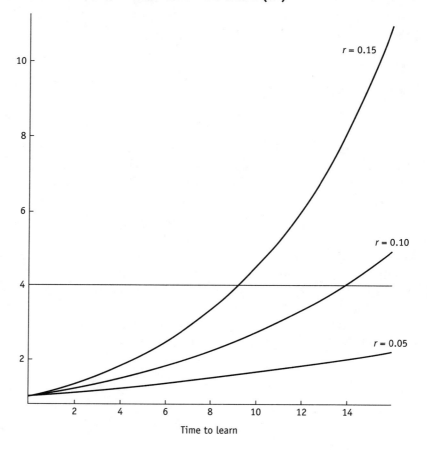

market-to-book ratios of four (the horizontal line plotted in the figure) or even higher.[18]

Conclusion

Lev's proposal moves us in the right direction. I do not know how much fine-tuning it needs before it can be implemented, but his broad message is exactly right: measure our intangible capital properly, and do it soon.

18. For evidence of learning at the plant level, see Bahk and Gort (1993).

Comments by Jack E. Triplett

Baruch Lev's volume on intangibles is a stimulating and outstanding discussion of an important problem. As an economist I am very sympathetic to the issues he raises.[19]

Defining Intangibles

The very intangibility of intangibles is a great barrier to measuring them. The absence of data on intangibles, in turn, inhibits cogent discussion and consensus on Lev's policy proposals.

Obtaining an operational definition of intangibles is vital to measurement.

How are data on *tangible* investments gathered? Products that are investments are listed, and then it is determined who makes these products, how many of them are made, and what their prices are. In parallel, gathering statistical information on intangibles requires first that there is agreement on what statistics are needed.

Several definitions of the term *intangibles* exist. Lev proposes that intangible assets are claims to future benefits that do not have physical or financial (stocks or bonds) embodiments. Alternatively, he proposes that intangible assets are nonphysical sources of value (claims to future benefits) generated by innovation, unique organizational designs, or human resource practices. Note that the future claims part of these definitions is simply the definition of an investment or an asset.

Lev distinguishes three classes of intangibles (which I regroup into four):

—Innovations that may be protected by patents, trademarks, or copyrights

—Unique organizational structures or designs

—Brands

—Human resources practices that enhance the value of the human resource–related intangibles by increasing employee productivity

An Organization for Economic Cooperation and Development publication notes that intangibles are often defined negatively as "not tangible" or, alternatively, as the cost of products that are not tangible. It points

19. Jack Triplett is a visiting fellow in the economic studies program at Brookings and an expert on macroeconomic data and measurement issues, especially in the area of services and their contributions to productivity.

out that such definitions do not say "what actually constitutes an intangible investment."[20]

The 1993 System of National Accounts (hereafter, SNA 1993) calls for capitalizing intangible investments in national accounts.[21] In SNA 1993, *produced* intangibles are defined by classification, and four groupings are listed: mineral exploration, computer software, literary and artistic originals, and "other." Most of what Lev discusses undoubtedly falls into that miscellaneous (and undefined) "other" classification.

SNA 1993 explicitly excludes R&D from the definition of intangible investments, and it regards "patented entities" as *nonproduced* intangibles. My understanding is that these decisions represent a compromise of sorts, but even so they leave the SNA 1993 interpretation of intangible investments looking more than a bit bizarre.

M. M. Croes provides data on intangible investment for fifteen OECD countries.[22] His working definition was also generated implicitly from a classification. His list of intangibles includes R&D, computer software, education, media advertising, and payments for international transfers of technology. An explicit criterion for inclusion on this list is that expenditures data for items in the category already exist, which is far too restrictive a definition of intangible investment.

In Croes's definition, total intangible investment ranges between 7 and 11 percent of gross domestic product (GDP) in OECD countries, and the United States has by no means the highest percentage. In terms of separate components, the largest of Croes's elements is education and training (5–7 percent of GDP across these countries). Among the other components, the United States is the highest only in media advertising expenditures, while Sweden seems to have the largest proportions of GDP devoted to R&D and computer software.

One conclusion from the Croes study is that even a narrow definition of intangibles indicates that they account for a sizable portion of GDP. I presume they would account for a still larger proportion of GDP in Lev's definition.

20. Werner Clement, Gerhard Hammerer, and Karl Schwarz, "Intangible Investment from an Evolutionary Perspective" (www.oecd.org//dsti/sti/industry/indcomp/prod/paper2.pdf [1998]).

21. SNA 1993 is a joint publication of the Commission of the European Communities, the International Monetary Fund, the OECD, the United Nations, and the World Bank.

22. Croes (1999).

The major point I draw from these examples is the ambiguity in the definition of intangible investments. I am not unsympathetic to the idea "By their fruits shall ye know them." However, the ambiguity about what to include in the definition of intangibles, the absence of a concrete list of the activities on which data are to be collected, makes everything else more difficult.

It is also true that there is a sort of vicious circle with respect to measuring intangibles. Statistical agencies, and especially compilers of national accounts, make great direct use of accounting data, company reports, and so forth. Additionally, it is exceedingly hard to collect survey information from enterprises for data that are not kept in company records in some form. So, to an extent, statistical agency programs depend on accounting conventions, either directly or indirectly. But as Lev makes clear, the absence of national statistical estimates inhibits understanding of the importance of intangibles and thus inhibits as well changes in accounting procedures that might ultimately make it possible to collect statistical information. There is nothing unique about intangibles in this respect. The paradox that you must first have data in order to decide how to collect data comes up in other aspects of economic statistics as well.[23]

Pursuing the policy objectives discussed by Lev will generate reservations when the categories of intangible investments are not clear, because there will be a great amount of uncertainty about the effects of capitalizing them in accounting rules and in economic data. Simon Kuznets once remarked, "The human imagination abhors the vacuum of ignorance and, for lack of facts, fills it with speculation."[24] The sound policy corollary is, Do not act too fast when speculation serves for facts. I suspect that this is one force for conservatism with respect to the treatment of intangible investments.

The Economic Impact of Computers

The topic of computers is by no means central to Lev's study, but computers often come up in discussions of intangibles. There is a widely held belief that computers create intangible outputs, and in consequence the economic contribution of computers and information technology equipment is greater that what is estimated with conventional economic statistics. For example, Robert Hall contends that college-educated workers,

23. Parker and Grimm (2000); OECD (2000); Carson and others (1994).
24. Creamer, Dobrovolsky, and Borenstein (1960, p. xxvi).

using computers, create what he calls e-capital.[25] E-capital, in turn, explains why the stock market is so high and also why the earnings of college-educated workers have grown faster than the earnings of less educated workers.

The alternative view of computers is associated with Dale Jorgensen, who claims that computers are just another investment good.[26] The overall evidence is strongly in favor of the Jorgensen view. Information technology capital has increased both output and labor productivity in the United States throughout the forty-five-year history of computers in this country and has had similar impacts in other OECD countries. Computers contribute to output and to labor productivity, so there is no need to invoke some phantom, unmeasured output in the form of intangibles in order to find an economic contribution from computers.

Service industries provide an exception to that statement. The top service industry users of computers include (in order): finance and banking, wholesale trade, business services, communications, and insurance. The output of most of these industries is hard to measure.[27] Are these industries also more likely to produce intangibles? I suspect they are, compared with, say, the stone, clay, and glass industry. If there is an untold story behind the computer's contribution to output, it is very likely in this area of hard-to-measure service industries. If services output has been missed, it may well lie disproportionately in some of the intangible investments that Lev discusses.

Capital Questions

It is common to associate intangibles with the stock market boom of the 1990s. The value of U.S. companies rose greatly, relative to the valuation of their physical plant and equipment. The value of Tobin's q (the ratio of a company's stock market value to the value of its capital equipment) rose from approximately 1.2 in 1995 to 2.4 in 1999. This rise in q is consistent with a large proportion of intangibles in the firm's capital assets. Of course, if the stock market declines, on this reasoning we have destroyed a large quantity of intangible capital, but that is not the point I want to make.

25. Hall (2001).
26. Jorgensen is reviewed in Barry P. Bosworth and Jack E. Triplett, "What's New about the New Economy? IT, Economic Growth, and Productivity" (www.brookings.org/scholars/jtriplett.htm [2000]).
27. Triplett and Bosworth (2001).

I do want to express some reservation about reasoning backward in order to ascertain levels of productive investment from stock market values. An old, simple capital theory equation relates the present price of an asset to the discounted stream of returns from the asset:

$$P_k = \Sigma(p_t q_t) / (1 + r)^t.$$

In the equation, P_k is the value of a piece of capital equipment (or an intangible asset), q_t is the quantity of capital services this asset yields in period t (this q is not Tobin's q), p_t is the price of this capital service in period t, and r is the discount rate. A capital service for tangible capital can be thought of as machine hours (of constant quality), the capital input to production, which matches labor hours as the labor input. An investment will have a high value when it contributes a large stream of qs over future periods. Thus for the usual kind of (tangible) capital good, if we see that the price of the capital good (P_k) is high, we infer that it must yield a large number of future capital services; that is, it must be very productive.

A few attempts have been made to use this equation to value intangible capital. For example, one study values Australian movies by estimating their future streams of receipts, because the potential value of a motion picture is not well estimated by the cost of production.[28] This is especially true in the Australian case, because Australian motion pictures are heavily subsidized, most of them never return their total production cost, and they are in effect produced just to earn the subsidy. However, the study finds that an estimate of flow of services made soon after a movie's release will require substantial upward or downward revision if the movie proves either very popular or very unpopular. Lev talks about uncertainty: this must surely be a serious problem in valuing intangible capital assets.

But a more serious difficulty arises with intangibles. Many start-up e-business companies are trying to attain market share; their investments are investments in rent seeking. If they are successful, they will enjoy high p_t in future periods. A high stream of p_t will also produce a high value of P_k, even if the investment has relatively low capital services, or q_t.

In the case of intangibles, the capital good may be unique to an owner. The organizational design of an e-commerce firm (organizational design is one of Lev's categories of intangibles) is not intended necessarily to produce great quantities of capital services but to obtain some future

28. Australian Bureau of Statistics (1997).

monopoly price on providing those services. The company might not have invented a system for producing tremendously high q, but if it got in line at the right spot at the right time it would find a way to ensure that it would obtain a future high p_t.

So if intangible investment is rent seeking, we might have a high valuation on the intangible because of high future ps, even if the q is not making much of a contribution to production or to the economy. Ownership of monopoly rents is very valuable on the stock market and very valuable to the firm, but it does not make a tremendous contribution to national productivity. Timothy Bresnahan, Paul Milgrom, and Jonathan Paul, for example, conclude that the computer lowers the cost of rent seeking in capital markets, particularly in the stock market, and as a result raises the amount of it.[29] Increasing the amount of rent-seeking behavior in the economy is not necessarily a good thing.

This is not a major problem for tangible investments. One cannot expect to get high prices for capital services from, say, computers or machine tools, because many people can invest in those assets. Competition ensures that there cannot be a large rent associated with simple ownership of some capital good. Ownership of a tangible capital good is transparent, in Lev's language.

Much research is required to confirm that the returns to intangible investments represent higher social products (high levels of q_t in the equation) as opposed to returns to rent seeking (high levels of p_t). The need for a list of intangibles for such research is obvious.

Conclusion

For this discussion of intangibles to go forward very far, it is important to put together a better list of what intangibles are.

Comments by Wayne Upton

Baruch Lev's study on intangible assets and other intangible sources of business value is an important contribution to the business reporting literature.[30] His work shows a level of intellectual rigor that is missing from

29. Bresnahan, Milgrom, and Paul (1992).
30. Wayne Upton is a senior project manager for the Financial Accounting Standards Board. The FASB encourages the expression of views by members of the board and its staff. The views expressed in this commentary are those of Upton and do not represent FASB's official positions.

much of the popular writing on this topic. One may disagree with some of his observations, and I do, but one cannot help but admire the quality of the work.

The problem that confronts businesses, users of business reporting information, standard setters, and regulators is how best to understand and communicate the difference between the value of a company (usually expressed as the market capitalization based on quoted prices) and the accounting book value of that company. One might simply attribute the entire difference to some notion of intangibles and be done with the exercise. But that approach is essentially circular and provides little feedback information to users of financial and business reporting information. There must be more going on and more that can be said. We can observe the market capitalization of a traded stock and observe the accounting book value. We do not know exactly why they are different, but we can make some reasonable speculations. A company's market capitalization might be decomposed along the lines below:

Accounting book value	**$XXX**
± Market assessments of differences between accounting measurement and underlying value of recognized assets and liabilities	XXX
± Market assessments of the underlying value of items that meet the definition of assets and liabilities but that are not recognized in financial statements (for example, patents developed through internal research and development)	XXX
± Market assessments of intangible value drivers or value impairers that do not meet the definition of assets and liabilities (for example, employee morale)	XXX
± Market assessments of the entity's future plans, opportunities, and business risks	XXX
± Other factors, including puffery, pessimism, and market psychology	XXX
Market capitalization	**XXXX**

In a perfect world, financial statements would include all items that meet the definition of assets and liabilities and provide decision-useful information about their values. Business reporting outside of financial statements and notes would provide information and metrics about other value drivers and impairers of value and about plans, opportunities, and risks. The last adjustment might be labeled with the admonition found on old maps: *Here be monsters!*

Proposals to address the perceived problem in business reporting center on three propositions, each stated in terms of a solution to the problem.

—*Proposition 1.* Traditional financial statements focus on the entity's ability to realize value from existing assets and liabilities. Proponents argue that financial statements are largely backward looking. A new financial reporting paradigm is needed to capture and report on the entity's creation of value. This paradigm would supplement, or might replace, existing financial statements.

—*Proposition 2.* The important value drivers in the new economy are largely nonfinancial and do not lend themselves to presentation in financial reports. However, a set of measures could be developed that would allow investors and creditors to evaluate entities and compare them with one another.

—*Proposition 3.* The importance of intangible assets is the distinguishing feature of the new economy. By and large, existing financial statements recognize those assets only when they are acquired from others. Accounting standard setters should develop a basis for the recognition and measurement of internally generated intangible assets.

Total Value Creation, a system developed by the Canadian Institute of Chartered Accountants, is the best example of the first proposition, or at least the best example of which I am aware. Lev's "value chain scoreboard" seems to fit the second proposition, as do the Financial Accounting Standards Board's Business Reporting Research Project and efforts in several European countries. Much of Lev's earlier work focuses on the third proposition. His present study represents a significant shift in emphasis and, perhaps, a recognition of the obstacles to any comprehensive recognition of intangibles in financial statements.

In this work, Lev proposes a useful three-way classification of intangibles: discovered intangibles, like those resulting from R&D; organization intangibles, like brands; and human resource intangibles, like employee satisfaction. As the author acknowledges, those three categories are fundamentally different. Given the differences, it may be that one reporting system cannot fully communicate information about all three. Lev's value chain scoreboard seems to focus primarily on discovered intangibles, an important and much-discussed element of the so-called new economy. This reporting scheme has much to recommend it.

—The information is presented in the form of metrics. Each metric can be described in a reasonably concise manner and presented consistently from period to period.

—The metrics can be standardized to some degree, as Lev suggests, or they can be entity-specific. Many argue that nonfinancial metrics should reflect the information that managers use to run companies. In this view, companies should not be required to develop business reporting metrics solely for purposes of disclosure. Publishing the information used to run the business allows readers to "get inside the manager's brain."

—The metrics are grouped in a single presentation, rather than scattered through annual reports and other information, and the presentation is designed to communicate the relation of metrics to one another.

But what of financial statements? Lev acknowledges the role of accounting information as a reality check on nonfinancial metrics. Would financial statements not be more useful if they captured more intangible assets in the statement of financial position (the balance sheet)?

The answer is obviously yes, but the solution is not simple. A business entity's statement of financial position should be a home for assets, liabilities, and owners' equity—and nothing else. If an intangible is to be included in the statement of financial position, it must satisfy the four criteria described in paragraph 63, FASB Concepts Statement 5, *Recognition and Measurement in Financial Statements of Business Enterprises:*

—Definitions: The item meets the definition of an element of financial statements.

—Measurability: The item has a relevant attribute measurable with sufficient reliability.

—Relevance: The information about the item is capable of making a difference in user decisions.

—Reliability: The information is representationally faithful, verifiable, and neutral.

Paragraph 25, FASB Concepts Statement 6, *Elements of Financial Statements,* defines an asset this way: "Assets are probable future economic benefits obtained or controlled by a particular entity as a result of past transactions or events." Paragraph 49(a) of the International Accounting Standards Committee's *Framework for the Preparation and Presentation of Financial Statements* provides a similar definition: "An asset is a resource controlled by the enterprise as a result of past events and from which future economic benefits are expected to flow to the enterprise."

Both definitions include the same essential characteristics of an asset. It represents future economic benefits, is a consequence of a past transaction or event, and is controlled by the entity. Both definitions are derived from sensible economics and everyday use of the language. Both serve an important function of all definitions—they circumscribe the population that satisfies the definition and exclude the population that does not.

Many see the control characteristic as the greatest conceptual obstacle to recognition of intangibles in financial statements. (Control is closely related to what Lev describes as excludability.) Many intangible factors are critical to business success but are not controlled by the entity. A successful beach resort probably should be located in a temperate climate. The climate, however, is not an asset in the accounting sense because the entity cannot control others' access to it. Happy, well-trained workers and satisfied customers are important, but the entity cannot prevent workers from going to work elsewhere or customers from buying a competitor's product. However, many intangibles—patents, customer lists, brands, databases—satisfy the control characteristic.

Note that the definition does not require that an asset arise from a transaction. It refers to a past transaction or event. I disagree with Lev's characterization of the structure of accounting as reflecting legally binding transactions with third parties. A transaction is the most common trigger for accounting recognition; tying accounting recognition to exchange transactions provides important accounting control. Still, past practice is just that—practice. The fact that accountants have not recognized intangible assets in financial statements does not suggest that they should not or cannot. Lev properly describes the gap between efforts to create an intangible (transactions that create costs to the entity) and realization through future sales. He also describes the gaps between effort, costs, and the knowledge that the effort has resulted in an asset. Those gaps suggest that accountants should at least consider whether some alternative event-driven recognition trigger is appropriate. The gaps do not suggest, in themselves, that accountants should abandon the notion of recognizing internally generated intangible assets.

Note also that costs are not assets. The cost of a building, a patent, or a software program is not the asset. The asset is the future use benefit that the entity obtains from having the asset; the cost is one attribute of that asset. This leads to the second conceptual obstacle to recognition. Do intangibles that meet the definition of an asset have "a relevant attribute measurable with sufficient reliability?"

Many intangible assets have determinable cost, but some people question whether cost is a relevant measurement for internally generated intangibles. They argue that there is a degree of correlation (in the general, not the mathematical, sense) between cost and future benefits of a purchased asset. The price (the initial cost) of an aircraft, a drill press, or a patent reflects the ability of that asset to produce future benefits. If that correlation did not exist, no business would pay the price asked by the seller. The same cannot be said of discovered assets. Two drug projects may cost the same to develop but may produce radically different revenue streams. There is an old saying for this in the oil business: What you spend does not matter; what you find does.

If not cost, then what measurement? Some suggest that the relevant measurement attribute is fair value. Here, Lev observes that "the belief that managers have sophisticated internal systems to measure and value intangibles is a myth." It is not clear who believes that "myth," but many comments on recent FASB projects articulate the difficulties in measuring even the intangibles that a company acquires when it buys another company. The problems of valuing internally generated intangibles are even more significant. Indeed, the measurement problem may go beyond measurement. Many companies may not know what intangible assets they own. Any well-run company has a fixed-asset register—but a customer list register?

The obstacles to greater recognition of intangible assets are also cultural and behavioral. Lev's discussion of "the politics of intangibles" is insightful. He observes, properly in my view, that the reaction against recognizing intangibles "is not a diabolical scheme to obscure relevant information. Rather, it reflects expected attitudes, given the economic characteristics of intangible investments."

Lev's study makes a good case for the harm created by lack of information about intangibles and the need for better information. It may be that his value chain scoreboard, or something like it, is the best first step to meeting that need. Enhanced reporting of nonfinancial metrics could help all participants in the business reporting process. Managers could learn more about the role of intangibles in their own operations. Analysts and other users could gain comfort in both the usefulness and the reliability of that information. Standard setters and regulators could learn more about which metrics are most important and whether recognition of intangible assets would, as many believe, enhance the usefulness of financial statements.

References

Australian Bureau of Statistics. 1997. "Australian National Accounts: Implementation of SNA93 Changes to Gross Fixed Capital Formation and the Asset Boundary." Paper prepared for OECD Capital Stock Conference, Canberra, March 10–14.

Bahk, Byong-Hyong, and Michael Gort. 1993. "Decomposing Learning by Doing in New Plants." *Journal of Political Economy* 101 (4): 561–83.

Bresnahan, Timothy F., Paul Milgrom, and Jonathan Paul. 1992. "The Real Output of the Stock Exchange." In *Output Measures in the Service Sectors*, edited by Zvi Griliches, 195–216. NBER Studies in Income and Wealth 56. University of Chicago Press.

Carroll, Glen, and Michael Hannan. 2000. *The Demography of Corporations and Industries*. Princeton University Press.

Carson, Carol S., and others. 1994. "A Satellite Account for Research and Development." *Survey of Current Business* 74 (11): 37–71.

Comin, Diego. 1999. "An Uncertainty-Driven Theory of the Productivity Slowdown: Manufacturing." Working Paper. Harvard University, Department of Economics.

Creamer, Daniel, Sergei Dobrovolsky, and Israel Borenstein. 1960. *Capital in Manufacturing and Mining: Its Formation and Financing*. Princeton University Press.

Croes, M. M. 1999. "Intangible Investments in Fifteen OECD Countries." OECD, March.

Ernst & Young. 1994. *Survey of Corporate Managers, Financial Analysts, Portfolio Managers, and Investors*. Boston: Center for Business Innovation.

Gates, Stephen. 1999a. *Aligning Performance Measures and Incentives in European Companies*. Research Report 1252-99-RR. New York: Conference Board.

———. 1999b. *Aligning Strategic Performance Measures and Results*. Research Report 1261-99-RR. New York: Conference Board.

Gompers, Paul A., and Josh Lerner. 1998. "Risk and Return in Private Equity Investments: The Challenge of Performance Assessment." *Journal of Private Equity* 1 (Winter): 5–12.

Gort, Michael, and Stephen Klepper. 1982. "Time Paths in the Diffusion of Product Innovations." *Economic Journal* 92:630–53.

Greenwood, Jeremy, and Boyan Jovanovic. 1999. "The IT Revolution and the Stock Market: Preliminary Evidence." *AEA Papers and Proceedings* (May): 116-22.

Hackett, Brian. 1997. *The Value of Training in the Era of Intellectual Capital*. Research Report 1199-97-RR. New York: Conference Board.

———. 2000. *Beyond Knowledge Management: New Ways to Work and Learn*. Research Report 1262-00-RR. New York: Conference Board.

Hall, Robert E. 2001. "E-Capital: The Link between the Stock Market and the Labor Market in the 1990s." *BPEA* (forthcoming).

Hobijn, Bart, and Boyan Jovanovic. 1999. "The IT Revolution and the Stock Market: Evidence." New York University, October.

Horsley, Phillip. 1997. *Trends in Private Equity.* San Francisco: Horsley/Bridge.

Huntsman, Blaine, and James P. Hoban. 1980. "Investment in New Enterprise: Some Observations about Risk, Return, and Market Structure." *Financial Management* 9 (Summer): 44–51.

Jovanovic, Boyan. 1982. "Selection and the Evolution of Industry." *Econometrica* 50:649–70.

Jovanovic, Boyan, and Yaw Nyarko. 1995. "A Bayesian Learning Model Fitted to a Variety of Learning Curves." *BPEA: Microeconomics,* 247–306.

OECD. 2000. "Software in the National Accounts: Recent Developments." Paper prepared for OECD Meeting of National Accounts Experts, Paris, September 26–29.

Parker, Robert, and Bruce Grimm. 2000. "Software Prices and Real Output: Recent Developments at the Bureau of Economic Analysis." Paper prepared for NBER Program on Technological Change and Productivity Measurement, Cambridge, March 17.

Triplett, Jack E., and Barry P. Bosworth. 2001. "Productivity in the Services Sector." In *Services in the International Economy,* edited by Robert M. Stern. University of Michigan Press.

Yorukogklu, Mehmet. 1998. "The Information-Technology Productivity Paradox." *Review of Economic Dynamics* 1 (2): 551–92.

Index

Aboody, David, 98

Accounting issues: accounting periods, 85–86; activity-based costing, 33; assets, 68, 69–70, 76, 102, 123, 124–25; cost accounting, 33, 88; deficiencies, 18n20, 19; financial information and statements, 81–82, 84, 92, 99–101, 121, 126, 195–99; generally accepted accounting principles, 87, 88–89, 114, 123, 135–50, 181; human capital, 76, 131, 183; innovation revenues, 106; off-balance-sheet liabilities, 76; overhaul of, 122–27; performance and sales indicators, 114; period expenses, 33; physical and financial assets, 8; quarterly earnings, 58n20; risk, 41–42, 82–83; rules, regulation, and standardization, 120–22; usefulness of financial information, 36; valuation, 195; value chains, 118–19

Accounting issues, intangibles: accounting deficiencies, 1–2, 3, 17, 18–19; costs, 83n7, 89, 116, 123, 126, 198; disclosure of, 79–103, 119–20; earnings, 123; expensing, 83, 88–92, 101, 103, 123, 124; generally accepted accounting principles, 135–50; international

accounting standards, 150–54, 197; management of earnings, 101–03; measurement and reporting, 69–70, 83–84; recognition of intangibles as assets, 7, 36, 42, 123–27, 198; research and development, 54–55, 87–88, 91–92, 95–98, 103, 124–27; risks, 37–42, 123–24; rules and regulations, 135–54; structure and limitations, 84–85; tangibles-intangibles accounting asymmetry, 7, 80, 81–85; undervaluation of intangibles, 96–98

Accounting Principles Board (APB), 135–36, 138, 142, 144, 145

Actioneer Incorporated, 30–31

A. D. Little, 162

Airports, 146, 153

Alliances. *See* Networks

Amazon.com: computer systems, 64; customer acquisition costs, 68; employees, 73; as intangible asset, 6; international spillover, 34; non-rivalry attribute, 26; stock price, 130n5; visitors on Internet, 72

American Airlines, 24, 27, 32

American Institute of Certified Public Accountants, 91, 120

American Telephone and Telegraph (AT&T), 34–35

America Online (AOL): customer acquisition and base, 67, 68, 83*n*7; as intangible asset, 6; penetration strategies, 28; percent of Internet users, 25; success of, 83
Amihud, Yakov, 95
Amir, Eli, 100–01
AMR Corporation. *See* American Airlines
AOL. *See* America Online
APB. *See* Accounting Principles Board
Assets: accounting issues, 83, 84, 89, 123, 135–38, 152, 181; benefits of, 33; commissions, 68; as commodities, 1; cost and, 198–99; criteria of, 68, 69, 74, 197–99; definition, 5, 197–98; intangible or intellectual, 1, 5–7, 13, 24, 123, 132; investment risks, 39; leveraging of, 23–24; management of, 32–33; media creative assets, 142–44; physical and financial, 1, 7, 12*n*13, 54; production research, 40; recognition of, 121; rivalry and scalability, 24–26; service value, 161; value of, 66*n*43, 193. *See also* Intangibles
Aston Martin, 10. *See also* Ford Motor Company
AT&T. *See* American Telephone and Telegraph
Atari, 29
Australia, 193
Automobile industry, 185

Bell, Alexander Graham, 14
Bell Laboratories, 34–35
Banking, 15, 137–38, 139–40, 149–50, 154
Barad, Jill, 90
Bonfield, Peter, 133*n*10
Books and publications, 142, 153
Boone, Jeff, 95
Brands and trademarks: accounting issues, 144; acquisition, valuation, and management, 70, 71, 72; commercialization and, 113–14; feasibility, 113; Ford new business model, 10–11; Internet and, 10–11; as nexus of intangibles, 6; value chains, 116
Bresnahan, Timothy, 194
Bridgestone/Firestone, 82*n*4
Bristol-Myers Squibb Company, 93*n*29
British Telecom, 133*n*10
Broadcasting industry, 146, 153
Brynjolfsson, Erik, 63, 64
Business and corporate issues: business processes, 112; corporate investment in R&D, 52–53, 87–88; corporate value, 64, 65–66, 70, 77; cost of capital, 95–98; customer base, 67–68; decisionmaking, 108, 158–59; diversification, 64–65; earnings as measure of performance, 85; failures, 86–91, 183–86; human capital, 13–14, 183; industrial-era corporations, 11; information and data, 62*n*32, 79–103; intangibles, 17, 46–47, 51–52, 65, 79–103; innovations, 46–47; investment, 54, 55, 63, 131; leadership, 179; market value, 57, 59, 62–63, 131; mergers and acquisitions, 159–61; network markets, 31; organizational capital, 62–66; patents and patent royalties, 34, 59, 61, 62, 116; proxies for company attributes, 70; reporting of performance and value, 7, 97–98; research and development, 55–57; resource allocation, 133; restructuring, 11, 17; risk, 37–42; twenty-first-century corporation, 12; vertical integration, 11, 12–13, 17; virtual firms, 31–33. *See also* Accounting issues; Brands and trademarks; Employment issues; Innovation; Investment issues; Manufacturing; Production; Productivity; Value chains

Cable television, 140–41
Canadian Institute of Chartered Accountants, 196
Canary Wharf (London, U.K.), 39
Capital, human. *See* Human resources
Carroll, Glen, 185
Case studies, 51–55, 117–18, 159–65. *See also* individual companies
Cellular telephones. *See* Technology
Cerent Corporation, 46*n*61
Chemical industry, 52–55
Christensen, Clayton, 38, 109
Cisco Systems: *2001* economic downturn, 129; acquisitions, 46*n*61, 87–88, 89; as business process, 112; decisionmaking, 108; Internet and, 13, 25; organizational design, 6; physical and financial assets, 31; success of, 83; value creation, 24–25
Coca-Cola, 6, 8
Communication technologies. *See* Technology
Communities of practice, 179
Computer-aided tomography (CT), 40–41, 59
Computers: computer capital, 63, 194; as disruptive innovation, 109; economic impact of, 191–92; employee issues, 73; organizational change and, 63–64; purchase of, 26*n*10. *See also* Internet; Software; Technology
Conference Board, 182
Consumers and customers: acquisition and retention, 67, 68–69, 83*n*7, 116–17, 125, 138–39, 152–53; customer lists and databases, 141, 152; satisfaction, 70; selection of technologies, 27; standards, 27, 28
Contractual arrangements, 144–46, 153
Corning, 16
Council for Chemical Research, 52
Council on Knowledge Management, 177

Credit and credit cards, 139–40
Croes, M. M., 190
CT. *See* Computer-aided tomography
Customers. *See* Consumers and customers

Dell, 6, 66, 108
Deregulation, 9, 11
Devitt, Jason, 30
Dow Chemical Company, 161–63
Drilling and mineral rights, 148, 154
Drugs. *See* Pharmaceuticals

Eastman Kodak, 102
eBay, 25
Economic issues: *2001* economic downturn, 129–30; business cycles, 95, 96*f*, 130; capitalist market system, 16*n*19; capital markets, 12*n*13, 57, 90, 107–08; competition, 17, 28, 131, 132, 158; contracts, 43–44; costs and benefits, 21, 22–24; deficiencies in disclosures of intangibles, 4, 79–103; excessive cost of capital, 19; innovation, 16*n*18, 39–40; of intangibles, 2–3, 9, 21–49, 190; investment in R&D, 53–55; knowledge-based economies, 119; leveraging, 23–25; major forces, 107; markets and market share, 25–27, 32, 57–59, 60; monopoly profits, 16*n*19; pricing, 28; rational expectations environment, 86*n*12; rivalry, scarcity, and scalability, 22–26; spillovers, 33–34, 112; theories, 86, 90, 93, 120, 131; value drivers, 196. *See also* Business and corporate issues; Employment issues; Investment issues; Stocks and stock market; Value chains
Economist magazine, 23*n*3, 24, 129*n*1
Edison, Thomas, 14
Emerging Issues Task Force, 88–20, 139

Employment issues: *2001* economic downturn, 130; benefits of ideas and development, 35–36, 75; creative workers, 14–15; employees as assets, 181–82; employer-employee bonds, 13; incentive compensation, 179, 182; selling of projects to employees, 160; stabilization of work force, 13–14; training, 33, 179, 186–88. *See also* Business and corporate issues; Human resources; Management; Productivity
Encyclopedia Britannica, 44–45
Enron, 16, 65
Entrepreneurs and entrepreneurship, 16*n*19. *See also* Innovation
Environmental issues, 52, 144–45
Eureka system, 36*n*35
Europe, 181, 182, 196

Failures. *See* Business and corporate issues
Fairchild, 35
Farnsworth, Philo, 35
FASB. *See* Financial Accounting Standards Board
FCC. *See* Federal Communications Commission
FDA. *See* Food and Drug Administration
Feasibility. *See* Technology
Federal Communications Commission (FCC), 146, 148
Federal Express, 66
Financial Accounting Standards Board (FASB): Business Reporting Research Project, 196; costs of internally developed software, 142; fraudulent financial reports, 19; information disclosure, 86–87; recognition of intangibles as assets, 42, 124; roles of, 120–21; servicing of credit, 149*n*27; software capitalization requirement, 91–92; standardizing information on

intangibles, 121–22; statements of financial position, 197
Financial World, 70
Fiorina, Carly, 163
Food and Drug Administration (FDA), 66
Forbes, 9
Ford Motor Company, 10–12, 26, 82*n*4
Fox, Stephen P., 164

Gap, 66
Gates, Stephen, 180–83
GE. *See* General Electric
General Electric (GE), 26, 106*n*2
Generally accepted accounting principles issues (GAAP). *See* Accounting issues
General Motors (GM), 12
Glosten, Lawrence, 94
GM. *See* General Motors
Gompers, Paul, 184
Goodwill, 137–38, 139, 149, 152. *See also* Accounting, intangibles; Intangibles
Grossman, Gene, 25

Hackett, Brian, 177–80
Hall, Bronwyn, 60
Hall, Robert, 191–92
Hamel, Gary, 131
Hannan, Michael, 185
Helpman, Elhanan, 25
Hewlett-Packard, 163–65
Hoban, James, 184
Horsley, Phillip, 184
Human resources: as an asset, 74, 181–82; biotechnology companies, 76; disclosure of information, 181; human capital, 12*n*13, 13–14, 76, 131, 183, 186–88; intangibles and, 6–7, 75; measurement and valuation, 73, 74–76; value chains and, 180–82. *See also* Employment issues

Huntsman, Blaine, 184

IBM. *See* International Business Machines
ICM. *See* Intellectual capital management
ICM Gathering (ICMG), 155, 156, 158
Inc. 500 list, 13, 35
Information and information technology (IT): corporate insiders versus outsiders, 19; costs, 40*n*48; decentralization of decisionmaking, 107–10; effects of, 9, 11, 192; information asymmetry, 93–99; information revelation principle, 86–91, 122; information sharing, 35–36; information structure, 122; innovations of, 14*n*16; investment in, 63, 64; regulation and standardization, 120–22; value chain disclosure, 119–20. *See also* Accounting; Computers; Intangibles; Internet; Investment issues
Information systems, 3–4, 33, 106–27
Innovation: commercialization of, 113–14, 124; competitive role of, 131; contracts, 43–44; as corporate activity, 16, 46; creative workers and 14–15; disruptive innovation concept, 109; intangibles and, 2, 16, 17, 39–42, 141–42; intellectual capital and, 156–57; international accounting standards, 153; inventor incentive program, 164–65; investment in, 59; as output measures, 70; performance measures, 182–83; process innovation, 40; revenues, 114; risks of, 37–42, 59; sources of new ideas and knowledge, 112; urgency for, 14–16; valuation, 156–58; value chain scoreboard, 110–27. *See also* Brands and trademarks; Business and corporate issues; Patents;

Research and development; Value chains
Insurance issues, 145
Intangibles: capital, 24, 62–66, 132; changes in, 8–12; classification of, 196; computer-related, 64; constituencies of, 19–20; costs and benefits, 40*n*48, 44–45, 47–49, 126, 136–37, 152, 198–99; customer-related, 66–73, 138–41; definitions and synopsis, 1–4, 5, 20, 31, 180, 183, 189–91; deverticalization and innovation, 17; diversification and, 65; expansion of intangible assets, 31–33; employee-related, 13; information regarding, 1, 2, 17–20, 79–103; intellectual capital, 21; market issues, 8, 42–47; network effects, 29–30, 61; nondisclosure, 54, 55; nonrivalry of, 22–23, 26; organizational capital, 13; patents, 61; risks of, 37–42, 82–83, 84, 89–90, 113, 123–24; scalability, 22–31, 61; spillovers and excludability, 33–37; standards, 124; value issues, 51–55, 65–66, 77, 96–98, 132, 193–94, 199. *See also* Accounting issues, intangibles; Economic issues; Investment issues; Management; Measurement; Research and development; Value chains
Intangibles, measurement and reporting: customer-related intangibles, 67–71; disclosure of intangible assets, 182–83; expensing of, 7; human resources, 74–75; Internet traffic, 71–73; output measures of market value and patents, 57–61; performance measures and, 177–80; plans for, 81, 83–85, 92–93, 103; proposed information system, 107–27, 196, 199; recognition and measurement, 151–54,

181–82, 191; undisclosed performance indicators, 105–07
Intel Corporation, 25, 30, 35, 129
Intellectual capital management (ICM). *See* Intellectual capital and property
Intellectual capital and property: case studies, 159–65; definition, 5, 24; management best practices, 155–65; protection of, 34–37, 70; trading of, 84; use of, 105–06; value chains, 116. *See also* Brands and trademarks; Patents
International Accounting Standards Committee, 197
International Business Machines (IBM), 65, 87, 88*t*, 89
Internet: *2001* economic downturn, 129; brands of, 6; business organization and, 6, 10–11; business use of, 106; commercialization and, 113, 114; customer acquisition and base, 67, 68–69, 116–17; effects on intangibles, 9, 43; e-tailers and dot.coms, 83, 193–94; feasibility, 113; IBM and, 65; individual investors and, 107–08; markets, market value, and market share, 32, 47, 69, 72, 114; research and development, 62; retailing, 132; stock prices, 69; successes in online selling, 31–32; traffic measures, 71–73. *See also* Amazon.com; America Online; Cisco Systems; Computers; Information and Information technology; Technology
Intranet systems, 65, 74, 112, 113
Investment issues: analysts, 56, 90, 93–94, 100–01, 107–08, 127, 134; basic research, 56; benefits of assets, 33; commercialization, 106, 110; costs, 95, 102; customer acquisition costs, 68–69, 125, 138–39; customer issues, 70, 97–98; decisionmaking issues,

107–09; failures and losses, 184; financial statements, 81, 89; function of markets, 42–43; individual investors, 107–09; information and data, 51–77, 79–81, 84–85, 93–102, 105–09, 134; insiders, 93–94, 98, 102, 103; in intangibles, 42–47, 51–77, 79–81, 84, 124–25, 131; litigation, 120; market-to-book value, 8, 9*f*, 58, 60, 72, 183, 184, 187; market share and values, 57–59, 60, 86, 89, 102, 114; mortgage-backed securities, 44; organizational capital, 62–66; patents, 59–60; performance indicators, 105–07; price-to-sales value, 72; private and social returns, 36–37, 57; research and development, 44, 52, 55, 58, 62, 97; risk and risk assessment, 41, 83*n*7; trademarks and, 71. *See also* Stocks and stock market
Iridium satellite, 58, 82, 90*n*20
IT (information technology). *See* Information and information technologies

Jaguar, 10. *See also* Ford Motor Company
Java. *See* Software
J. C. Penny, 31–32, 113
Jorgensen, Dale, 192
Jovanovic, Boyan, 183–88

Knowledge, 25, 155–65, 178–79
Krugman, Paul, 131, 132
Kuznets, Simon, 191
Kyle, Albert, 93, 94

Lamoreaux, Naomi, 45–46
Land Rover, 10. *See also* Ford Motor Company
Lazear, Edward, 75
Lear Corporation, 11*n*10
Learning Company, 90*n*20
Lerner, Josh, 184

Lotus Development Corporation, 30, 87, 88*t*, 89

Mahoney, Richard, 56*n*16
Management: accounting issues, 19, 122–23; adaptive capacity, 36; of brands, 70; compensation, 89; customer satisfaction, 70; efficiency gains, 23n3; of enormous organizations, 11; externalization of decisionmaking processes, 108–10; financial statement information, 81–82; information issues, 99, 106, 119–20, 126–27; of innovations, 41; intellectual capital management best practices, 155–65; internal measurements, 182, 182–83; litigation, 120; partial excludability, 35; of risk, 41, 49, 84
Management, intangibles: accounting, 88–89; assessment of expected returns, 133; difficulties of, 32–33, 43; earnings and, 101–02; excludability and spillovers, 33–37; information and, 1–2, 3, 17, 80; intellectual capital, 155–65; of knowledge, 105, 178–79; marketability, 43–45; methods, 48–49, 132
Manufacturing, 11–12, 54, 132. *See also* Production; Productivity
Markets. *See* Economic issues; Investment issues
Market-to-book value. *See* Investment issues
Mattel, 90*n*20
McCaw Cellular, 35
Media creative assets, 142–44
Media Metrix, 71, 116–17
Mendelson, Haim, 95
Merck and Company, 6, 8, 13, 108
MFP (multifactor productivity). *See* Productivity
Microsoft, 30, 31, 45, 91–92
Milgrom, Paul, 94, 194
Mineral rights, 148

Minnesota Mining and Manufacturing. *See* 3M
Monsanto Company, 56*n*16, 82–83
Morck, Randall, 65
Mortgages, 149–50, 154
Motion pictures, 142–44, 150, 154, 193
Motorola, 58, 82, 90*n*20
Movies. *See* Motion pictures
Multifactor productivity (MFP). *See* Productivity

Nakamura, Leonard, 15
Nasdaq, 129
National Cash Register Company (NCR), 90
National Institutes of Health (NIH), 56
NCR. *See* National Cash Register Company
NES (Nintendo Entertainment System). *See* Nintendo
Neste Oy, 159–61
Netscape, 28
Networks: alliances, 30; broadcasting, 146–48, 153–54; effects of, 26–31, 67; information issues, 109, 110; intangibles, 30; management of, 32; markets, 28; standards, 27, 28; tipping, 28
Nielsen/Netrating, 71, 72, 116–17
NIH. *See* National Institutes of Health
Nintendo, 29, 30
Nokia Corporation, 30
Nortel Networks, 134*n*11

OECD. *See* Organization for Economic Cooperation and Development
Oil and gas industries, 148
Online operations. *See* Internet
Oracle, 91–92
Organization for Economic Cooperation and Development (OECD), 189–90
Outsourcing. *See* Production

Palm, 30–31

Patents: accounting issues, 144; audits and reviews, 160–61, 162–63; backward and forward citations, 59, 60; as business indicators, 116; feasibility, 113; infringement, 34, 59n25; innovation process, 59; network effects, 29–30; as nonproduced intangibles, 190; as output measure, 57, 70; patent agents, 46; prior art, 59n25; protective effects of, 14, 16, 84; R&D contribution, 34, 58–61, 62; sales, trading, and licensing, 36, 43, 45–47, 61, 62, 84, 105, 116, 133; spillovers, 33–34; transistors, 34; value of, 38. *See also* Innovation

Paul, Jonathan, 194

Performers, 43

Pharmaceuticals and pharmaceutical companies: clinical testing, 84, 113; costs and returns, 23; intangible investment, 132; intranets, 65; network effects, 28; preproduction organizing, 185; value chain of, 66

Pharmacia, 82–83

Pocket Sensei, 30–31

Policy and policymakers: corporate financial information, 19–20; economic objectives, 108–09; Financial Accounting Standards Board, 42; information regarding intangibles, 80; intangible excludability and spillovers, 36–37; investment in innovation, 41; role in accounting policy, 120–21; standardization, 127

Political issues, 3, 80, 85–91

Production, 2, 11–12, 14, 40. *See also* Business and corporate issues; Innovation; Manufacturing; Productivity

Productivity: chemical R&D, 52–55; computers and, 192; human resource issues, 6–7, 74–75; of intangibles, 52; multifactor productivity, 14n16; research and development, 55–56, 58; training and, 186–88. *See also* Business and corporate issues; Innovation; Manufacturing; Production

Property rights. *See* Intellectual property

Public policy. *See* Policy and policymakers

R&D. *See* Research and development

Rajan, Raghuram, 15

Raman, K. K., 95

RCA-NBC, 35

Regulations, 120–21, 122–23; Regulation FD (Selective Disclosure and Insider Trading, SEC), 90, 108n3

Research: basic research, 40, 55–56; data availability, 62n32, 77; on intangible assets, 3; risks of, 40, 56; stocks and securities, 96–97

Research and development (R&D): acquisition of technology, 112; bid-ask spread of stocks, 95–96; chemical industry, 52–55, 132; commercialization, 106, 110; costs of, 23, 96; effects on earnings, 101–03; expenditures, 52n2, 58, 62–63, 92; government-sponsored, 56; growth of business enterprises, 55–57; information issues, 65, 95, 106; in-process R&D, 87, 89; insider gains, 98; investment issues, 44, 52, 55, 61, 62, 103, 115–16; Merck and Company, 6, 108; as nexus of intangibles, 6; organizational issues, 62–66; output and output indicators, 57–61, 62; patent issues, 34, 58–61, 62; probabilities of success, 41n49; R&D intensity, 52n5, 57; reporting, 97–98; return on, 61–62; risks of, 39, 41; spillovers, 112; subsidies, 37; transistor, 34; U.S. corporate expenditures, 16, 92n28; value chain scoreboard, 115–16. *See also*

Accounting, intangibles; Innovation; Intangibles; Value chains
Risk. *See* Accounting issues; Intangibles
Rivalry. *See* Economic issues
Romer, Paul, 131
Ryanair, 23*n*3

S&P. *See* Standard and Poor
Sabre. *See* American Airlines
Safe harbor rules, 120
Safelite Glass Corporation, 75
Sarnoff, David, 35
Scalability. *See* Economic issues
Scarcity. *See* Economic issues
Scherer, F. M., 38–39
Schumpeter, Joseph, 186
SEC. *See* Securities and Exchange Commission
Securities and Exchange Commission (SEC), 19, 83*n*7, 93*n*29, 98, 120, 121
Seethamraju, Chandra, 70, 71
Senate, U.S., 7
SFAS. *See* Statement of Financial Accounting Standards
Shane, Hilary, 59–60
Smullyan, Raymond, 81
SNA. *See* System of National Accounts
Social effects, 80, 94, 97–98, 99, 103, 194
Software: accounting issues, 91–92; alpha and beta testing, 84, 91, 113; capitalization requirement, 91–92; costs and returns, 23, 79*n*1, 91, 123*n*29, 142; customer support, 140; for hand-held devices, 30; Java, 26; open-source, 108; standards, 124; values, 125. *See also* Computers
Sokoloff, Kenneth, 45–46
Sony Corporation, 6, 30
Standard and Poor (S&P), 8, 9*f*, 58, 63, 98*n*42
Standards: accounting issues, 120–22; consumers and customers, 27, 28;

information, 120–22; intangibles, 124; international accounting standards, 150–54, 197; networks, 27, 28; policies, 127; software, 124. *See also* Financial Accounting Standards; Statement of Financial Accounting Standards
Statement of Financial Accounting Standards (SFAS): banking and thrift industry, 139; cable television, 141; contractual arrangements, 144–45; customer lists and databases, 141; media, 142; other specific industries, 146–48, 150; rules of, 137
Statoil, 159
Stocks and stock market: *2001* losses, 129; bid-ask spread, 94, 95–96; capital markets, 57, 108–09, 133–34, 183, 192–94; computers and e-capital, 191–92, 193–94; customer acquisition costs, 68, 116; effects of Internet, 10; expenses, 68*n*49; information issues, 94, 96–97, 99–101; insider trading, 93–94, 98–99; intangible capital, 183; investment of corporate sector, 17; patent issues, 60–61; price/earnings ratio, 10; prices and valuation, 8, 57–58, 69, 86, 98*n*42, 133–34; Tobin's *q*, 60, 187, 192; values of R&D, 125; volatility of, 131. *See also* Investment issues
Sun Microsystems, 129
Supply chains, 10, 13, 132
Sweden, 190
System of National Accounts (SNA), 190

Technology: acquisition of R&D, 87–88; audits, 159–61; business cycles and, 130; cellular telephones, 35, 67–68; communication, 12*n*13; consumer selection of, 27, 28; contracts, 43–44; creative

destruction, 186; disk drives, 38; feasibility, 66, 124–25; investment issues, 54, 132, 183; markets in, 46–47; network effects, 26–31; Nintendo, 29; research and, 40, 56; semiconductors, 60; standards, 28; stock values, 57–58; tech factor valuation method, 162; television, 35; transistors, 34–35. *See also* Information and information technology; Intellectual property; Patents
Teece, David, 44
Television, 142–44
3M, 38, 65
Tipping. *See* Networks
Tobin, James, 161
Tobin's *q* measures. *See* Stocks and stock market
Total Value Creation, 196
Trade issues, 13, 17
Trademarks. *See* Brands and trademarks
Trajtenberg, Manuel, 59
Transportation industry, 148–49, 154
Triplett, Jack E., 189–94

United Airlines, 22
United States, 190
Upton, Wayne, 194–99

Value chains: accounting issues, 118–19; decisionmaking issues, 110; disclosure of, 119–20; example, 117–18; human resources and, 180–82; intangibles, 67–68, 69–70, 196; knowledge-based enterprises, 66; litigation and safe harbor rules, 120; movement up and down, 11*n*10, 84; reporting, 122; scoreboard, 110–18, 127, 196–97
Value issues: accounting valuation, 66*n*43, 156–58, 193, 195; brands, 70; corporate value, 7–8, 64, 65–66, 70, 77; creation of, 24–25; intangibles, 23, 26, 51–55, 65–66, 77, 96–98, 132, 193–94, 199; market-to-book ratio, 8, 9*f*, 58, 60, 72, 183, 184, 187; market value, 57, 59, 62–63, 131; patents, 38; price-to-sales value, 72; reporting of, 7, 97–98; research and development, 125; service value, 161; software, 125; stock, 57–58; valuation criteria, 122; value drivers, 196
Vanlev, 93*n*29
Vertical integration. *See* Business and corporate issues
Vindigo, 30
Visa credit cards, 30
Visteon, 10. *See also* Ford Motor Company
Volvo, 10. *See also* Ford Motor Company

Wal-Mart, 16, 64, 85, 108
Wall Street Journal, 85, 102
Williams Company, 66

Xerox, 6, 38, 112

Yahoo!, 6, 68
Yang, Shinkyu, 63, 64
Yeung, Bernard, 65

Zingales, Luigi, 15

Cited Author Index

Aaker, David, 70n56
Aboody, David, 52n5, 52n6, 53n8, 79n1, 84n8, 92n26, 94n30, 98n43, 99n45, 123n29, 125n36, 126n41
Acs, Zoltan, 55n15
Aghion, Philippe, 51n1
AICPA. *See* American Institute of Certified Public Accountants
AIMR. *See* Association for Investment Management and Research
Akerlof, George, 94n33
American Institute of Certified Public Accountants (AICPA), 91n25
Amihud, Yakov, 95n34
Amir, Eli, 68n47, 68n48, 100n47, 125n38
Association for Investment Management and Research (AIMR), 92n27
Audretsch, David, 55n15
Austin, David, 60n26
Australian Bureau of Statistics, 193n28
Azoulay, Pierre, 28n17

Bahk, Byhong-Hyong, 188n18
Barth, Mary, 70n58, 125n38
Bassi, Laurie, 73n66
Becker, Brian, 75n68
Ben Zion, Uri, 58n22
Berger, Philip, 64n40

Bernard, Victor, 97n39
Berndt, Ernst, 28n17
Bhide, Amar, 13n15, 35n33
Bobrow, Daniel, 7n3
Bond, Stephen, 66n43
Boone, Jeff, 95n35
Borenstein, Israel, 191n24
Bosworth, Barry P., 192n26, 192n27
Botosan, Christine, 90n21, 96n38
Boulton, Richard, 66n44
Bresnahan, Timothy F., 194n29
Brown, Stephen, 100n46
Brynjolfsson, Erik, 63n36, 64n37, 70n59
Bublitz, B., 58n22
Bushee, Brian, 102n49

Cappelli, Peter, 75n68
Carson, Carol S., 191n23
Castagna, Michael J., 155–65
Chan, Louis, 97n41
Chan, Su, 58n20
Chandler, Alfred, 11n11
Chang, James, 100n46
Chauvin, Keith, 58n23
Cheslow, Robert, 7n3
Christensen, Clayton, 38n41, 109n4, 109n5
Clement, Werner, 190n20
Clinch, Greg, 125n38
Coase, Ronald, 46n60

Cohen, Wesley, 34n28
Comin, Diego, 185
Conference Board, 182n8
Creamer, Daniel, 191n24
Crepon, Bruno, 114n12
Croes, M. M., 190n22
Cummins, Jason, 66n43

Daley, Lane, 64n40
Darby, Michael, 76n71, 117n21
Darrough, Masako, 101n48
De Bondt, Werner, 97n39
Deloitte & Touche, 92n26
Demers, Elizabeth, 62n30, 69n51,
    72n62, 72n63, 113n9, 116n16,
    117n20
Deng, Zhen, 46n61, 59n25, 60n27,
    62n31, 87n14, 89n19, 112n7,
    116n17
Dobrovolsky, Sergei, 191n24
Duguet, Emmanual, 114n12

Easton, Peter, 85n10
Eccles, Robert, 110n6
Economides, Nicholas, 27n11
Elfenbein, Dan, 112n8
Ernst & Young, 179n6
Ettredge, M., 58n22

Farrell, Joseph, 28n18
FASB. *See* Financial Accounting
    Standards Board
Feldman, Maryann, 55n15
Financial Accounting Standards
    Board (FASB), 36n37, 85n11,
    87n13, 91n24, 110n6, 114n13,
    118n22, 120n24, 121n25,
    124n31, 124n32, 124n33,
    125n34, 126n40, 135n2, 136n3,
    137n4, 139n6, 139n7, 140n8,
    140n9, 140n10, 141n12, 142n13,
    142n14, 142n15, 142n16,
    144n17, 144n18, 144n19,
    145n20, 145n21, 146n22,
    146n23, 148n25, 148n26,
    149n27, 149n28, 150n29

Fox, Stephen P., 164n7
Francis, Jennifer, 100n46
Freeman, Chris, 34n31, 52n4

Garicano, Luis, 106n2
Glosten, Lawrence, 94n31
Gompers, Paul, 184n12
Goolsbee, Austan, 26n10
Gordon, Robert, 14n16
Gort, Michael, 188n18, 186n15
Greenwood, Jeremy, 183n10
Griliches, Zvi, 42n51, 55n13, 55n15,
    57n19
Grimm, Bruce, 191n23
Grossman, Gene, 25n7
Gu, Feng, 61n29, 116n19

Hackett, Brian, 179n2, 179n3, 179n4,
    179n5
Hall, Bronwyn, 34n29, 55n14, 57n18,
    57n19, 60n26, 116n17
Hall, Robert, 8n6, 8n7, 63n35,
    66n43, 192n25
Ham, Richard, 34n29
Hamel, Gary, 131n8
Hammerer, Gerhard, 190n20
Hand, John, 69n51, 72n63
Harhoff, Dietmar, 38n42, 41n49
Harrison, Suzanne, 155–65
Harrison, Trevor, 85n10
Healy, Paul, 126n39, 126n41
Helpman, Elhanan, 25n7
Herschey, Mark, 58n22, 58n23,
    60n27
Hoban, James P., 184n11
Hobijn, Bart, 183n10
Homer-Dixon, Thomas, 39n44
Horsley, Phillip, 184n12
Howe, Chris, 126n39, 126n41
Howitt, Peter, 51n1
Huntsman, Blaine, 184n11
Huselid, Mark, 75n68

IASC. *See* International Accounting
    Standards Committee
ICM Group, 155–65

Ijiri, Yuji, 81*n*3
International Accounting Standards Committee (IASC), 124*n*33, 150*n*30
Ittner, Christopher, 70*n*57

Jaffe, Adam, 57*n*19, 60*n*26, 116*n*17
Jorgensen, Dale, 192*n*26
Jovanic, Boyan, 183*n*10, 186*n*16

Kaplan, Steven, 106*n*2
Katz, Michael, 28*n*18
Kelm, Kathryn, 58*n*21
Kesinger, John, 58*n*20
Klenow, Peter, 26*n*10
Klepper, Stephen, 186*n*15
Kline, David, 36*n*36, 46*n*61, 61*n*28
Klock, Mark, 60*n*26
Kothari, S. P., 39*n*45, 94*n*30
Kukies, Joerg, 38*n*42, 41*n*49
Kyle, Albert, 93*n*29

Laento, Kari, 159*n*1
Laguesse, Ted, 39*n*45, 94*n*30
Lakonishok, Josef, 97*n*39, 97*n*41
Lamoreaux, Naomi, 46*n*58, 46*n*59
Lanjouw, Jean, 59*n*25
Larcker, David, 70*n*57
Lazear, Edward, 75*n*69, 75*n*70
Leone, Andrew, 39*n*45, 94*n*30
Lerner, Josh, 46*n*61, 112*n*8, 184*n*12
Lev, Baruch, 2*n*2, 52*n*5, 52*n*6, 53*n*8, 79*n*1, 84*n*8, 112*n*7, 113*n*9, 36*n*38, 43*n*54, 46*n*61, 59*n*25, 60*n*27, 61*n*29, 62*n*30, 62*n*31, 68*n*47, 68*n*48, 69*n*51, 72*n*62, 72*n*63, 76*n*73, 85*n*10, 87*n*14, 89*n*19, 92*n*26, 94*n*30, 97*n*40, 98*n*43, 99*n*45, 100*f*, 100*n*46, 100*n*47, 116*n*16, 116*n*17, 116*n*19, 117*n*20, 118*n*22, 119*n*23, 123*n*29, 123*n*30, 125*n*35, 125*n*36, 125*n*38, 126*n*41
Libert, Barry, 66*n*44
Liebowitz, Stanley, 28*n*20
Liu, Qian, 76*n*71, 117*n*21

Lo, Kin, 100*n*46
Lys, Tom, 100*n*46

Mahoney, Richard, 56*n*16
Mairesse, Jacques, 114*n*12
Mansfield, Edwin, 41*n*49, 55*n*15, 56*n*17
Margolis, Stephen, 28*n*20
Martin, John, 58*n*20
Megna, Pamela, 60*n*26
Mehrotra, Vikas, 64*n*40
Mendelson, Haim, 95*n*34
Milgrom, Paul, 94*n*32, 194*n*29
Morck, Randall, 64*n*39, 65*n*41
Myers, Stewart, 126*n*39, 126*n*41

Nadiri, Ishaq, 45*n*57
Nakamura, Leonard, 15*t*, 16*n*19, 37*n*39, 62*n*32, 63*n*33
Narayanan, V., 58*n*21
Narin, Francis, 59*n*25, 60*n*27, 116*n*17
Nelson, Richard, 34*n*28
Neumark, David, 75*n*68
Nyarko, Yaw, 186*n*16

OECD. *See* Organization for Economic Cooperation and Development
Ofek, Eli, 64*n*40
Ohlson, James, 85*n*10
Organization for Economic Cooperation and Development (OECD), 74*n*67, 92*n*28, 191*n*23
Oriel, Sharon, 163*n*6

Parker, Robert, 191*n*23
Patel, Pari, 59*n*24
Paul, Jonathan, 194*n*29
Pavitt, Keith, 59*n*24
Petrash, Gordon, 161*n*2, 162*n*3, 162*n*4, 163*n*5
Pinches, George, 58*n*21
Pindyck, Robert, 28*n*17

Rajan, Raghuram, 15n17
Raman, Kris, 95n35
Rangan, Srinivasan, 101n48
Richardson, Vernon, 60n27
Rivette, Kevin, 36n36, 46n61, 61n28
Romer, Paul, 16n18, 22n1, 40n46, 131n7
Rosett, Joshua, 76n73

Samek, Steve, 66n44
Sarath, Bharat, 97n40, 123n30
Schankerman, Mark, 59n25
Scherer, Frederick, 38n42, 41n49
Scheutze, Walter, 42n52
Schipper, Katherine, 100n46
Scholz, Susan, 60n27
Schumpeter, Joseph, 16n19
Schwartz, Aba, 76n73
Schwarz, Karl, 190n20
Seethamraju, Chandra, 70n59, 70n60, 71n61
Sengupta, Partha, 90n21, 96n38
Shane, Hilary, 60n26
Shapiro, Carl, 11n12, 26n9, 27n14, 27n16, 28n18, 29n21, 30n23, 32n26, 39n43, 40n48, 45n56, 127n42
Shi, Charles, 95n37
Shleifer, Andrei, 97n39
Sivakumar, Ranjini, 64n40
Smullyan, Raymond, 81n3
Soete, Luc, 34n31, 52n4
Sokoloff, Kenneth, 46n58, 46n59
Sougiannis, Theodore, 97n40, 97n41, 100n47, 123n30, 125n35
Stephan, Paula, 76n72
Stewart, Thomas, 1n1

Sullivan, Patrick H., Sr., 155–65

Tasker, Sarah, 110n6, 114n14
Teece, David, 44n55
Thaler, Richard, 97n39
Thomas, Jacob, 97n39
Tolstoy, Leo, 105n1
Trajtenberg, Manuel, 57n19, 60n26, 116n17
Triplett, Jack E., 192n26, 192n27
Trueman, Brett, 72n63
Tsai, Alexander, 46n61

Vallabhajosyula, Shyam, 135–54
Varian, Hal, 11n12, 26n9, 27n14, 27n16, 29n21, 30n23, 32n26, 39n43, 40n48, 45n56, 127n42
Vishny, Robert, 97n39

Wagner, Samuel, 41n49
Walsh, John, 34n28
Weber, Bruce, 24n4
Weygandt, Jerry, 58n22
Whalen, Jack, 7n3
Wong, Franco, 72n63
Wu, Min, 43n54

Yang, Shinkyu, 63n36, 64n37, 70n59
Yeung, Bernard, 64n39, 65n41
Yorukoglu, Mehmet, 186n17

Zarowin, Paul, 36n38, 100f, 100n46, 118n22, 119n23
Zhang, Xiao-Jun, 72n63
Zingales, Luigi, 11n11, 12n13, 13n14, 15n17
Zucker, Lynne, 76n71, 117n21